Education and International Development:
theory, practice and issues

Education and International Development:
theory, practice and issues

Clive Harber

SYMPOSIUM
BOOKS

Symposium Books Ltd
PO Box 204, Didcot, Oxford OX11 9ZQ, United Kingdom
www.symposium-books.co.uk

Published in the United Kingdom, 2014

ISBN 978-1-873927-47-2

Printed and bound in the United Kingdom by Hobbs the Printers, Southampton
www.hobbs.uk.com

Contents

Dedication

This book is dedicated to my nephew Matthew Graham who has recently started out on an academic career in African history – and to his sister Rachael so that there is no sibling rivalry.

Acknowledgements

I have worked closely with a number of academic colleagues over the last thirty plus years and regular discussions and collaboration with them have certainly contributed to my thinking on education in general, and education and development in particular. These are Roland Meighan, Lynn Davies and Michele Schweisfurth of the University of Birmingham; Jeff Serf of the University of Wolverhampton; David Stephens of the University of Brighton and, most recently, Vusi Mncube of the University of South Africa. The ideas of other many other colleagues in Britain and Africa have also undoubtedly rubbed off on me over the years, as have those of master's and doctoral students. I thank them also. Finally, I would like to thank my wife, Mary Harber, who herself has a background in development studies, for painstakingly reading through each draft chapter and telling me what was wrong with it.

Preface

When I was teaching on courses on, and supervising research students in, education and international development at the universities of Birmingham, United Kingdom and Natal (now KwaZulu Natal), South Africa in the 1990s and 2000s, it was clear that there was no longer a single, reasonably up-to-date book that provided an introductory overview of the field of study. It was thus difficult to recommend to new students what they should read before commencing their studies to get a feel of the field – or indeed what they should refer to when a new topic arose on their course. I therefore set out to write a book primarily with the following students in mind: one-year master's students pursuing a course on, or that involved, education and international development, second or third year undergraduate students doing courses in the area of education and international development, and doctoral students doing academic research in a context of education and international development. I am also aware of a number of staff in universities who have been asked to teach such courses without their having a strong background in the area and I hope this will be of use to them as well.

Education and international development is now a very large field of academic and practical endeavour. My selection of major theories, goals, practicalities and issues is only one possible selection, and others may well have different priorities, but I have tried to cover educational topics that seem directly or particularly relevant to development. No single book can cover every detail and nuance of such a large field of study. It is also true that the main, though by no means exclusive, focus of the book is primary and secondary education and thus to a certain extent teacher education. Each chapter sets out an introduction to some of the main ideas and debates of the topic that it covers and provides sources for considerable further reading both in the references at the end of the chapter and in a section suggesting further readings.

I began writing the book about a year after I retired from university employment. Indeed, writing such a book while in employment would have been difficult because anything remotely resembling a textbook tends to be frowned on in the UK context of what is known as the 'Research Excellence Framework' (REF). Under this regime all university departments are graded and ranked – and funds distributed accordingly – based on the 'quality' of each department's academic publications. As was made clear time and time again in meetings on the REF, books or

9

articles aimed at being helpful to students by providing a scholarly overview of a topic based largely on secondary literature were to be given a zero or very low rating and not entered into the REF. This is a major disincentive in what are known as 'research-intensive' universities, where at times, and as a direct result of the REF, there seems to be an inverse relationship between what is valued and what might actually be useful to others.

However, all this having been said, I hope that the book nevertheless does provide readers with a useful, reasonably comprehensive, but concise introduction to an academic area that I still find fascinating and have been professionally engaged with since 1977.

CHAPTER 1

Education and Development: introductory ideas

What is Development?

Concern with the idea that societies and states 'develop' over time, usually with the assumption that development means that matters are improving in some way, goes back at least as far as Aristotle and has occurred in many different cultures (Fägerlind and Saha, 1989, ch. 1). However, this book is primarily concerned with post-1945 debates and theories. The end of the Second World War was a catalyst for anti-colonial movements, leading eventually to independence in a wide range of formerly colonial countries, particularly in Asia, Africa and the Middle East, and thereby creating a focus on the difference between the newly independent, 'developing' states and the 'developed' states of Europe and North America.

Views and theories on the history, nature, causes and purposes of 'development' are many, varied and often controversial (e.g. Rist, 2008; Haynes, 2008; Pieterse, 2010). However, the present book is not a book on development studies per se, as the main foci are the relationships between education and development and the nature and practice of education in 'developing' countries. Thus, for example, the theories of development discussed here are those most directly concerned with the role of education in development. Nevertheless, it is important to begin with a discussion of development in order to provide a context for the ensuing discussion of the role of education in development.

Post-Second World War discussions of development were originally primarily concerned with economic development – the growth of wealth and output as measured by indicators of national wealth such as the gross national product. The main division was therefore initially between the industrialised countries of the northern hemisphere and the poorer, more agriculturally based countries of the southern hemisphere. In effect this meant that the category of 'developing' countries would include the whole of Africa, Latin America, the Caribbean and most of Asia excluding Australia, New Zealand and Japan, while 'developed' would include North America, Europe, the countries of the former Soviet Union and Japan, Australia and New Zealand. Built into this twofold categorisation of international development was also the notion that the richer nations had a responsibility to help poorer, low-income countries to develop.

However, over time, attempts to measure development have become increasingly more diverse and sophisticated, with a whole range of different social indicators such as health, education, gender, well-being and environmental protection being added. While attempts to classify states as 'developed' or 'developing' are fraught with difficulty and controversy, perhaps the most authoritative international statement on issues surrounding human development is the annual publication of the United Nations Development Programme (UNDP), entitled the *Human Development Report*. This is an attempt to move away from sole reliance on economic indicators of development to 'ones that put people at the centre', defining human development as:

> the expansion of people's freedoms to live long, healthy and
> creative live; to advance other goals they have reason to value;
> to engage actively in shaping development equitably and
> sustainably on a shared planet. People are both the
> beneficiaries and the drivers of human development, as
> individuals and as groups. (UNDP, 2010, p. 2)

The *Human Development Report* ranks all the countries of the world from 1 to 187 according to a wide range of variables, but special emphasis is laid on what the UNDP terms the 'Human Development Index'. This is a composite index of what it considers to be the three key indicators of human development. These are life expectancy at birth, years of enrolment in schooling and gross national income per capita. In 2012, for example, Norway topped the index and Niger was bottom (UNDP, 2013). However, the rate at which developing countries have improved in terms of wealth, health and education has varied considerably, with some countries improving rapidly and others much more slowly. In terms of health, for example, some countries have gone backwards – in 2010 the UNDP noted a reversal in the level of health of the population in 19 countries and in nine of these, due primarily to HIV/AIDS, life expectancy was below 1970 levels (UNDP, 2010, p. 3). Moreover, it is important to remember that in terms of wealth and social welfare, the gap between those countries at the top of the HDI and those at the bottom remains very large indeed despite (at the time of writing) 68 years having elapsed since the end of the Second World War, and that there is often – in fact usually – significant inequality within countries as well. The UNDP summed up the situation as follows:

> In sum, we see great advances, but changes over the past few
> decades have by no means been wholly positive. Some
> countries have suffered serious setbacks – particularly in
> health – sometimes erasing in a few years the gains of several

decades. Economic growth has been extremely unequal – both in countries experiencing fast growth and in groups benefitting from national progress. And the gaps in human development across the world, while narrowing, remain huge. (UNDP, 2010, p. 4)

More graphically, Collier, in *The Bottom Billion*, comments that

For forty years the development challenge has been a rich world of one billion people facing a poor world of five billion people ... Most of the five billion, about 80%, live in countries that are indeed developing at an amazing speed. The real challenge of development is that there is a group of countries at the bottom that are falling behind and often falling apart. The countries at the bottom coexist with the twenty-first century but their reality is the fourteenth century: civil war, plague, ignorance. They are concentrated in Africa and Central Asia, with a scattering elsewhere ... We must learn to turn the familiar numbers upside down: a total of five billion people who are already prosperous, or at least on track to be so, and one billion who are stuck at the bottom. (Collier, 2007, p. 3)

In terms of the subject of the present book, it is important to note here in relation to the widely used UNDP's Human Development Index that while greater longevity and higher wealth may be more direct or obvious goals of development, enrolment in formal education is more of an indirect means to an end. Simply putting more young people into school is not in itself necessarily beneficial to society. It is the assumed results or benefits of schooling which explain why this indicator is included in the HDI. This will be further discussed below, both in this chapter and throughout the book. At this point it is simply necessary to caution against any automatic assumption that education directly or necessarily leads to benefits for individuals and societies in any straightforward manner. Indeed, as we shall see, the opposite is often the case. Even the *Human Development Report* notes that such relationships are problematic: 'One of the surprising results of human development research in recent years ... is the lack of significant correlation between economic growth and improvements in health and education' (UNDP, 2010, p. 4).

However, the UNDP Human Development reports, since their inception in 1990, have increasingly tried to broaden the range of indicators they use to measure development to include more social, political and environmental ones in line with their emphasis on human capabilities and also to refine the indicators that they use. For example, in the twentieth report (UNDP, 2010), three new indices were included – the Inequality-adjusted Human Development Index, the Gender Inequality Index and the Multidimensional Poverty Index. The first takes into account the level of inequality in a society – the extent to which any improvement in the HDI is shared equally or not. In 2012, for example, America was third in the HDI ranking but only sixteenth in the inequality-adjusted ranking (UNDP, 2013). The Gender Inequality Index does the same but specifically takes into account the extent to which women and girls share equally, or not, in improvements in human development. The multidimensional measure of poverty takes into account the different, multiple deprivations of poverty such as access to education and health, rather than just money-based measures. Other numerical indices used by the UNDP to rank countries globally include, for example, empowerment (levels of human rights and democracy), sustainability (nature of energy supply and consumption, access to water and sanitation and levels of pollution), human security (refugees, war fatalities and undernourishment), perceptions of individual well-being and happiness (e.g. the extent to which people feel they have a purposeful life, are treated with respect and have a social support network), civic and community well-being (crime and safety, affordable housing, healthcare, air and water quality).

Nor is the UNDP the only body to construct indices of development. The New Economics Foundation has constructed what it terms the 'Happy Planet Index' where countries are ranked by life satisfaction, life expectancy and ecological footprint. On this index Costa Rica (sixty-ninth in the UNDP's Human Development Index for 2011) comes top (http://www.happyplanetindex.org). Bhutan even has its own Gross Happiness Index which presents an alternative model of human development rooted in Buddhist philosophy (Kendall, 2009, p. 419). Freedom House (www.freedomhouse.org) rates all countries in the world as 'free', 'partly free' and 'not free' and records the direction in which they seem to be moving. In 2012, for example, many were moving in what they would perceive as a negative direction from free to partly free to not free.

Nevertheless, classification of countries as 'developed', 'less developed' or 'developing' and as being situated in the 'North' or 'South' remains difficult and by no means clear cut, and no terms are completely satisfactory. This is partly because ranking and categorising is inevitably to some extent subjective – change the indicator(s) regarded as important and you change the ranking. It is also problematic because significant change can occur quite rapidly so that some countries, such as Singapore, Brunei or South Korea, originally regarded as 'developing', have now become 'developed'. Some 'developed' countries (Japan, New Zealand and Australia, for example), are located geographically in the South, which is why two terms that are now increasingly used are the 'Global South' (developing countries geographically in the South) and the 'Global North' (developed countries geographically in the North and South). Moreover:

> All of these binary labels, in fact, assume and fix the focus of developmentalist debates on states at a time when divisions between rich and poor, 'North' and 'South' are as great or greater within countries as across them, thus concealing the issue of how inequality and poverty affect 'Northern' geographical spaces as well as 'Southern', and how people, groups, and development-like resources flow within and across state boundaries. (Kendall, 2009, p. 421)

Perhaps reflecting this problem of a binary division between 'developed' and 'developing', the UNDP now both ranks countries and classifies them into four groups – very high, high, medium and low human development (UNDP, 2011).

There are other problems with the notion of 'development'. One is the assumption that there is a clear and single path of development upon which all people and states must embark to enhance their well-being and that this path must be identical to the historical experience of the 'developed' or industrialised countries. Also, by using the labels 'developed' and 'less developed', unequal power and authority are firmly established in global economic and political relationships. Through unequal trade and aid relationships, which often benefit the richer, donor countries as much the poorer, recipient ones, there is also a form of Western cultural homogenisation ('Coca Colonisation') of the world. Traditional forms of development have also been criticised for the environmental destruction that they have brought in their path. Such criticisms of development have even gone beyond debates about alternative interpretations of development to a rejection of the very notion of development because of in-built notions of neo-colonialism by the richer nations: 'it is not the failure of development which has to be feared, but its success' (Sachs, 1992, p. 3). Such 'post' or 'anti' development theories have in turn been criticised for their lack of alternatives to development models and their failure to distinguish between the many different contemporary development discourses (see, for example, Kiely 1999; Pieterse, 2000; Kothari & Minogue, 2002; Rist, 2008).

While recognising these difficulties, the notion of development clearly persists and remains powerful in contemporary political and academic debates. In this book we are primarily concerned with countries below the top fifty in the UNDP's Human Development Index, i.e. generally not those countries that are ranked as 'Very High Human Development' but mainly with those countries classified as Medium and Low Human Development and in the lower reaches of the High Human Development category (UNDP, 2010, pp. 148-151). This corresponds closely with, for example, Smith's classification of about 100 states in Africa, Asia, the Middle East, Latin America and the Caribbean with a combined population of over 4.8 billion, accounting for 75% of the world's total and nearly 58% of the world's land area (Smith, 2009, p. 1).

Debates about the nature of development are controversial because they are intimately connected with different sets of ideas or theories about how development takes place or, perhaps more accurately, how it ought to take place. Although such theories purport to 'explain' how development takes place, they do so primarily either from a particular emphasis or priority (e.g. economic development rather than social or political development) or from a preferred ideological model such as capitalism, socialism, a particular religious belief or from a set of 'green' assumptions about sustainable development. It is often difficult to separate 'is' and 'ought' questions in discussions of development, since how it actually takes place cannot easily be separated from an understanding of its ultimate goal – the nature of a 'developed' society – and this is a matter of opinion, preference, judgement and power rather than fact.

The Role of Education in Development

As already noted, one key social institution believed to make a significant and positive difference in the way societies and individuals behave and develop is education. Formal education has been linked to different theories and practices of development because schools help to create the citizens and workforce of the future and therefore to define the direction of development. However, it is important to note that some form of indigenous education has always taken place in all societies in the sense of passing on, for example, economic practices, cultural expectations and rituals, food preparation, laws and health practices, whether learning by example or from written sources or from stories, songs, folklore, proverbs, dances or myths. Often this was a form of learning integrated into normal daily social practices – the young would observe, listen, copy and practise what they saw around them in their family, village or town and sometime improve upon on it (Aikman and May, 2003; Omolewa, 2007). However, this differs from the systems of formal education that were introduced through colonialism and then copied worldwide, with their separate institution of the school with its own school building and with specialist teachers and a planned curriculum that went beyond traditional knowledge.

Though there are many other forms and arenas for education (Meighan & Harber, 2007), it is this model of formal education, often with its roots in colonialism, that is the model of formal education often so heartily endorsed as one of the keys to development. Kendall (2009) argues that there is a near-hegemonic, bureaucratic model of formal, Western-style and state-provided schooling that defines and constitutes 'education' for development in the twenty-first century – as sanctioned at the global Education for All conferences at Jomtien and Dakar and as inscribed in the United Nations' (UN) Millennium Development Goals. The essential features of this taken-for-granted model of modern education are that children learn primarily from adults about high-stakes academic subjects, on a fixed schedule, in an indoor setting that includes particular features (desks, chairs, chalkboards, written teaching and learning materials). Moreover, there is an imagined linear development model, from informal, family-provided education concerning daily tasks and survival skills to 'modern' schooling systems:

> The international development model of education posits that mass, state-sponsored schooling is: (1) central to the creation of a 'modern' nation-state; (2) central to the development of 'modern' workers and families; and, thus (3) central to a state's 'modern' economic growth and international acceptance. The general conceptualisation of education and development has received critical attention since its inception, but has yet to be significantly challenged. (Kendall, 2009, p. 422)

Above are three examples of typical general statements about the assumed positive relationships between education and development. In 2006 the Center for Global Development in Washington, USA (www.cgdev.org) published the following statement in a document entitled 'Education and the Developing World':

> All children around the world have the right to an education. Investing in education is not just the right thing to do, it's the smart thing to do. Why? Because education gives people the skills they need to help themselves out of poverty and into prosperity.
>
> Better health: with education people are far better able to prevent disease and to use health services effectively. For example, young people who have completed primary education are less than half as likely to contract HIV as those who have little or no schooling.
>
> Higher wages and economic growth: in many poor countries, people with just one additional year of schooling earn 10% higher wages. These earnings in turn contribute to national economic growth. No country has ever achieved continuous and rapid growth without reaching an adult literacy rate of at least 40%.
>
> Democracy and political stability: education supports the growth of civil society, democracy and political stability

allowing people to know their rights and acquire the skills and knowledge necessary to exercise them.

The World Bank has also, for example, stated that

The expansion of educational opportunity, which can promote income equality and growth, is a win-win strategy that in most societies is far easier to implement than the redistribution of other assets such as land or capital. In short, education is one of the most powerful instruments known for reducing poverty and inequality and for laying the basis for sustained economic growth, sound governance and effective institutions. (Cited in Mundy, 2006, p. 33)

Most recently Colclough (2012, p. 1) wrote in relation to education and development:

Most people believe that education brings important benefits ... those with more education have better job prospects. They tend to have higher earnings from work and better standards of living. Education is also seen to help people participate in society and control their environment more easily, brining benefits for their health, nutrition and family life.

Thus, it is regularly and often assumed that enrolment in formal education is necessarily and inherently a 'good thing' for development, that it is a key indicator of development and that what happens inside schools and higher education is automatically of benefit to both individuals and society. This assumption is shared, most of the time, by national governments, global institutions like the World Bank and international aid agencies. It is why the achievement of universal primary education and gender equality in education are goals number 2 and 3 of the UN's Millennium Development Goals. This emphasis is reflected in the enormous global expenditure on formal education and the major conference held at Jomtien, Thailand in 1990 when most governments of the world met to plan how they would provide access to universal primary education for all children by the year 2000 – followed by a similar enormous conference held in Dakar, Senegal in 2000 where they met again to explain why they hadn't achieved their targets for 2000 but would do so by 2015.

Yet, despite such widespread faith and optimism, we need to be cautious about the assumed automatic benefits of formal education for development. As Crossley and Tikly note, 'many existing education systems still bear the hallmarks of the colonial encounter in that they remain elitist, lack relevance to local realities and are often at variance with indigenous knowledge systems' (2004, p. 149).

The Local and the Global: globalisation, culture and context

In this book we explore some of the major generalised ideas and theories about education and development. However, two key themes of the book that are made more explicit here are the importance of local culture and context in discussions of education and development on the one hand, and the importance of global patterns and trends affecting all countries and places on the other. This section begins with a discussion of globalisation and education before going on to discuss the importance of local context and culture in understanding education and development.

Though slightly ambiguous, globalisation is the term that is used to describe the increasing interconnectedness of the world. It is the idea that in many ways the world is now so interrelated and intertwined that it is becoming, or has become, one global economic, social and political system so that individual nation-states have decreased in importance (though not necessarily disappeared). Some even argue that this process began as early as the 1500s, as from then the internationalisation of trade and commerce was well under way (Robertson et al, 2007, p. 10) In fact, it might be more accurate to speak of *globalisations* in that globalisation has many strands:

- the economic – the spread of free-market, neoliberal or capitalist economic policies and trading patterns to most parts of the globe (this is discussed in more detail in chapter 7);
- the political – the spread of ideas of democracy and human rights to most parts of the globe (this is discussed in more detail in chapter 6);
- the increasing awareness of the ecological or environmental interconnectedness of the world – that environmental occurrences in one part of the world affect other parts and that the world is one large ecosystem (this is discussed in more detail in chapter 8);
- the actual, and immediate, interconnectedness of the world via information technologies such as the Internet, email, texting, Skype, mobile phones and 24-hour television news covering the globe – and the widespread use of the English language in using these forms of communication;
- the enormous increase in air travel and tourism so that the world becomes a smaller place geographically;
- the increase in global labour markets so that there is large, international-scale migration of labour between countries in search of work and a better standard of living, often, though not always, from poorer to richer nations;
- the power of transnational business corporations which operate globally across national frontiers and which can move physical and financial capital at will;

- the spread of common cultural patterns of consumption and behaviour as a result of the above – in terms of, for example, music, dress, food and films;
- the existence of 'global' governance through bodies such as the United Nations, the World Bank, the International Monetary Fund, the World Trade Organisation, the General Agreement on Trade in Services and regional bodies such as the European Union, the Organisation of American States, the Arab League and the African Union.

There are those on one end of a continuum who regard globalisation as an inevitable, consensual, mutual and even beneficial process stemming from the sort of factors outlined above while others on the other end of the continuum see this as an essentially unequal process of the more powerful countries of the industrialised 'North' forcing or imposing economic, political and social beliefs and behaviours on to the less powerful and less developed countries of the 'South' in their own interests (see, for example, Spring [2008] on four major interpretations of globalisation along this continuum).

What is the relationship between globalisation and education? First, there is the increasing importance of the 'knowledge economy' globally. This is the argument that in the twenty-first century the most important factors of production in a developed or rapidly developing economy are the skills and knowledge of people and constantly keeping them up to date. A study of successful engagement with the global economy in China, India, Sri Lanka and Kenya (defined as export-led growth with income equality and peace) found that education is an important factor in this success (Green et al, 2007). Five educational policies seemed to be common across the four countries in achieving successful global economic engagement:

1. high-quality mass education;
2. planned expansion of secondary, technical and higher education to create the skills necessary for sustained economic growth;
3. the development of communication skills that facilitate international economic transactions;
4. the equitable expansion of education to enhance its contribution to social equality; and
5. the awareness of the potential of schooling to promote both positive and negative contributions to national unity and social cohesion.

Second, as discussed above, formal education – school – is itself a global phenomenon. Schools exist in similar shape and form to each other in most countries of the world. Whether this is a universally beneficial global phenomenon or whether this is the product of a model spread essentially through the power of colonialism to serve certain purposes is discussed elsewhere in this book. Third, targets for education are increasingly set at a global level – for example, the UN's Education for All targets and their monitoring by UNESCO. Fourth, the performance of education systems is increasingly being measured and compared in studies such as PISA (the Programme for International Student Assessment), TIMSS (Trends in International Mathematics and Science Study) and PIRLS (Progress in International Reading Literacy Studies). Fifth, even within education systems there are increasingly common forms of governance globally – for example, decentralisation, school-based management, school choice and competition and an increasing role for both private education and fees paid by users (Sayed, 2010). This is partly the result of what is known as 'policy borrowing' or 'policy transfer' whereby countries import or copy, perhaps with some local adaptations, educational policies that have originated elsewhere (Phillips & Ochs, 2003; Rappleye, 2012). For example, Schweisfurth (2006) has shown how educational policies in post-genocide Rwanda have been influenced by dependence on aid from Britain, the exposure of Rwandan exiles to education in other, English-speaking, parts of Africa and the comparative field of genocide studies.

Spring (2008, pp. 348-352) adds two further ways that education is part of globalisation. First, he notes that some globalisation theorists argue that non-governmental and intergovernmental organisations (NGOs and IGOs) are key to creating a world culture in such areas as human rights education, environmental education and women's rights to and in education. Second, and as a result of historical imperialism, the study of the English language is part of a standardised global curriculum – by the mid 1980s, for example, 72% of the world's secondary schools taught English (Meyer et al, 1992 cited in Spring, 2008).

However, while there are increasingly global or supranational relationships affecting education everywhere, it is also important to remember that it is human beings who are involved in development – whether they are actively involved in development in their own countries, recipients of development aid or donors of aid. All these people bring with them their own cultures and ways of seeing and understanding the world. Everybody carries some cultural traits based on their shared customs, language, beliefs and assumptions about the world and how it functions. As Stephens (2007, p. 33) puts it in his detailed study of education, culture and development:

> at the basic level of one nation interacting with another,
> cultural factors play a fundamental part. Development, it is
> suggested, is therefore not 'culture-free' but is a process by
> which individuals rooted in one cultural tradition interact
> with individuals and agencies from another.

Therefore the context of development is important – where it is happening, development by whom and to whom. For development theories and policies to be useful and to work there is a need to understand how people actually behave in a specific context as well as providing generalised understandings, 'solutions' or 'answers' to the particular issue or problem. Harber and Davies (1997), for example, argue for the need to understand the specific contexts of developing countries in relation to the generalised statements of literature stemming from Western, industrialised nations about the nature and characteristics of school effectiveness and school management (Harber & Davies, 1997). Others, such as Bray (1992) and Crossley and Holmes (1999), argue that scale matters in that educational planning and development in the context of small states (defined by population rather than just area) is inherently different from that of larger states. This is because of factors such as economic vulnerability, dependency, isolation and administrative costs, as well as the fact that people tend to know each other better. Within developing countries, if a government, international organisation or NGO wishes to introduce an AIDS or health education programme in a particular country or region of a country, then it is important to understand the local sexual and health beliefs and practices of the population first if the project is to work. Indeed, a mismatch between the assumptions and policies of projects and the cultural beliefs and practices of local people often results in failure. Stephens (2007) is particularly critical of the dominance of economic models and theories in development in this regard both in terms of their one-size-fits-all application to developing countries and an insufficient awareness of both the nature of the local culture and the Western cultural assumptions behind many funded development projects. Generalised theories of, and debates about, the roles of education in development are important but so is an appreciation of the great variety of ways such roles play out in the wide range of different contexts and cultures that constitute 'developing countries'.

Conclusion

This book sets out to critically discuss some of the main themes and assumptions concerning the relationships between formal education and development that have been set out in this chapter. It begins by asking what we know about the nature of education and development in relation to access to, the quality of and outcomes from education in developing countries, including the crucial question of whether education can indeed help to reduce poverty. It then examines some of the key positive theories, and evidence underlying them, purporting to explain the relationships between education and development – that education is a form of human capital investment for all, leading to economic growth, that education helps to create a more 'modern' society, and that it contributes to political democratisation. Conversely, it also looks at theories and evidence suggesting that education does not provide equal opportunities for all but actively contributes to inequality and the continuing dependency of developing countries on their former colonisers and that education also socialises as much towards authoritarianism and violence in developing countries as it does to peace and democracy. It then explores ideological contexts for education – what are the purposes and practices of education when there is a wider context of how a particular country ought to develop? Can we talk of capitalist and socialist education systems? Is there a genuine green alternative? How does education function if there is a single religious goal for a country or educational institution? Finally, it discusses some of the key issues facing education in developing countries: gender equality; the role of international aid; health and HIV/AIDS; education in conflict and post-conflict societies; the role of private education; vocational education and employment; corruption; education following disasters and emergencies and the role and significance of literacy and language.

References

Aikman, S. & May, S. (Eds) (2003) *Comparative Education* 39(2), Special Issue on indigenous education.

Bray, M. (1992) *Educational Planning in Small Countries*. Paris: UNESCO.

Center for Global Development (2006) Education and the Developing World. Washington, DC: Center for Global Development. http://www.cgdev.org/publication/education-and-developing-world

Colclough, C. (2012) *Education Outcomes and Poverty: a reassessment*. London: Routledge.

Collier, P. (2007) *The Bottom Billion*. Oxford: Oxford University Press.

Crossley, M. & Holmes, K. (1999) *Educational Development in the Small States of the Commonwealth: retrospect and prospect*. London: Commonwealth Secretariat.

Crossley, M. & Tikly, L. (2004) Postcolonial Perspectives and Comparative and International Research in Education: a critical introduction, *Comparative Education*, 40(2), 147-156.

Fägerlind, I. & Saha, L. (1989) *Education and National Development: a comparative perspective*. Oxford: Pergamon.

Green, A., Little, A., Kamat, S.G., Oketch, M. & Vickers, E. (2007) *Education and Development in a Global Era: strategies for 'successful globalisation'*. London: Department for International Development.

Harber, C. & Davies, L. (1997) *School Management and School Effectiveness in Developing Countries*. London: Cassell.

Haynes, J. (Ed.) (2008) *Development Studies: a short introduction*. Cambridge: Polity Press.

Kendall, N. (2009) International Development Education, in R. Cowen & M. Kazamias (Eds) *International Handbook of Comparative Education*. London: Springer.

Kiely, R. (1999) The Last Refuge of the Noble Savage? A Critical Assessment of Post-development Theory, *European Journal of Development Research*, 11(1), 30-55.

Kothari, U. & Minogue, M. (2002) *Development Theory and Practice*. Basingstoke: Palgrave.

Meighan, R. & Harber, C. (2007) *A Sociology of Educating*. London: Continuum.

Mundy, K. (2006) Education for All and the New Development Compact, *Review of Education*, 52(1), 23-48.

Omolewa, M. (2007) Traditional African Modes of Education: their relevance in the modern world, *International Review of Education*, 53(5-6), 593-612.

Phillips, D. & Ochs, K. (2003) Processes of Policy Borrowing in Education: some explanatory analytical devices, *Comparative Education*, 39(4), 451-461.

Pieterse, J.N. (2000) After Post-development, *Third World Quarterly*, 21(2), 175-191.

Pieterse, J.N. (2010) *Development Theory*, 2nd edn. London: Sage.

Rappleye, J. (2012) *Educational Policy Transfer in an Era of Globalization: theory–history–comparison*. Frankfurt-am-Main: Peter Lang.

Rist, G. (2008) *The History of Development from Western Origins to Global Faith*. London: Zed Books.

Robertson, S., Novelli, M., Dale, R. Dachi, H. & Ndibelema, A. (2007) *Globalisation, Education and Development: ideas, actors and dynamics*. London: Department for International Development.

Sachs, W. (Ed.) (1992) *The Development Dictionary*. London: Zed Books.

Sayed, Y. (2010) Globalisation, Educational Governance and Decentralisation: promoting equity, increasing participation and enhancing quality, *Compare*, 40(1), 59-62.

Schweisfurth, M. (2006) Global and Cross-national Influences on Education in Post-genocide Rwanda, *Oxford Review of Education*, 32(5), 697-709.

Smith, B.C. (2009) *Understanding Third World Politics: theories of political change and development*. Basingstoke: Palgrave Macmillan.

Spring, J. (2008) Research on Globalisation and Education, *Review of Educational Research*, 78(2), 330-363.

Stephens, D. (2007) *Culture in Education and Development: principles, practices and policy*. Oxford: Symposium Books.

United Nations Development Programme (UNDP) (2010) *Human Development Report*. Basingstoke: Palgrave Macmillan.

United Nations Development Programme (UNDP) (2011) *Human Development Report*. Basingstoke: Palgrave Macmillan.

United Nations Development Programme (UNDP) (2013) *Human Development Report*. Basingstoke: Palgrave Macmillan.

Further Reading

Chisholm, L., Bloch, G. & Fleisch, B. (2008) *Education, Growth, Aid and Development: towards Education for All*. Hong Kong: Comparative Education Research Centre, University of Hong Kong.

Coulby, D. & Zambeta, E. (2005) *World Yearbook of Education 2005. Globalization and Nationalism in Education*. London: RoutledgeFalmer.

Cowen, R. & Kazamias, A. (2009) *International Handbook of Comparative Education,* vols 1 and 2. Dordrecht: Springer.

Little, A. (2000) Development Studies and Comparative Education: context, content, comparison and contributors, *Comparative Education*, 36(3), 279-296.

Peet, R. & Hardwick, E. (2009) *Theories of Development*, 2nd edn. New York: Guilford Press.

Phillips, D. & Schweisfurth, M. (2007) *Comparative and International Education* (particularly chapter 4). London: Continuum.

Sen, A. (1999) *Development as Freedom*. Oxford: Oxford University Press.

Shields, R. (2013) *Globalisation and International Education*. London: Bloomsbury.

UNESCO. Annual EFA Global Monitoring Reports.

Discussion and Activities

1. What criteria would you use in judging whether a country is 'developed' or 'less developed'? Do you agree with these terms or are there better terms?

2. In what ways do you think that education might contribute to development – or not?

3. Do you feel you live in a globalised world? Explain why this is or isn't the case.

4. If you are working or living in a developing (or any other) country, why is it important to know something about local context and culture?

CHAPTER 2

The Nature of Formal Education in Developing Countries: access, quality, outcomes and inequality

This chapter sets out to provide a relatively concise, and therefore inevitably selective, overview of the nature of formal education in developing countries and, in particular, what differentiates it from more 'developed' or richer countries. It contains a review of some of the evidence on, and factors affecting, access to education, the quality of education, the outcomes from education and educational inequalities in developing countries. The purpose is to review some of the evidence, ideas and sources of information so that later discussion of theories and issues of education and development is given a more informed basis and is grounded in educational realities in developing countries. Given the large amount of literature on these aspects of education in developing countries, examples of further reading are provided for each of the four main areas covered in addition to the references in the text.

Access to Education

> Access to education for all children in low-income countries is far from being achieved in many low-income countries. (Lewin & Little, 2011, p. 333)

The presumed benefits of formal education described in chapter 1 have meant that the right to education has long been recognised as a universal human right. Article 26 of the United Nations Universal Declaration of Human Rights (1948) said that everyone has the right to education and that it should be free, at least in the elementary and fundamental stages. The United Nations Convention on the Rights of the Child (1989) further stated that all children have the right to a primary education, that it should be free and that they should be eligible to go to secondary school. Lack of access to education, and issues of retention, drop-out and irregular attendance, are of particular significance in developing countries. Two major global conferences – one at Jomtien, Thailand in 1990 and the second at Dakar, Senegal in 2000 have committed all governments to achieving universal primary education, and the United Nations Millennium Development Goals further included a commitment to try to achieve primary education for all by 2015, including equality for boys and girls.

Each year UNESCO publishes an Education for All Global (EFA) Monitoring Report which summarises progress towards achieving universal primary education. In 2012 the UNESCO EFA Global Monitoring Report (UNESCO, 2012, p. 3) summarised progress to date. The good news is that since 1999 the number of primary-age children out of school fell from 108 million to 61 million. The bad news was that three-quarters of this reduction was achieved between 1999 and 2004, and between 2008 and 2010 progress stalled altogether. Between 1999 and 2008 the number of out-of-school children in South and West Asia fell by 26 million whereas in sub-Saharan Africa it fell by only 13 million. Between 2008 and 2010, the number of out-of-school children increased by 1.6 million in sub-Saharan Africa and decreased by 0.6 million in South and West Asia. Sub-Saharan Africa now accounts for half of the world's out-of-school children. Consequently, 'On current trends, the goal of universal primary education will be missed by a large margin' (UNESCO, 2012, p. 3). Gender parity, in terms of access, has improved significantly but there are still many countries where gender parity in education may not be achieved by 2015. This is further discussed in chapter 10. Dropping out from school before completing the full primary cycle is also a problem – in sub-Saharan Africa 10 million children drop out of primary school every year (UNESCO, 2011, p. 1). Indeed, Lewin and Little (2011, p. 333) add that if the definition of access is expanded to regular attendance at least 80% of the time, progression at an appropriate age with no child more than two years over age and achievement consistent with national attainment targets and within two years of the norm for the grade level, then perhaps as many as another 300 million children in developing countries are 'silently excluded' from school.

There are many factors hampering universal access to primary schooling and influencing drop-out and lack of regular attendance in developing countries, many of which are discussed in literature cited here and elsewhere in the book. Some of these are factors outside of school and some inside school:

- Poverty – families cannot afford to send their children to school because they cannot afford the fees; they cannot afford the other indirect costs of schooling such as uniforms, books, writing implements and travel costs; they cannot spare the household and agricultural labour of the children.
- Governments in developing countries do not have sufficient money to help to pay for education for all. This situation has been exacerbated by the global financial crisis and cuts in aid budgets in

donor countries. UNESCO (2011, p. 2) points out that 'Although low income countries have increased their share of national income spent on education from 2.9% to 3.8% since 1999, some regions and countries have continued to neglect education. Central Asia and South and West Asia invest the least in education'.

- The academic content of schooling is not seen as relevant to local needs and priorities, especially in a predominantly agricultural and rural area. Families and communities do not see education as a realistically viable route out of poverty, especially when there are few 'modern' sector jobs available locally and there are high rates of unemployment amongst educated young people

- Children are reluctant to attend school, and their families are reluctant to send them, because at school they experience harshness and violence from teachers. This is not uncommon in formal education systems globally and is certainly a feature of schools in developing countries where, for example, corporal punishment is still widely used.

- Access of females to formal education can be reduced by parental attitudes to schooling, i.e. seeing it as a poor investment of time and money for girls. Reluctance of girls to go to schools, or greater inclination to drop out, may also be caused by there not being separate toilet facilities for girls and boys or by their experiencing sexual harassment from male students and teachers. Moreover, girls who are pregnant can drop out of school because parents withdraw them, or schools are not prepared to continue to educate them. Ensuing childcare responsibilities may then affect the possibilities for attendance.

- There is no school within reasonable travelling/walking distance. In rural areas of developing countries the transport system is often poor and families do not own their own means of transport. Sometimes the distances are too far for access and sometimes young children have to walk considerable distances to and from school, thereby presenting an obstacle to more regular attendance.

- Armed conflict can close schools and make it dangerous to try to attend. From 1998 to 2008 thirty-five countries experienced armed conflict, of which thirty were low-income and middle-income countries. The average duration of violent conflict in low-income countries was 12 years. In conflict-affected poor regions, 28 million children of primary age are out of school – 2% of the world total (UNESCO, 2011, p. 2).

- Nomads and pastoralists can find it particularly difficult to access formal schooling as they tend to live in remote areas, with their children heavily involved in looking after cattle, and with ways of life that involve moving long distances. In Ethiopia, Kenya and

Uganda, for example, pastoralist groups are at the bottom of the distribution of educational opportunity (UNESCO, 2010, p. 143).

- Illness, for example from malaria or HIV/AIDS, can affect the attendance of children both by affecting them directly, and by the need to care for parents or other relatives. In eight countries of southern Africa, for example, the average prevalence rate of HIV/AIDS among young people aged 15-24 in 2009 was 14.3% (Harber, 2013, p. 25).
- Hunger and malnutrition can mean that children are unable to concentrate and benefit from schooling even if they attend school. In developing countries 195 million children under 5 – one in three – experience malnutrition (UNESCO, 2011, p. 1). School feeding programmes, i.e. providing free food for children who are hungry, have been introduced in a number of countries in order to try to improve attendance.
- Teaching and the quality of education provided can be of such poor quality that children learn very little. UNESCO (2011, p. 1) put it that 'The quality of education remains very low in many countries. Millions of children are emerging from primary school with reading, writing and arithmetic skills far below expected levels'. This therefore discourages parents from sending their children to school, especially given the direct and indirect costs of schooling referred to above.
- Low levels of transition from primary to secondary school – in many developing countries, for both financial reasons and reasons of political priorities, considerably less that 100% of children go on from primary to secondary school. For example, in 2007 the median figure for sub-Saharan Africa was 64%, for South and West Asia 86% and for Latin America and the Caribbean 94% (UNESCO, 2011, p. 324). However, within these median figures it is important to note that in some countries the figure is well under 50%. Yet, 'No country with low transition rates to secondary has ever universalised completion of primary school, nor did they ever achieve gender equality in enrolments. Widely available secondary schooling is necessary in order to produce enough graduates willing and able to become primary teachers' (Lewin & Little, 2011, p. 333).
- Disability can result in exclusion from school, either because of practical problems of access and functioning or because of a social stigma. This is further discussed in chapter 3.

Case Studies

At the end of this chapter is a list of suggested further reading on access to education in developing countries. However, in order to add some contextual flavour and detail to the above broad outline of factors inhibiting access to schooling, this chapter describes two research-based case studies. Apart from describing the complexities of access in a number of actual national settings, they also tend to re-emphasise an important point made in chapter – that, despite global efforts to achieve education for all, it cannot be automatically assumed that enrolment in school is a good thing for all children all of the time.

South-west China

Wu (2012) notes the huge emphasis given to formal education in China, both by government and by individuals, with the achievement of a 99% literacy rate. However, within this broader context not everybody is convinced about the importance of education. In South-west China in the rural ethnic Miao and Dong areas, over 30% of middle-school students drop out, often with tacit parental consent, even when the law stipulates that basic education is free and compulsory and when, officially, education is seen as a key route out of poverty and important for national economic growth. Carrying out participant observation and informal interviews, Wu found that one pupil had stopped going to school and started selling vegetables instead. The pupil's father said that they couldn't afford to have their child in school and that there were jobs to be done at home. The father said that even college graduates had a hard time finding jobs, let alone children, in his remote mountain village. Moreover, the teaching in schools was poor and the parents did not have the social connections to get their children jobs. Even if children stayed on at school the economic reality of the area was that they would end up working in a factory, so school was a waste of time and money – and besides, schooling made children lazy and incapable of farm work. Wu comments that this case echoed numerous cases where mediocre schooling did not justify either the monetary investment or time investment (often conflicting with significant life events such as marriage). Other negative factors reducing attendance at school were education as confinement, boredom and a recurring sense of failure, a difficult and uninteresting curriculum and repetitive drilling for tests. Wu argues that in this rural and poor context school drop-out can in fact be a way to achieve the social and economic self-reliance that schooling fails to bring – it is a rational act in response to economic and social dilemmas and a pragmatic critique of the limit-points of schooling.

Bangladesh and Malawi

The second case study makes another important point – that even when gender parity is achieved in terms of basic entry to formal schooling, this does not necessarily mean equity in access to the nature of the education provided. Chisamya et al (2012) studied education in Bangladesh and

Malawi where, even though rapid progress has been made in terms of gender parity in access to schooling, this has taken place in wider societies that continue to be marked by gender inequalities. In both countries, despite evidence of girls' equal academic capacity in terms of exams and grades, their schooling was marked by consistent discrimination from schools, families and communities. In Bangladesh, girls, parents and community members held more negative views about girls' rights compared to boys' to attend schools and to have a voice in family decisions about schooling. In response to the overall poor quality of schooling in Bangladesh a shadow education system of private tutoring has emerged, but families are more prepared to invest in this for boys than girls. Similarly, the resources provided to do schoolwork at home were greater for boys than girls. It was seen as more important that girls learn to cook, sew, clean and farm in line with what was perceived as their future roles. In Malawi, older female pupils received the message that they were no longer good students once they were physically mature, including being mocked if they tried to return to school after dropping out for marriage or pregnancy. Boys received more punishment and were treated more harshly than girls because male teachers wanted to engage in sexual relationships with the girls and thus treated them better. If girls did well, it was therefore seen as a result of sexual favours. Teachers made degrading comments to female students and girls' schooling was more disrupted by household chores. Education of females was seen by parents as a waste of money as the benefits would accrue to the husband, not the parents. Girls and women in Bangladesh were most concerned about sexual and/or domestic violence as this was widespread in schools and communities.

The Quality of Education

Getting young people into school is one thing, but what, then, is their experience once they are there? There is little point in children going to school unless it is of sufficient quality for them to benefit in some way. Indeed, simply getting more children into school in developing countries without actually increasing the number of school buildings has created a situation in some countries where schools have to operate a 'double shift' system, i.e. where some pupils attend in the morning and some in the afternoon. This in itself has raised concerns over the quality of education provided (Bray, 2008).

We can make judgements about the quality of education by the degree to which it achieves its desired outcomes, e.g. are children sufficiently literate or numerate as a result of schooling, or to what extent do young people pass examinations in the proportions that they would be expected to do so? We shall examine the outcomes of schooling more closely in the next section, but suffice it to say at present that there remain significant problems in achieving successful educational outcomes in many developing countries. However, here it is important to note that it is very difficult to get a clear definition of quality because people do not necessarily agree on what the desired outcomes of schooling should be, or what the weighting of, or priorities between, different outcomes should be. In the end, notions of 'quality' are ideological and depend to a certain extent on the values of the beholder. For example, a well-resourced and efficiently and professionally organised but authoritarian school where pupils are successful in traditional examinations, but have very little say, or participation, might be regarded as good quality by some but poor quality by an observer who favoured more democratic processes and outcomes in education.

Tikly and Barrett (2013), for example, distinguish between three overlapping approaches to quality which they term human capital, human rights and social justice approaches to quality in education in developing countries. A human capital approach focuses on the contribution education can make to economic growth – improving the quality of education improves its potential to facilitate economic growth. A human rights approach sees human rights as the purpose of development and takes human rights legislation such as the 1989 UN Convention on the Rights of the Child as the starting point. The focus of this approach to quality is on inclusion in terms of 'seeking out learners, acknowledging what the learner brings; the nature of the learning environment; content and the distribution of outcomes (2013, p. 12). A social justice approach is aligned with a human rights approach but has its origins in moral philosophy rather than international legislation. It sees the purpose of a quality education as overcoming injustice so that people can participate in life and decision-making on a more equal basis. This means removing institutional and economic structures that deny the resources to people that they need to interact with others equally and fairly. This applies particularly to those historically marginalised groups such as women, those in rural areas, those suffering from or affected by HIV/AIDS, orphans and vulnerable children, refugees and cultural and sexual minorities (2013, p. 13).

Since the purpose of this chapter is to provide a relatively concise overall picture of the state of play of education in developing as opposed to wealthier countries, here we will largely focus on the Dakar Forum on Education for All that met under UNESCO auspices in 2000. This identified several key elements as necessary for a quality education. Among them were: *well-nourished, motivated students, well-trained teachers using active learning techniques; adequate facilities and materials; and a welcoming, gender-sensitive, healthy, safe environment that encourages learning* (UNESCO, 2009, p. 108). In all developing countries there are schools where all or the majority of these elements are present. UNESCO (2005) provides examples of developing countries such as Cuba that have radically improved the quality of their education systems in these respects as well as those such as Senegal, Bangladesh, Sri Lanka, Egypt, South Africa, Brazil and Chile which are making major efforts at improving educational quality. However, what can distinguish schools in many developing countries is the very wide quality gap between well-resourced schools, often in urban areas, and very poorly resourced and very basic schools, often in rural areas. Serious issues therefore remain in terms of educational quality in many schools in developing countries. Here we shall examine the elements of quality in schools set out by UNESCO as necessary for a quality education.

Well-Nourished and Motivated Students

With regard to health and nutrition, UNESCO (2011, p. 24) notes that

> Millions of children enter primary school every year having experienced malnutrition in their early years. For many children, malnutrition starts in the womb as a result of poor maternal health. Hunger in the early years impairs cognitive development and damages learning potential in school. The problem is particularly marked in South Asia where 83 million children under the age of 5 suffer from malnutrition.

UNESCO further notes that 19 million children in developing countries are born underweight because of poor growth in the womb; about one-third of all children under 5 in the developing world are stunted or short for their age. Of these, 31% live in India and nearly one in two children in East and southern Africa are stunted. Such children have poorer learning outcomes and are more likely to start school late and drop out early. Undernourished, hungry children are much less likely to be motivated and to be able to concentrate in schools. This is why school feeding programmes that supplement the diets of children while they at school have been introduced into many countries. For example, such a programme was introduced into Kenya in 2009 and covers 1.9 million children (UNESCO, 2011, pp. 31, 114).

Well-Trained Teachers

While progress has been made in terms of providing access to primary education for all and many countries have increased their supply of teachers, there remains a serious problem of teacher shortages in developing countries. For example, in 2007 twenty-six countries out of 171 had primary school pupil–teacher ratios of above the widely used international ceiling of 1:40 – all but four of them in sub-Saharan Africa (UNESCO, 2010, p. 115). In 2010 the pupil–teacher ratio in primary schools in low-income countries was 43:1; in lower- and middle-income countries 31:1; in upper-middle-income countries 19:1 and in high-income countries 14:1. In secondary schools it was 26:1 in low-income countries; 21:1 in lower-middle-income countries; 16:1 in upper-middle-income countries and 12:1 in high-income countries (UNESCO, 2012, p. 122). In Malawi in 2006, for example, primary school pupil–teacher ratios varied from 36 to 120 pupils per teacher (UNESCO, 2011, p. 92). In terms of the ratio of pupils to *trained* teachers, the figures go over 1:80 in Madagascar, Mozambique, Sierra Leone and Togo and over 1:50 in Tanzania, Burundi, Eritrea, Congo and Burkina Faso (UNESCO, 2010, p. 115). Of 100 countries with data, 33 have less than 75% of their primary school teachers trained and in 12 the share is less than 50%, including Benin, Ethiopia, Honduras, Liberia, Mali and Sierra Leone (UNESCO, 2012, p. 123). The situation is considerably worse in rural areas where qualified teachers are less inclined to work because of issues of access to electricity, housing and the amenities of urban life as well as distance from family. Moreover, low salaries and poor working conditions for teachers often lower morale and force teachers to take on other work, thereby increasing teacher absenteeism and reducing the amount of time they actually teach. This has long been known to be a problem in schools in developing countries but, by its very nature, has been hard to quantify. However, in India pupils in randomly selected schools were given a camera to record the teacher at the beginning and end of the school day and teachers were only paid according to when they were there – absenteeism averaged 21% in these schools as opposed to 42% in control schools where this intervention did not take place (UNESCO, 2011, p. 94).

Active Learning Techniques

Do teachers in developing countries use active learning and participatory techniques in the classroom? The answer is both yes and no, but probably with the emphasis on the latter. This section will summarise a considerable amount of evidence for individual developing countries discussed in Harber and Mncube (2012). First, the good news. In 2009 a major, multi-method evaluation, including direct observation, took place of the UNICEF Child Friendly Schools (CFS) framework in 150 public or state schools in six developing countries – Nigeria, South Africa, the Philippines, Thailand, Guyana and Nicaragua (Osher et al, 2009). The evaluation found that most schools in the six countries encouraged students' active engagement with teachers using child-centred instructional techniques and by creating environments that encourage active learning as well as trust and respect. However, 'although teachers endorse active learning, traditional notions of effective instruction persist' (p. 74) and school heads and teachers identified the lack of trained teachers who can implement child-centred instructional methods

35

as a challenge in all six countries. Moreover, specific UNICEF/CFS in-service training on participatory and student-centred teaching seemed to have been the main catalyst for change and was necessary because of poor-quality initial teacher education in this respect. Student or learner support for the idea that they experienced various forms of child-centred teaching ranged from 73% to 92% across countries (p. 81).

The 2005 EFA Global Monitoring Report on the quality of education notes the desirability of more 'open-ended and discovery-based pedagogies' which are participatory, interactive, child-centred and characterised by cooperative learning and inquiry and which foster conceptual understanding, critical thinking and problem-solving skills. It cites a number of programmes that have adopted such pedagogies – for example, the Escuela Nueva programme in Colombia, the non-formal primary education programme of the Bangladesh Rural Advancement Programme, the Escuela Nueva Unitaria programme in Guatemala, the Fe y Alegria schools in Latin America, convergent pedagogy in Mali and the Aga Khan Foundation-supported Dar es Salaam Primary Schools Project. In addition, such programmes are also described as having some or all of the following characteristics: peer tutoring among learners, carefully developed self-guided learning materials, teacher – and student – constructed learning materials and a school focus on learning rather than teaching (UNESCO, 2005, p. 153).

However, it also describes the difficulty of moving away from the dominance of

> rigid, chalk-and-talk, teacher centred/dominated, lecture-driven pedagogy or rote learning ... Such pedagogy places students in a passive role, limiting their activity to memorizing facts and reciting them to the teacher ... Such teaching practices are the norm in the vast majority of classrooms in sub-Saharan Africa and elsewhere, even in the most affluent countries. (UNESCO, 2005, p. 152)

Evidence from a wide range of regions and countries reviewed in Harber (2004, ch. 2) and Harber and Mncube (2012, ch. 4) also strongly suggests that it remains true that, despite the examples of good practice cited above, the dominant teaching style in developing countries (and in many others) remains firmly teacher-centred.

Adequate Facilities and Materials

In terms of teaching and learning resources, many schools in developing countries lack both basic and adequate supplies of appropriate buildings, textbooks, teaching materials and toilets. The situation is consistently worse in rural than urban areas. UNESCO (2009, p. 116) talks of the 'parlous state' of the education infrastructure it has commented on in previous reports and provides the following examples.

- Half of the grade 6 pupils in Kenya, Malawi, Mozambique, Uganda, Tanzania and Zambia did not have a single book.
- In 25-40% of these and other countries teachers did not possess a manual in the subjects they taught.
- In Nigeria pupils in grades 4 and 6 reported lacking textbooks – 30% in English, 50% in mathematics, 65% in social studies and 75% in science.
- Poor school infrastructure is widespread in Latin America. Ecuador, Guatemala, Nicaragua, Panama, Paraguay and Peru have many primary schools lacking several or all of the following: sufficient toilets, potable water, libraries, books and computer rooms.
- In Peru, the Philippines and Sri Lanka half or more of school heads say that the school needs complete rebuilding or that some classrooms need major repairs.
- India, Peru, the Philippines and Sri Lanka suffer an acute shortage of seating.

A Healthy and Safe Environment

Examples such as those above also challenge the notion of 'healthy and safe environments' for all children, as does the widespread persistence of corporal punishment in schools in developing countries, which is discussed in more detail in chapter 6.

Gender Sensitivity

While, as we have seen, there have been improvements in gender equality in terms of access to schooling, the treatment of girls by male pupils and staff cannot in many cases be described as 'gender sensitive' and is often better described as sexual harassment. For example, in 2008 Amnesty International published a report tellingly entitled *Safe Schools: every girl's right.* In the introduction it states:

> Every day, girls face being assaulted on their way to school,
> pushed and hit in school grounds, teased and insulted by their
> classmates, and humiliated by having rumours circulated
> about them through whisper campaigns, mobile phones or the
> internet. Some are threatened with sexual assault by other
> students, offered higher marks by teachers in return for sexual
> favours, even raped in the staff room. Some are beaten or
> caned in the name of school discipline ... . Violence against
> girls takes place in and around many educational institutions
> all over the world. It is inflicted not only by teachers, but also

> by administrators, other school employees, fellow students
> and outsiders. The result is that countless girls are kept out of
> school, drop out of school, or do not participate fully in
> school. (2008, pp. 1-2)

While the phenomenon is certainly not only located in developing countries (Harber, 2004, ch. 7), Plan (2008, pp. 22-33) cites evidence of significantly high levels of sexual violence against girls by students and staff in Uganda, South Africa, Zambia, Botswana, Ghana, Malawi, Zimbabwe, Ecuador, the Dominican Republic, Honduras, Guatemala, Mexico, Nicaragua, Panama, Thailand and Nepal.

Explanations of schooling as a violent experience will be further discussed in chapter 6, and gender and education are further discussed in chapter 10.

Educational Outcomes

Outcomes are, of course, in the end what education is all about, as the whole point of education is to have an impact on individuals and societies and the degree to which desired outcomes are achieved is related to the quality of education provided. In this section we see the distinction between direct and longer-term outcomes. The former is basically the learning of students as often measured in tests and examination results. The latter concerns the longer-term impact upon the lives and livelihoods of people, such as their employment and income.

However, it is important to note that this section focuses only on some of the more positive outcomes of schooling, and that schooling can also have negative consequences. For example, in one study, discussed further below, there is evidence of corporal punishment in Ghana and that fear, lack of confidence and school drop-out are the outcomes. There is also evidence of vulgar language being used by teachers when addressing pupils as well as the presence of sexual violence (Colclough, 2012, p. 128). These are actually very far from being unusual occurrences and negative outcomes of schooling, such as anxiety, pain, embarrassment and anger (as well as fear and lack of confidence), can be both short- and long-term consequences of education. This is also further discussed in chapter 6.

In relation to direct outcomes in the form of tests and examinations, UNESCO notes that 'Incomplete country coverage in international learning assessments and the non-comparability of national surveys make it difficult to extrapolate global trends (2011, p. 85). However, if there are issues of educational quality in developing countries, as discussed earlier, it would be expected that this would be reflected in educational assessments. UNESCO (2012, p. 124) states that of the 650 million children of primary school age, some 130 million fail to learn basics expected at their level of education and that the situation is particularly more marked and prevalent in low-income, developing countries. In Africa, for example:

> Less than one third of the children of school leaving age currently acquire the knowledge and skills specified in their national primary education curriculum ... In many schools in Africa, learning achievement is so low that after several years of schooling, the students have not obtained basic literacy and numeracy skills. (Verspoor, 2008, pp. 13, 16)

Indeed, research has supported the link between educational quality and the resulting outcomes. Lee and Zuze (2011), for example, found strong links between material and human resources and grade 6 student achievement in reading and mathematics in four African countries. Bouhlila (2011) studied the maths and science results of countries in the Middle East and North Africa and concluded that one of the factors explaining poor results was a lack of resources. Reporting on research on a project to improve quality in schools in three African countries (Ethiopia, Zambia and Zimbabwe), Harber and Stephens (2009) found that outcomes tended to be better in schools where the project had taken place than in those schools where it had not.

One key indicator of both access to education and quality of education is the rate of literacy. The nature of literacy will be discussed more fully in chapter 17 but it is important to note here that in 1946 UNESCO put literacy at the top of its education and human rights agenda. While there have been major improvements in literacy in developing countries and there are regional and country-by-country variations, the difference in the aggregate figures between developed and less developed countries is still noteworthy and reflects the above discussion on access and quality. In 2000-04 the literacy rate of the population aged 15+ in developed countries was 98.7% whereas in developing countries it was 76.4% ((Wagner, 2011, p. 74). By 2005-8 the respective figures were 99% and 79% (UNESCO, 2011, p. 280). In 2000-07, the regional average adult illiteracy rate in Arab states was 29%, while it was 36% in South and West Asia and 38% in Sub-Saharan Africa (Wagner, 2011, p. 122).

Within these figures there are still high proportions of adults in developing countries who have *completed* primary schooling but still report not being able to read, as set out in Table I. This raises serious questions about the quality of education being provided.

UNESCO (2011, pp. 84-87) provides a useful summary of learning outcomes. In 2006 the Progress in International Reading Literacy Study (PIRLS) assessed reading skills in 40 high- and middle-income countries against a series of international benchmarks – advanced, high, intermediate, low and below low. In developed, high-income countries the majority of students performed at or above the intermediate benchmark. However, in middle-income countries, such as South Africa and Morocco, the majority of students had not acquired basic reading skills even after four years of primary schooling.

Country	%
Lao PDR	3
Bolivia	3
Sao Tome/Principe	3
Burundi	9
Comoros	11
Rwanda	11
Cameroon	13
Cote d'Ivoire	13
Equatorial Guinea	14
Madagascar	14
Uzbekistan	19
Central African Republic	20
Tajikistan	22
Sierra Leone	29
Niger	34
Chad	35

Table I. Proportions of adults in developing countries who have completed primary schooling but still report not being able to read. *Source*: Wagner, 2011, pp. 74, 124.

In 2007 the Southern and Eastern African Consortium for Monitoring Educational Quality (SACMEQ) carried out assessments in 14 countries. In Malawi and Zambia a third of grade 6 students had failed to acquire even the most basic literacy skills, implying that many were unable to read fluently after five or six years of primary education. A nationwide survey of rural India in 2009 found that only 38% of grade 4 students could read a text designed for grade 2 students. Similar results were found in rural Pakistan. However, SACMEQ do note in relation to trends in mathematics achievement in SACMEQ countries during the 2000-07 period that there have been both improvements and declines in performance despite an expansion of school access across the region. This calls into question the widespread claim that increased enrolment has automatically been accompanied by a steep decline in quality, thereby implying a necessary trade- off between learning outcomes and access.

Nevertheless, in terms of more global comparisons, as Harber (2013, p. 12) notes, the average SACMEQ maths score for eight of the SACMEQ countries in 2007 was 494.2. This was very similar to that of South Africa, which was ranked in the middle of the eight countries. In 2002 the South African Human Sciences Research Council administered the Third International Mathematics and Science Study test to a sample of grade 8 learners in South Africa. The South African learners (representing the average for the SACMEQ countries) achieved 264 on this test as opposed to the global international average of 467 (Bloch, 2009, pp. 63-64), suggesting that mathematical achievement in southern Africa is on the low side by international comparisons.

In terms of the longer-term outcomes of education, one key overall outcome is poverty eradication or, perhaps more realistically in the foreseeable future, poverty reduction. Education is seen to have the potential to contribute to this through enabling both greater individual prosperity, health and well-being and national economic growth:

> becoming non-poor seems to require at least achieving literacy, and primary schooling has properly become a recurrent part of the international human rights commitments that have been reaffirmed by all nations over the past half-century.
> (Colclough, 2012, p. 165)

Cremin and Nakabugo (2012) provide a useful review of some of the evidence of the role of education in development and poverty reduction, in the light of support for education as a key instrument for poverty reduction by such bodies as the World Bank and the Organisation for Economic Cooperation and Development (OECD). They point out that international comparative studies have found that higher levels of education result in higher average earnings: 'In every country studied it has been found that workers with education tend to earn more than those with less education, with the wage premium depending on the level of education (p. 503). They also note that, according to a synthesis of studies by the World Bank, the estimated 'rates of return' from investing in education (i.e. the extra wealth earned by individuals and the state as a result of investing a certain amount of money in education) are typically more than 10%, with the highest rates of return coming from the lowest levels of formal education, i.e. primary education. Other studies have established the link between education and economic growth in developing countries, including one that found that for the period 1850-1960 none of the world's richest countries had achieved significant economic growth without universal primary education. Moreover, higher education has also been found to have a positive relationship with earnings compared to those with only secondary education. Within work, education can contribute to productivity – for example, farmers with education are more likely to adopt new technologies and get a higher rate of return from their land and there is evidence that poor, self-employed people have a wider and more profitable range of earning possibilities when they have had a basic education. Also, educating children of the poor greatly increases their chances of escaping poverty.

Some studies have also indicated that the rate of return of investing in women's education is higher than that of men in most developing countries. There is also evidence that education for girls and young women is important for development – it increases a woman's ability to participate in society, to improve her quality of life and her standard of living. A mother's level of schooling is also linked to the health and survival of her children. Overall, Cremin and Nakabugo conclude that

> Education, and particularly literacy, contributes to health gains, lower fertility, improved infant survival, higher labour productivity, as well as more rapid GDP growth, but also makes a contribution to social integration through equipping individuals for participation in all aspects of social, political, economic and cultural life. Education is both a goal of development and a means to its achievement. (2012, p. 505)

A further useful overview of the relationship between education and poverty reduction is provided by Colclough (2012), though this wide-ranging empirical study based on South Asia and sub-Saharan Africa also raises some questions about the changing nature of the relationship. For example, while wage returns to primary education remain positive, secondary and higher education now seem to be producing higher returns:

> Taking a fresh look at the results of recent studies from more than 30 countries, and combining these with those from more than 100 studies published prior to the mid-1990's, a compelling picture of steep decline in the wage returns to primary schooling across the developing world over the past half-century emerges. (2012, p. 156)

Moreover, while better fertility and health behaviour still appears responsive to the number of years women spend in school, the threshold needed for such change appears to be increasing, with some secondary education needed in addition to primary education.

However, one of the key conclusions of this study of outcomes is also that, while there are important positive relationships between education and poverty reduction, these are often mediated by social and contextual factors such as urban/rural location and gender, with family and social networks regularly being more important in determining actual patterns of employment than education. Indeed, the study is as much about how poverty prevents people from accessing and benefiting from education, i.e. its socially reproductive role, as about education's impact on poverty, and it is to inequalities in education that we turn our attention in the next section.

Inequality

> Schools do not operate in isolation. Learning outcomes are
> influenced by household circumstances and by the inherited
> disadvantages that come with poverty and extreme inequality
> ... children enter school carrying disadvantages linked to
> household poverty and parental illiteracy [and] schools can
> mitigate these disadvantages though they often have the
> opposite effect. (UNESCO, 2011, p. 88)

Education is not a level playing field. Globally, the enormous
inequalities in wealth between countries also mean that there is a vast
gulf in educational opportunities between young people in richer and
poorer countries. For example, in 2003, per student public expenditure
in low-income countries was $48 at the primary level and $87 at the
secondary level, in middle-income countries it was $555 and $660 and in
high-income countries it was $3263 and $4279 (Bing, 2008, p. 91). The
significantly different levels of access and quality mean that,
internationally, schooling also helps to reproduce inequality between
nations, which is why the 2009 Global Monitoring Report on Education
for All was titled *Overcoming Inequality* (UNESCO, 2009).

Within countries, certain households tend to be educationally
disadvantaged in terms of access, quality and outcomes – children from
these households have less chance of going to school than others, more
chance of dropping out, receive a poorer quality of education and
achieve less successful outcomes. Education often, therefore, reproduces
the existing inequalities of the wider society rather than providing equal
opportunities for all, whether this be inequality based on socio-economic
status, region, ethnicity, disability, gender or religion (Watkins, 2000). As
UNESCO (2011) demonstrates, the existence of both large numbers of
out-of-school children and children who drop out of school prior to
completion in developing countries is significantly influenced by gender
(more girls than boys), wealth (more from poorer backgrounds than
better-off backgrounds) and area (more from rural than urban areas):

> In sub-Saharan Africa alone, about 10 million children drop
> out of school each year. Household poverty, inequalities
> linked to language and ethnicity, and rural–urban differences
> all contribute to the problem, along with the poor quality of
> education in schools where classrooms are overcrowded,
> books are scarce and teachers are under-qualified and poorly
> motivated. (UNESCO, 2011, p. 47)

Table II demonstrates inequality of access to levels of education in
relation to wealth, within certain developing countries. As the writer of
the article from which the figures in Table II are taken acknowledges, the

schooling actually provided to the poor is also likely to be of lower quality.

Country	Richest 20%	Poorest 20%
Bangladesh	8.1	3.7
Burkina Faso	5.6	0.8
Ethiopia	7.4	1.6
Ghana	9.2	3.2
Guatemala	8.3	1.9
India	11.1	4.4
Mali	4.8	0.4
Mozambique	5.0	1.9
Nicaragua	9.2	2.5
Nigeria	9.9	3.9
Peru	11.1	6.5
Philippines	11.0	6.3
Tanzania	8.1	3.9
Zambia	9.0	4.0

Table II. Average years of education for richest and poorest 20% of 17-22-year-olds. *Source*: Elliott (2008).

Holsinger and Jacob (2008, pp. 1-3) use an education gini coefficient (a measure of economic inequality) to measure the gap between the actual distribution of educational access and resources within countries compared with what would be full equality of distribution. While there are inequalities in all regions of the world, the highest inequalities of educational distribution are in sub-Saharan Africa, South Asia, the Middle East and North Africa, Central America and the Caribbean, Oceania and South America – the main geographical regions of developing countries. Moreover, overall inequality in educational provision was highly correlated with low overall school attainment.

In terms of inequality of outcomes, UNESCO (2012, p. 127) reports a survey of both more affluent countries of the OECD and 40 other countries, including less affluent ones. In every country, the higher the socio-economic origin and status of the student, the better the academic performance, but within less wealthy countries such as Argentina, Chile, Colombia and Jordan, the gap in terms of achievement between those of higher socio-economic status and those of lower socio-economic status was much larger. UNESCO (2011, pp. 83-97) further provides data from 15 southern African SACMEQ countries that shows a consistent pattern of children from richer households doing better in reading than those from poorer households. This pattern holds true for urban over rural areas but not so for male/female differences. UNESCO adds that in India there are significant differences in reading abilities between regions, reflecting regional levels of wealth and poverty. While, as UNESCO (2011) points out and provides evidence for, when poor children attend good-quality schools their learning achievement can be as high as those from richer households, the reality is that children from poorer and more rural backgrounds in developing countries tend also to go to poorer quality schools in terms of, for example, teacher qualifications, teacher motivation, resources and class sizes.

Case Study

Post-apartheid South Africa provides a good example of a country that has tried to end the socio-economic and racial inequalities of the past in education, and the difficulties faced in doing so. Despite a relatively strong performance in terms of economic growth since 1994, South Africa still has one of the most unequal societies in the world with between 45% and 55% of the population categorised as poor and between 20% and 25% as in extreme poverty, and there are spatial, racial and gender dimensions to this poverty (McGrath & Akooje, 2007, pp. 422-423).

Has education helped to reduce this inequality or to perpetuate it? Soudien (2007) sets out some of the achievements of educational policy since the end of apartheid such as ending the old racialised education departments, attempting to bring disaffected parents back into the system, redressing imbalances in teacher–pupil ratios inherited from apartheid, achieving figures approaching 100% in terms of enrolment for the compulsory phase of schooling and significantly increasing the national budget allocation to education. It terms of outcomes, pass rates for the Senior Certificate Examination rose from 47.4% in 1997 to 73.3% in 2003 and black student enrolment in higher education grew from 191,000 in 1993 to 449,000 in 2003.

However, such achievements mask serious continuing inequalities in education and perpetuated by the education system. At the same time that efforts have been made to redistribute resources from the rich to the poor there has also been an acceptance that some of the funding burden will have to be borne by users of education in the form of fees. Whatever the reasons for this, the result has been to perpetuate or even exacerbate inequality rather than to reduce it. Schools serving well-off communities can charge high fees to maintain excellent facilities and employ more teachers, while schools in poorer communities will not be able to do so. Admission on the grounds of race is now illegal, but high fees may well have the same net effect. It seems very likely that public schools will be increasingly divided between a minority of relatively affluent and well-resourced schools and a majority of poorer schools much more dependent on state funding. In their detailed study of two provinces, tellingly entitled *Elusive Equity*, Fiske and Ladd (2004, pp.233-234) conclude that South Africa has made progress on equal *treatment* in terms of allocation of state resources, but the country has been less successful in terms of equal educational *opportunity* because of the very unequal access to good-quality schooling, and has not been successful at all in terms of educational *adequacy* in that repetition and drop-out rates among black students remain high and matriculation pass rates low with little evidence of improvement. This is a similar conclusion to that reached by Spreen and Vally (2006, pp. 354-357), who also point out that many children go to school hungry and that 27% of schools have no running water, 43% have no electricity, 80% have no library and 78% have no computers. A study of rural schools in South Africa graphically brings home the way poverty both prevents access to education and success within it, concluding that 'For many, education cannot compensate for much deeper economic and social inequalities – it is not a ladder out of poverty, it simply confirms one's status in life' (Nelson Mandela Foundation, 2005, p. 142).

Conclusion

The purpose of this chapter has been to provide an introduction to, and overview of, some of the key features of education in developing countries. Each country, or region of a larger country, will have some of these features and not others. A useful exercise, therefore, would be to take a particular developing country or region of interest to examine access, quality, outcomes and inequality, to see what the particular situation is in that country or region. This chapter has primarily presented a broad description of the situation and has briefly noted some of the factors that have contributed to that situation. The following section of the book examines some key theories of education and development – how might we begin to *explain* how education affects development and vice versa? We will do this by critically examining three broad thematic aspects of the relationship between education and development – economic, social and political – and the theories that purport to explain them as well as explaining why education might also sometimes be harmful to development.

References

Amnesty International (2008) *Safe Schools: every girl's right.* London: Amnesty International Publications.

Bing, W.K. (2008) Education and Inequality in the Developing World, in D. Holsinger & W. Jacob (2008) *Inequality in Education: comparative and international perspectives.* Comparative Education Research Centre, University of Hong Kong, vol. 24. Hong Kong: Springer.

Bloch, G. (2009) *The Toxic Mix* (Cape Town: Tafelberg).

Bouhlila, D. (2011) The Quality of Secondary Education in the Middle East and North Africa: what can we learn from TIMMS' results?, *Compare*, 41(3), 327-352.

Bray, M. (2008) *Double-Shift Schooling: design and operation for cost-effectiveness.* Paris/London: UNESCO/Commonwealth Secretariat.

Chisamya, G., DeJaeghere, J., Kendall, N. & Khan, M. (2012) Gender and Education for All: progress and problems in achieving gender equity, *International Journal of Educational Development*, 32(6), 743-755.

Colclough, C. (2012) Education Outcomes Reassessed, in C. Colclough (Ed.) *Education Outcomes and Poverty: a reassessment.* Abingdon: Routledge.

Cremin, P. & Nakabugo, M. (2012) Education, Development and Poverty Reduction: a literature critique, *International Journal of Educational Development*, 32(4), 499-506.

Fiske, E. & Ladd, H. (2004) *Elusive Equity: education reform in post-apartheid South Africa.* Cape Town: HSRC Press.

Harber, C. (2004) *Schooling as Violence: how schools harm pupils and societies.* London: RoutledgeFalmer.

Harber, C. (2013) Education in Southern Africa: patterns and issues, in C. Harber (Ed.) *Education in Southern Africa.* London: Continuum.

Harber, C. & Mncube, V. (2012*) Education, Democracy and Development: does education contribute to democratisation in developing countries?* Oxford: Symposium Books.

Harber, C. & Stephens, D. (2009) *From Shouters to Supporters: the Quality Education Project.* Oslo: Save the Children.

Holsinger, D. & Jacob, W. (Eds) (2008) *Inequality in Education: comparative and international perspectives.* Comparative Education Research Centre, University of Hong Kong, vol. 24. Hong Kong: Springer.

Lee, V. & Zuze, T. (2011) School Resources and Academic Performance in Sub-Saharan Africa, *Comparative Education Review*, 55(3) 369-397.

Lewin, K. & Little, A. (2011) Access to Education Revisited: equity, dropout and transitions to secondary school in South Asia and Sub-Saharan Africa, *International Journal of Educational Development*, 31(4), 333-337.

McGrath, S. & Akoojee, S. (2007) Education and Skills for Development in South Africa: reflections on the accelerated and shared growth initiative for South Africa, *International Journal of Educational Development*, 27(4), 421-434.

Nelson Mandela Foundation (2005) *Emerging Voices.* Cape Town: HSRC Press.

Osher, D., Kelly, D., Tolani-Brown, N., Shors, L. & Chen, C-S. (2009) *UNICEF Child Friendly Schools Programming: Global Evaluation Final Report.* Washington, DC: American Institutes for Research.

Plan (2008) *The Global Campaign to End Violence in Schools.* Woking: Plan.

Soudien, C. (2007) The 'A' Factor: coming to terms with the question of legacy in South African education, *International Journal of Educational Development*, 27(2), 182-193.

Spreen, C. & Vally, S. (2006) Education Rights, Education Policies and Inequality in South Africa, *International Journal of Educational Development*, 26(4), 352-362.

Tikly, L. & Barrett, A. (2013) Education Quality and Social Justice in the Global South: towards a conceptual framework, in L. Tikly & A.M. Barrett (Eds) *Education Quality and Social Justice in the Global South.* Abingdon: Routledge.

UNESCO (2005) *The Quality Imperative.* EFA Global Monitoring Report. Paris: UNESCO.

UNESCO (2009) *Overcoming Inequality: why governance matters.* EFA Global Monitoring Report. Paris: UNESCO.

UNESCO (2010) *Reaching the Marginalized.* EFA Global Monitoring Report. Paris: UNESCO.

UNESCO (2011) *The Hidden Crisis: armed conflict and education.* EFA Global Monitoring Report. Paris: UNESCO.

UNESCO (2012) *Youth and Skills: putting education to work.* EFA Global Monitoring Report. Paris: UNESCO.

Verspoor, A. (2008) The Challenge of Learning: improving the quality of basic education in sub-Saharan Africa, in D. Johnson (Ed.) *The Changing Landscape of Education in Africa.* Oxford: Symposium Books.

Wagner, D. (2011) *Smaller, Quicker, Cheaper: improving assessments for developing countries.* Paris: UNESCO/IIEP.

Watkins, K. (2000) *Education Now: breaking the cycle of poverty.* Oxford: Oxfam.

Wu, J. (2012) Disenchantment and Participation Limits of Compulsory Education: lessons from Southwest China, *Compare*, 42(4), 621-646.

Further Reading

Access

Annual UNESCO EFA Global Monitoring Reports.

Binder, S. (2009) Why are some Low-Income Countries Better at Providing Secondary Education?, *Comparative Education Review*, 53(4), 513-534.

Ghuman, S. & Lloyd, C. (2010) Teacher Absence as a Factor in Gender Inequalities in Access to Primary Schooling in Rural Pakistan, *Comparative Education Review*, 54(4), 539-554.

Korinek, K. & Punpuing, S. (2012) The Effect of Household and Community on School Attrition: an analysis of Thai youth, *Comparative Education Review*, 56(3), 474-510.

Kosack, S. (2009) Realising Education for All: defining and using the political will to invest in primary education, *Comparative Education*, 45(4), 495-523.

Lewin, K. & Kyeampong, K. (2009) *Education in Sub-saharan Africa: researching access, transition and equity,* Special Issue of *Comparative Education* 45(2).

Lewin, K. & Little, A. (2011) *Access, Equity and Transitions in Education in Low Income Countries,* Special Issue of the *International Journal of Educational Development,* 31(4).

Omwami, E. & Keller, E. (2010) Public Funding and Budgetary Challenges to Providing Universal Access to Primary Education in Sub-Saharan Africa, *International Review of Education,* 56, 5-31.

Tsujita, Y. (2013) Factors that Prevent Children from Gaining Access to Schooling: a study of Delhi slum households, *International Journal of International Development* 33(4), 348-357.

Quality

Annual UNESCO EFA Global Monitoring Reports, particularly UNESCO (2005) *The Quality Imperative.* Paris: UNESCO.

Anderson, J. (2005) Improving Latin America's School Quality: which special interventions work?, *Comparative Education Review,* 49(2), 205-229.

Chapman, D. & Miric, S. (2009) Education Quality in the Middle East, *International Review of Education,* 55, 311-344.

Dembele, M. & Oviawe, J. (2007) Introduction: Quality Education in Africa – international commitments, local challenges and responses, *International Review of Education,* 53, 473-483.

Hawes, H. & Stephens, D. (1990) *Questions of Quality: primary education and development.* Harlow: Longman.

Nikel, J. & Lowe, J. (2010) Talking of Fabric: a multi-dimensional model of quality in education, *Compare,* 40(5), 589-605.

Sayed, Y. & Ahmed, R. (2011) Education Quality in Post-apartheid South African Policy: balancing equity, diversity, rights and participation, *Comparative Education,* 47(1), 103-118.

Tikly, L. (2011) Towards a Framework for Researching the Quality of Education in Low-income Countries, *Comparative Education,* 47(1), 1-23.

Tikly, L. & Barrett, A.M. (Eds) *Education Quality and Social Justice in the Global South.* Abingdon: Routledge.

Tikly, L. & Barrett, A. (2011) Social Justice, Capabilities and the Quality of Education in Low Income Countries, *International Journal of Educational Development,* 31(1), 3-14.

Outcomes

Alexander, A., Broadfoot, P. & Phillips, D. (Eds) (1999) *Learning from Comparing – Part 3.* Oxford: Symposium Books.

Annual UNESCO EFA Global Monitoring Reports.

Bonal, X. (2007) On Global Absences: reflections on the failings in the education and poverty relationship in Latin America, *International Journal of Educational Development,* 27(1), 86-100.

Clive Harber

Colclough, C. (Ed.) *Education Outcomes and Poverty: a reassessment.* Abingdon: Routledge.

Colclough, C. (2012b) Education, Poverty and Development – mapping their interconnections, *Comparative Education*, 48(2), 135-148.

Compare (2012) 42(3) – Forum on learning assessments in developing countries.

International Journal of Educational Development (2012) 32(4) – Special Issue on Education, Policy and Poverty Reduction.

International Journal of Educational Development (2007) – Special Issue on Beyond Basic Education and Towards an Expanded Vision of Education – For Poverty Reduction and Growth?

Kamens, D. & McNeely, L. (2010) Globalisation and the Growth of International Testing and National Assessment, *Comparative Education Review*, 54(1), 5-25.

Inequality

Annual UNESCO EFA Global Monitoring Reports.

Barron, T. & Amerena, P. (Eds) (2007) *Disability and Inclusive Development.* London: Leonard Cheshire International.

Buchmann, C. & Hannum, E. (2001) Education and Stratification in Developing Countries: a review of theories and research, *American Review of Sociology*, 27, 77-102.

Colclough, C. (Ed.) *Education Outcomes and Poverty: a reassessment.* Abingdon: Routledge.

Compare (2012) 42(2) – Special Issue on Developing Education, Challenging Marginalisation.

Holsinger, D. (2005) Inequality in the Public Provision of Education: why it matters, *Comparative Education Review*, 49(3), 297-310.

Pridmore, P. & Jere, C. (2011) Disrupting Patterns of Educational Inequality and Disadvantage in Malawi, *Compare*, 41(4), 513-532.

Reiter, B. (2009) Inequality and School Reform in Bahia, Brazil, *International Review of Education*, 55, 345-365.

Zuze, T. & Leibbrandt, M. (2011) Free Education and Social Inequality in Uganda Primary Schools: a step backward or a step in the right direction?, *International Journal of Educational Development*, 31(2), 169-178.

Discussion and Activities

1. What do you think would be the best three policies to improve access to education in developing countries?
2. What would be your definition of 'quality' in education? What problems do you think developing countries might face in actually achieving your definition for all pupils?
3. Which outcomes from schooling do you think are the most important ones to measure? Why?

50

4. What do you think are the main forms of inequality that affect education in developing countries?

CHAPTER 3

Economic Development: human capital or dependency and socio-economic reproduction?

Introduction

Debates about the nature of development are intimately connected with different sets of ideas or theories about how development takes place or, perhaps more accurately, how it ought to take place. Although such theories purport to 'explain' how development takes place, they do so primarily either from a particular emphasis or priority (e.g. economic development rather than social or political development) or from a preferred ideological model such as capitalism or socialism. It is often difficult to separate 'is' and 'ought' questions in discussions of development, since how it actually takes place cannot easily be separated from an understanding of its ultimate goal – the nature of a 'developed' society – and this is a matter of opinion, preference, judgement and power rather than fact. In this section of the book we examine the nature of areas of development theory that purport to explain important ways in which education is a key factor in development. This chapter begins with education and economic development.

Human Capital Theory

Education imparts skills and knowledge, which augments productivity and yields higher economic returns to individuals. Overall, returns are high in all countries and higher in developing countries than developed countries because educated workers are scarcer in the former.
(Bing, 2008, p. 87)

One major and enduring emphasis within development theory has been the concern with economic development and, in particular, economic growth. Even within the broader understanding of development now espoused, for example, by the United Nations, gross national income continues to be given conceptual importance as one of three essential components of development, along with life expectancy at birth and mean years of schooling (United Nations Development Programme [UNDP], 2011, p. 127). A key theory in relation to the role of education vis-à-vis the economy is human capital theory, which is based on the idea that investment in education is needed as a fundamental aspect of a country's strategy for achieving development. The World Bank, for example, has stated that human capital theory 'has no genuine rival of equal breadth and rigour', and it is used by them to explain the economic success of East Asia (Samoff, 1999, p. 68).

The idea of human capital goes back at least as far as Adam Smith and his classic study *The Wealth of Nations*, published in 1776, in which he defined it as human skills, dexterity (physical, intellectual and psychological) and judgement. More recently, human capital theory was developed in the early 1960s by writers such as Schultz (1961) and Becker (1964). It is based on the idea that the key to economic development is to see the increased education of the human workforce as a capital investment rather than as a form of economic consumption. Not only is education a good investment for individuals (in terms of future returns in the form of higher income) but an educated population is necessary for industrial development and economic growth because such a population is more productive. The skills and motivation for productive behaviour are therefore imparted through formal education. Increased educational expenditure and increased participation rates in education would therefore improve economic productivity and set the economy on a path of growth. One important implication of this is that both the causes of, and the cure for, lack of economic development lie within countries themselves.

A key aspect of human capital theory is rates of return analysis, which assumes that it is education that is mainly responsible for the fact that the more educated earn more than the less educated. The rate of return is the rate of interest on what has been invested – how much more will I earn in my lifetime by staying on in each stage of education as opposed to going into the labour market? How much better off in terms of national wealth and economic growth will a country be by investing a certain amount in education?

As we saw in chapter 2, there is considerable evidence of the relationship between education and both greater individual prosperity and national economic growth, and globally there have been many studies of rates of return (Psacharopoulos & Patrinos, 2004). However, even if it is accepted that there is a relationship between levels of education and productivity and economic growth, the theory is nevertheless questionable on a number of grounds. One is the problem of the variation of rates of return to different levels of education over time – was earlier research on the high rates of return to primary education because universal primary education had not yet been achieved? Does the rate of return to a level of education decrease over time as it more people attain it, so that it becomes less of a scarce commodity and therefore its market value declines?

Another problem with human capital theory is the assumption that the higher earnings of more educated people are a consequence of their greater productivity. This assumes a perfect fit between education and the labour market in that the better educated get the better jobs and higher salaries. Yet certain occupations may have higher incomes simply for historical reasons, perhaps maintained by restricting the number of new entrants (e.g.in medicine and accountancy), or more educated people may come from better-off families which have good contacts and social networks in the world of employment. Income differentials are also affected by social structures – in many societies racial, caste, gender and other forms of discrimination affect both employment and promotion prospects. Moreover, even if more schooling does lead to higher earnings, is this 'because those who emerge from schooling have learned things that are more useful to employers, or is it that such people can more quickly or easily acquire vocational skills that employers need?' (Colclough, 2012, p. 141).

'Screening theory' goes further and argues that, while it is true that more educated people earn more, this is not because education makes people more productive, but because people differ in their innate productive potential. Education does not add to the market value of its products but simply provides a screening or filtering mechanism to identify and select those with the natural potential, abilities and personal attributes for future employers (Dore, 1976; Oxenham, 1984, pp. 31-33).

Other criticisms of human capital theory have been set out by Little (2003). One is that there are methodological problems with calculating the 'rates of return' to different levels of educational investment as well as practical ones of getting reliable data in developing countries. Also, there is too much emphasis on the economic benefits of education as opposed to effects on health, fertility and mortality as well as general well-being, i.e. it is argued that economic growth should be seen as a means to an end and not an end in itself and that there are other motivations for learning apart from the economic.

However, perhaps the biggest problem with human capital theory is one of cause and effect. Simply because high levels of education have been associated with economic growth and employment in certain countries does not mean, first, that this is a universal phenomenon, or, second, that education causes economic growth – indeed, it may just as well be that economic growth allows a country to afford education. Chang (2011, pp. 180-181) argues that in fact the evidence linking education to productivity is not as strong as is suggested and points out that in East Asia the Philippines had a much higher literacy rate than

Clive Harber

Taiwan, but the latter has done significantly better in terms of economic growth since 1960. Similarly, Argentina has had a much higher literacy rate than South Korea but the economic performance of the latter has been much better since 1960. He also points out that despite growing literacy rates in sub-Saharan Africa between 1980 and 2004, the per capita income of the region actually fell by 0.3%. Many developing countries spend a high proportion of their national budgets on education yet the result is simply more people who are both educated and unemployed or underemployed. This is because, with the changed expectations that result from formal schooling, the relatively small and modern, urban sectors of the economy cannot absorb them unless the economy is growing rapidly:

> Education is not easily converted into human capital and well-being in low-income countries because these countries do not have a high degree of economic and labour market differentiation that makes it possible to convert acquired knowledge and skills. (Daun, 2010, p. 409)

One further result of the mismatch between investment in education and the labour market in developing countries is the emigration of more highly qualified personnel from the poorer to the richer countries – a 'south to north' brain drain. For example, it was estimated that there were about 100,000 highly educated African professionals working in the USA alone in the late 1990s and this was linked by the International Monetary Fund to an upsurge in absolute poverty in sub-Saharan Africa because investment in education was not being translated into a catalyst for economic growth (Kigotho, 1999).

For many children in rural primary schools in developing countries, the poor quality of education (too little money being spread too thinly over the school-age population), the selective nature of each stage of the educational pyramid (where only a proportion of learners progress from one level to the next) and the lack of useful social and economic contacts in the labour market simply means that they leave schools ill equipped for the world of work and often with a sense of failure. Indeed, one study of human capital and educational expansion in Ghana (Rolleston & Okech, 2008) found that, while the basic tenets of human capital theory held, educational expansion and the lack of growth in wages and employment squeezed the benefits to education. Rapid expansion of education may have contributed to qualification inflation where the private benefit of education is eroded in financial terms. Rolleston and Okech conclude:

> Moreover, rapid educational expansion de-linked from economic opportunity may be associated with a number of negative effects including increasing difficulty for the poorest in accessing the 'educational route' out of poverty, an

56

increasing psychological sense of 'underdevelopment' and 'disadvantage', and an inflationary cycle which devalues educational credentials while further increasing demand for education. (2008, p. 338)

Increased expenditure on, or investment in, education in itself is not therefore necessarily a guarantee of economic growth and personal prosperity. It is the economy which must generate economic growth, with education perhaps best being seen as either hampering or facilitating this growth through the quantity, nature and quality of provision.

Dependency Theory

While human capital theory emphasises the role of education in generating within-country economic growth as the basis for national development, dependency theory (Baran, 1957; Frank, 1967) rejects the possibility of countries developing independently. Based on Marxist ideas of the exploitation of the poor by the rich (further discussed below), dependency theory does not see all poorer countries as 'developing' towards some future developed goal. It argues that poorer countries are underdeveloped because other, industrial, countries are developed. It posits that the relationship between the 'metropole' or rich and powerful northern countries and the 'periphery' of poorer southern countries is based on exploitation and domination. Rather than poor countries being poor because they are not economically developed or 'modern', they remain poor because the more powerful capitalist countries of the 'metropole' (Western Europe and North America) can use their financial, organisational and technological supremacy to control the terms of trade. This means that they can buy primary goods (agricultural and mining products) at low prices and sell manufactured goods at prices favourable to themselves. Within the underdeveloped societies, ruling elites are not so much post-independence as neo-colonial in that they retain attitudes, interests and allegiances consistent with the countries of the metropole. As a result, imported consumer goods are favoured over locally produced ones, and the interests of multinational corporations are favoured over small local producers and employers. Therefore both poorer countries and rich elites within the countries become dependent on the more powerful countries.

An example in educational terms is that:

because of the power of world languages such as English, developed country publishers are able to sell textbooks and educational resources at competitive rates, undermining the establishment of indigenous publishing firms. The textbooks and northern examining boards drive the curriculum and local assessment, and schools become more locked in a cycle of neo-colonial education which may not fit the culture of their people. (Harber & Davies, 1997, p. 86)

There are a number of criticisms of dependency theory, the most important of which are of its deterministic and static nature and its resultant failure to provide a coherent strategy for change:

> Perhaps the most serious difficulty with dependency theory has been its failure to provide a viable strategy for development ... the important question is what kind of dependency and what kind of development should be pursued in any given context. The dependency theorists have given very few guidelines in this regard. (Fägerlind & Saha, 1989, p. 25)

It also notably fails to explain the economic growth and development of the 'peripheral' capitalist countries of South-East Asia like Singapore, Hong Kong, Taiwan, South Korea, China and parts of India.

More recently Tikly (2004) has written of a new form of dependency based on Western imperialism that incorporates developing countries into its global interests. Through this imperialism the attitudes of a dominating metropolitan centre predominate in a distant territory. Economic globalisation has meant:

> imposing trade liberalisation measures with the object of opening up new markets in low-income countries for western goods and services; the emergence of a system of global economic regulation in which the more powerful nations have been able to determine terms of trade in goods and services; locating manufacturing production wherever in the peripheral global economy production costs are lowest; and ... imposing a system of debt peonage (servitude) on low-income countries that has served to oil the wheels of the global financial markets. (Tikly, 2004, p. 176)

A key aspect of this is the way in which Western economic discourses on education, particularly human capital theory, have been imposed on developing countries via institutions like the World Bank, despite its Western cultural bias. Thus, as a result of rates of return analysis, priority has been given within loans and aid to primary education:

> the over-emphasis on primary education at the expense of other levels of education removes the indigenous capacity for research and innovation which is centrally important if countries are to link education to indigenously determined future development priorities. (Tikly, 2004, p. 190)

Also, given the continued hegemony of Western textbooks, materials and resources, he argues that it is likely that education will continue to serve as a basis for a Eurocentric kind of education for most of the world's children.

Socio-economic Reproduction

Within countries, human capital theory has an underlying assumption of meritocracy – those who do best in, and because of, education have better absorbed the knowledge, skills and attitudes of schooling and are therefore more successful in the labour market, both in terms of getting jobs and getting better paid for them. So, inequality is the result of equal competition, with the more 'able' getting their rewards. However, as we began to see in chapter 2, there is much evidence of inequality within the education system, so that the reasons why people succeed or fail may have less to do with innate ability and effort than both their social origins and their experiences of schooling. In a nutshell, the argument is that those who begin life in poorer and/or less advantaged groups tend to go to lower status and poorer schools and end up in lower status and less well-paid occupations – or no occupation at all. The reverse is true for those from upper and middle level groups in society. While there may be exceptions of people who succeed despite their disadvantaged backgrounds, the experience of upward social mobility for a few masks the fact that the majority stay in the socio-economic group in which they began their lives. From this perspective, education is essentially a mechanism of socio-economic reproduction rather than one of equality of opportunity.

There are many reasons why education systems favour certain groups over others (see Holsinger & Jacob [2008, p. 5] for a useful and extensive list of the factors involved and for relevant literature). While much has been written on the role of education in social and economic reproduction, perhaps the most wide-ranging theoretical explanation is from a Marxist or neo-Marxist (i.e. new or revived) perspective, though not all writers on reproduction are necessarily Marxist. Karl Marx saw nineteenth-century capitalist society as divided into unequal and eventually antagonistic economic classes where the rich bourgeoisie, or middle class, who owned the means of production (land, factories, commerce, etc.), exploited the poorer proletariat, who sold their labour and worked for them. In terms of this analysis, those who had economic power because they owned the means of production also had political power at the level of the state. However, control of the state by the economic ruling class did not just mean control of the proletariat or working class by force through bodies such as the police, the judiciary and the army. It also meant control through institutions that influenced how people thought by the transmission of an ideology or a particular system of thought that taught people to accept their place in society and take for granted the given and unequal social and economic order.

Marx himself wrote little on education, though he did see relationships in schools, as much as those in factories, as serving the needs of the ruling class: 'a schoolmaster is a productive labourer, when in addition to belabouring the heads of his scholars, he works like a horse to enrich the school proprietor. That the latter has laid out his capital in a teaching factory, instead of a sausage factory, does not alter the relation' (Marx, 1867, cited in Hill et al, 2008, p. 59).

The role of education was given more attention by the Italian Marxist writer Antonio Gramsci (1977), who used the term 'hegemonic' ideas; that is, the dominant ideas in a society that support the ruling group and which are given far greater credence than other ideas in the media and in the education system. Examples might include dominant religious values, nationalism and patriotism, authoritarianism, the identification of a particular enemy, competition, individualism, monarchy, meritocracy and patriarchy. The aim is to create predispositions to certain values and beliefs supportive of existing ruling groups in the minds of learners so that they are given more weight than others and indeed become taken for granted and seen as natural and inevitable.

Indeed, it has been argued that socio-economic control and reproduction of the status quo has been a feature of formal schooling since its inception. Green's historical study of the origins of formal schooling systems in England, France, the United States and Prussia in the nineteenth century argues that a key purpose of their construction was the formation and consolidation of national consciousness but with different implications for different levels of the social order:

> The nineteenth century education system came to assume a primary responsibility for the moral, cultural and political development of the nation. It became the secular church. It was variously called upon to assimilate immigrant cultures, to promote established religious doctrines, to spread the standard form of the appointed national language, to forge a national identity and a national culture, to generalise new habits of routine and rational calculation, to encourage patriotic values, to inculcate moral disciplines and, above all, to indoctrinate in the political and economic creeds of the dominant classes. It helped construct the very subjectivities of citizenship, justifying the ways of the state to the people and the duties of the people to the state. It sought to create each person as a universal subject but it did so differentially according to class and gender. (1990, p. 80)

Schooling thus provided a means of social and political control, in particular to counter the threat to the state of increasingly industrialised, urbanised and potentially organised working populations. As Green's study argues, 'The task of public schooling was not so much to develop new skills for the industrial sector as to inculcate habits of conformity, discipline and morality that would counter the widespread problems of social disorder' (1990, p. 59).

Schooling for the majority would be organised accordingly to prepare future workers with the subordinate values and behaviours necessary for the modern bureaucratic, mass production workplace and the existing social order – regularity, routine, monotonous work and strict discipline. Its organisational form would therefore need to be authoritarian in order to inculcate habits of obedience and conformity. As Marten Shipman put it in his study of the history of education and modernisation:

> Punctuality, quiet orderly work in groups, response to orders, bells and timetables, respect for authority, even tolerance of monotony, boredom, punishment, lack of reward and regular attendance at place of work are the habits to be learned at school ... Education not only prepares for new ways of living it also stresses attitudes to authority that help to preserve the existing distribution of power. (1971, pp. 47, 54-55)

This authoritarian model of schooling with its origins in state formation, modernisation and social and political control gradually extended globally from European societies through colonisation, where the key purpose of schooling was to help to control indigenous populations for the benefit of the colonial power. By the 1930s colonialism had exercised its sway over 84.6% of the land surface of the globe (Loomba, 1998, p. 15). When formal education was eventually provided, missionary schools and those of the colonial state were used to control local populations by teaching the superiority of the culture of the colonising power and by supplying the subordinate personnel necessary for the effective functioning of the colonial administration (Altbach & Kelly, 1978). Even if it was not always entirely successful in this, and indeed in the end helped to sow the seeds of its own destruction, the organisational style of schooling bequeathed by both the needs of industrialised mass production and then colonialism remains as a firm legacy in many postcolonial societies.

In a study of the ex-British colony of Trinidad and Tobago, for example, London argues that

> Schooling was intended to inculcate into the colonised a worldview of voluntary subservience to the ruling groups, and a willingness to continue to occupy positions on the lowest rungs of the occupational and social ladder. A number of

effective strategies were used in the process, but the most significant among these was the instructional programmes and teaching methodologies used in colonial schools ... Values, attitudes and behaviour were highlighted such as the habits of obedience, order, punctuality and honesty. (London, 2002, p. 57)

Some of the characteristics of colonial schooling in Trinidad and Tobago outlined by London include mindlessness, verbatim repetition, character development, mastery of rules as a prerequisite for application, use of abstract illustrations, monotonous drill, inculcation of specified norms for cleanliness and neatness, and harsh discipline. He concludes by arguing that schooling is one of the places where colonial forms and practices have persisted and remained essentially the same throughout the postcolonial period.

A similar authoritarian stress on conformity and obedience existed, for example, in British India (Alexander, 2000, p. 92), francophone Africa (Moumouni, 1968) and Portuguese Mozambique (Barnes, 1982). In a study of contemporary schooling in India, Mali, Lebanon, Liberia, Mozambique, Pakistan, Mongolia, Ethiopia and Peru for the Department for International Development/Save the Children the authors note that

Almost all the systems were essentially modelled on those of the colonial powers (Britain, France, Portugal and Spain) and still use styles of classroom discipline and teaching methodology that were current a hundred years ago or more in the colonial country. (Molteno et al, 2000, p. 13)

The Mechanisms of Reproduction of Educational Inequality

If we are to understand how economic and social reproduction takes place via education then we need to examine the mechanisms by which it actually takes place. First, there are clearly out-of-school factors in developing countries that influence who actually goes to school in the first place, who drops out early, as well as who actually benefits from schooling. It might be that social and cultural practices exclude certain groups from education more than others. For example, parents who have to pay school fees may prefer to keep girls at home to help with domestic work and send boys to school. In some countries nomadic or pastoralist groups may find it much more difficult to access schooling than more geographically settled communities. In countries affected by disasters such as flooding, earthquakes, drought or war those communities affected most – usually the poorest – will have difficulty accessing schooling. High school fees will also deter the poorest groups from attending school. In rural areas the need for agricultural labour, large distances between home and school and a poor transport infrastructure may deter children from attending school (see, for example, the annual UNESCO Education for All Global Monitoring Reports on these and related factors).

However, there are also factors which certain children bring with them that give them an advantage from the beginning. Children from more affluent homes bring with them what has been termed 'cultural capital' (Bourdieu & Passeron, 1977); that is, their home provides an advantage in schooling because it has access to books, travel, the Internet and parents who are educated and can help, guide and encourage children. They can also provide extra help in the form of paying for extra tuition (UNESCO, 2011, p. 89). Moreover, children from such backgrounds may well also be more successful in school because they possess attributes favoured by teachers, are 'labelled' as good students and are expected to perform successfully as such – with the opposite being the case as well (Meighan & Harber, 2007, ch. 25).

The type of school a child attends can also have an effect. For example, if parents can afford the fees of the more expensive, high-status private schools this can provide an advantage. In Africa, the children of political elites have tended to go to certain schools modelled on the British public (independent) schools, or the French *lycées*. One example would be Kamuzu Academy in Malawi founded by the then President of Malawi, Dr Hastings Kamuzu Banda. This school, which was highly selective, was closely based on a British public school. Classics (the study of the ancient Greek and Latin languages) was compulsory and all instruction was in English; pupils heard speaking Chichewa were liable to be punished. The school was deliberately and explicitly created for the minority that Banda hoped would go on to become the leaders of Malawi (Harber, 1989, pp. 6-9; 1997, p. 9; Carroll, 2002). In the postcolonial period Boyle (1999) explores how the growth of expensive private schools in Cameroon, Congo and Kenya have contributed to social class formation and reproduction. Likewise, in Nigeria, expensive private schools have enabled the rich to purchase educational advantage (Rose & Adelabu, 2007).

In India a higher proportion of upper-caste children are enrolled in fee-paying private schools and the same schools are not a factor favouring gender or other forms of social equity (Mehrotra & Panchamukhi, 2007, p. 136). What these fees buy for more affluent groups in many developing countries are better school facilities, a more personalised approach to learning, and better teachers, and the result is both better academic achievement and, importantly, better social and organisational skills (Kitaev, 2007, p. 102). In Nepal the difference in academic results is stark: in 2005 29% of 171,440 government school students passed the School Leaving Certificate while 80% of the 44,863 private schools' entrants passed (Caddell, 2006, p. 463). Caddell argues that elite schools in Kathmandu tend to emphasise the cosmopolitan school environment – their international staff, the choice of non-Nepalese curricula and examinations and the range of international colleges and universities that their graduates have attended. Principals emphasise how attending their institution allows young people to become doctors or engineers and enables them to move away from their village. Conversely, and as evidence from a wide range of African and other developing countries strongly suggests, the postcolonial educational experience for most young people outside of an elite school continues to be authoritarian, designed for those who take orders, and follow rather than give orders (Harber, 2004, ch. 2). This will be further discussed in chapter 5.

Experiences within school can be unequal for different groups as well. Those from an ethnic minority in a country might be at a disadvantage if the language of instruction is the national language with which they are not familiar, and children from poorer backgrounds may be at a disadvantage if the language of instruction in school is the ex-colonial language used competently only by elites (Brock-Utne, 2008). Children from ethnic minorities might suffer discrimination by and prejudice from both fellow students and teachers, which affects their academic performance (Harber, 2004, ch. 6). Discrimination against girls in the form of sexual harassment and violence by both other male students and male teachers is not uncommon in schools and can lead to underperformance and school drop-out (e.g. Leach & Mitchell, 2006). Language and gender are discussed in more detail in chapters 17 and 10, and education and ethnicity is further discussed in chapter 6.

Finally, disability can be a factor in the way that schools reproduce inequality. Four out of five children with disabilities globally are in developing countries. In Malawi, Tanzania and Burkina Faso, being disabled doubles the chance of not attending school. Within schools children with disabilities face institutionalised discrimination, stigmatisation and neglect. In Ghana the Ministry of Education, for example, has said that the education of children with disabilities is undervalued by families and that children with disabilities in mainstream schools receive less attention from teachers. Many schools continue to be physically inaccessible to pupils with disabilities, and their families and schools lack the financial support that would help with fuller educational participation (UNESCO, 2010, pp. 181-183).

While there is much truth in social reproduction theory, as there is with theories of both human capital and dependency, it too has its problems. The main problem with theories of social reproduction is the danger of over-determinism – that they explain a situation in which certain groups (the poor, the disabled, females, etc.) and the individuals within them can never succeed, despite their abilities and best efforts. The layers of social stratification are fixed and unchanging and education merely serves to faithfully reproduce them from one generation to the next for everybody. Clearly there are many exceptions to an 'iron law' of reproduction and individuals from disadvantaged groups do succeed in education and beyond despite their backgrounds. Indeed, there are times, such as in the immediate postcolonial period and in times of rapid educational expansion, when levels of upward social and economic mobility may be high, even though elements of social reproduction are also present.

Conclusion

In post-Second World War discussion of development the economic dimension of development – economic growth – has tended to be given priority until relatively recently. As this chapter has suggested, for the past fifty years education has been seen as having an important role in economic development by producing more skilled, knowledgeable and ultimately productive workers for the economy. However, educational opportunities are not spread equally and some groups in developing countries – the affluent, the more powerful, males and the able bodied, for example – have enjoyed better access to education and had more successful experiences within it. In this way education is also a site of economic and social reproduction as well as one that offers opportunities for all. A parallel, more sociological, theory of development to that of human capital theory is modernisation theory and it is to this that we turn in the next chapter.

References

Alexander, R. (2000) *Culture and Pedagogy: international comparisons in primary education*. Oxford: Blackwell.

Altbach, P. & Kelly, G. (1978) *Education and Colonialism*. London: Longman.

Baran, P. (1957) *The Political Economy of Growth*. New York: Monthly Review Press.

Barnes, B. (1982) Education for Socialism in Mozambique, *Comparative Education Review*, 26(3), 406-419.

Becker, G. (1964) *Human Capital: a theoretical and empirical analysis with special reference to education*. Princeton: Princeton University Press.

Bing, W.K. (2008) Education and Inequality in the Developing World, in D. Holsinger & W. Jacob (Eds) *Inequality in Education: comparative and international perspectives*. Comparative Education Research Centre, University of Hong Kong, vol. 24. Hong Kong: Springer.

Bourdieu, P. & Passeron, J. (1977) *Reproduction in Education, Society and Culture*. London: Sage.

Boyle, P. (1999) *Class Formation and Civil Society: the politics of education in Africa*. Aldershot: Ashgate.

Clive Harber

Brock-Utne, B. (2008) Language and Democracy in Africa, in D. Holsinger & W. Jacob (Eds) *Inequality in Education: comparative and international perspectives.* Comparative Education Research Centre, University of Hong Kong, vol. 24. Hong Kong: Springer.

Caddell, M. (2006) Private Schools as Battlefields: contested visions of learning and livelihood in Nepal, *Compare,* 36(4), 463-480.

Carroll, R. (2002) The Eton of Africa, *The Guardian,* 25 November.

Chang, H-J. (2011) *23 Things They Don't Tell You about Capitalism.* London: Penguin.

Colclough, C. (2012) Education, Poverty and Development: mapping their interconnections, *Comparative Education,* 48(2), 135-148.

Daun, H. (2010) Childhood Learning, Life Skills and Well-being in Adult Life: a Senegalese case, *Comparative Education,* 46(4), 409-428.

Dore, R. (1976) *The Diploma Disease.* London: Allen & Unwin.

Fägerlind, I. & Saha, L. (1989) *Education and National Development: a comparative perspective.* Oxford: Pergamon.

Frank, G. (1967) *Capitalism and Underdevelopment in Latin America.* New York: Monthly Review Press.

Gramsci, A. (1977) *Selections from the Prison Notebooks of Antonio Gramsci,* ed. and trans. Q. Hoare & G. Nowell Smith. London: Lawrence & Wishart.

Green, A. (1990) *Education and State Formation.* London: Macmillan.

Harber, C. (1989) *Politics in African Education.* London: Macmillan.

Harber, C. (1997) *Education, Democracy and Political Development in Africa.* Brighton: Sussex Academic Press.

Harber, C. (2004) *Schooling as Violence: how schools harm pupils and societies.* London: RoutledgeFalmer.

Harber, C. & Davies, L. (1997) *School Management and School Effectiveness in Developing Countries.* London: Cassell.

Hill, D., Greaves, N. & Maisura, A. (2008) Does Capitalism Inevitably Increase Inequality?, in D. Holsinger & W. Jacob (Eds) *Inequality in Education: comparative and international perspectives.* Comparative Education Research Centre, University of Hong Kong, vol. 24. Hong Kong: Springer.

Holsinger, D. and Jacob, W. (2008) *Inequality in Education: comparative and international perspectives.* Comparative Education Research Centre, University of Hong Kong, vol. 24. Hong Kong: Springer.

Kigotho, W. (1999) IMF Links African Slump to Brain Drain, *Times Higher Education Supplement,* 9 July.

Kitaev, I. (2007) Education for All and Private Education in Developing and Transitional Countries, in P. Srivastava & G. Walford (Eds) *Private Schooling in Less Economically Developed Countries.* Oxford: Symposium Books.

Leach, F. & Mitchell, C. (Eds) (2006) *Combating Gender Violence in and around Schools.* Stoke-on-Trent: Trentham Books.

Little, A. (2003) Motivating Learning and Development, *Compare,* 33(4), 429-436.

London, N. (2002) Curriculum Convergence: an ethno-historical investigation into schooling in Trinidad and Tobago, *Comparative Education*, 38(1), 53-72.

Loomba, A. (1998) *Colonialism/Postcolonialism*. London: Routledge.

Mehrotra, S. & Panchamukhi, P.R. (2007) Universalising Elementary Education in India: is the private sector the answer?, in P. Srivastava & G. Walford, (Eds) *Private Schooling in Less Economically Developed Countries*. Oxford: Symposium Books.

Meighan, R. & Harber, C. (2007) *A Sociology of Educating*. London: Continuum.

Molteno, M., Ogadhoh, K., Cain, E. & Crumpton, B. (2000) *Towards Responsive Schools: supporting better schooling for disadvantaged children*. London: Department for International Development/Save the Children.

Moumouni, A. (1968) *Education in Africa*. London: Andre Deutsch.

Oxenham, J. (1984) *Education versus Qualifications?* London: Allen & Unwin.

Psacharopoulos, G. & Patrinos, H. (2004) Returns to Investment in Education: a further update, *Education Economics*, 12(2), 111-134.

Rolleston, C. & Okech, M. (2008) Educational Expansion in Ghana: economic assumptions and expectations, *International Journal of Educational Development*, 28(3), 320-339.

Rose, P. & Adelabu, M. (2007) Private Sector Contributions to Education for All in Nigeria, in P. Srivastava & G. Walford, (Eds) *Private Schooling in Less Economically Developed Countries*. Oxford: Symposium Books.

Samoff, J. (1999) Institutionalising International Influence, in R. Arnove & C. Torres (Eds) *Comparative Education: the dialectic of the global and the local*. Oxford: Rowman & Littlefield.

Schultz, T. (1961) Investment in Human Capital, *American Economic Review*, 51, 1-17.

Shipman, M. (1971) *Education and Modernisation*. London: Faber.

Tikly, L. (2004) Education and the New Imperialism, *Comparative Education*, 40(2), 173-198.

UNESCO (2011) *The Hidden Crisis: armed conflict and education*. EFA Global Monitoring Report. Paris: UNESCO.

UNESCO (2010) *Reaching the Marginalised*. EFA Global Monitoring Report. Paris: UNESCO.

United Nations Development Programme (2011) *Human Development Report*. Basingstoke: Palgrave Macmillan.

Further Reading

Buchmann, C. & Hannum, E. (2001) Education and Stratification in Developing Countries: a review of theories and research, *Annual Review of Sociology*, 27, 77-102.

Compare (2004) 34(1) – Special Edition, 'Towards a Comparative Economics of Education'.

Hartog, J. (2000) Human Capital as an Instrument of Analysis for the Economics of Education, *European Journal of Education,* 35(1), 7-20.

Leach, F. & Little, A. (1999) *Education, Cultures and Economics.* London: RoutledgeFalmer.

Resnick, J. (2006) International Organisations, the Education-Economics Black Box and the Development of World Education Culture, *Comparative Education Review,* 50(2), 173-195.

Walker, M. (2012) A Capital or Capabilities Education Narrative in a World of Staggering Inequalities, *International Journal of Educational Development,* 32(3), 384-393.

Discussion and Activities

1. Chang (2011, p. 189) writes that 'Education is valuable, but its main value is not in raising productivity. It lies in its ability to help us develop our potentials and live a more fulfilling and independent life'. Do you agree with this statement?
2. Pupils at school are often told, 'work hard and you will do well'. Does the truth of this depend primarily on who you are?
3. Karl Marx wrote that 'The tradition of all dead generations weighs like a nightmare on the brains of the living'. In what ways do you think that the colonial experience might still manifest itself in schools in postcolonial countries?

CHAPTER 4

Modernisation or the 'Prismatic' Society and Institution?

And the history of developing societies in the last 30 years
suggests that it would be foolhardy to ignore some of the
insights of that large body of theoretical and empirical
scholarship on modernisation. (Leftwich, 1996, p. 21)

Introduction

Modernisation theories of development were at the height of their
influence in the 1960s and 70s. Modernisation theory sees all societies as
moving from less complex, undifferentiated and agrarian social systems
to modern, industrial societies. Wealth and economic growth are linked
to the degree of development along this continuum. If societies are poor
or 'underdeveloped', it is because they have not evolved the social,
cultural, economic and political structures for industrialisation and
economic take-off. An institution seen as central to the process of
modernisation, or becoming modern, is the school.

A key critique of modernisation theory was its Western bias – its
assumption that all societies needed to develop in the same historical
manner and direction as Western Europe and North America. However,
while this remains a serious criticism of modernisation theory in general,
the introduction of formal schooling through European colonialism in
Africa was nevertheless the introduction of an essentially Western and
modern system and organisation into less modern societies. The
postcolonial period has witnessed an enormous expansion of this
organisational form of learning. This chapter examines whether
schooling actually operates in the modern way in which it is supposed to
by drawing on ideas of a 'prismatic' society and organisations and as a
case study of educational decentralisation in Uganda.

Modernisation and Education

A 'modern' society, according to modernisation theory, is one
that has such features as an ethic of science and rationality,

industrialisation, urbanisation, bureaucratisation, differentiation and specialisation of social structures, the principles of individualism and political stability. (Leftwich, 1996, pp. 6-11)

Peet and Hartwick (2009, p. 122) put it that:

in the economic sphere, modernisation meant specialisation of economic activities and occupational roles and the growth of markets; in terms of socio-spatial organisation, modernisation meant urbanisation, mobility, flexibility and the spread of education; in the political sphere, modernisation meant the spread of democracy and the weakening of traditional elites; in the cultural sphere, modernisation meant growing differentiation between the various cultural and value systems (for example, a separation between religion and philosophy), secularisation, and the emergence of a new intelligentsia. These developments were closely related to the expansion of modern communications media and the consumption of the culture created by centrally placed elites, manifested as changes in attitudes, especially the emergence of an outlook that stressed individual self-advancement.

A key example of modernisation theory was the work of McLelland (1961) on the 'achievement motive' where the values of hard work, punctuality, competition and capability of divorcing work from family ties would lead to economic and technological development.

However, of particular concern for present purposes are the characteristics of individual modernity – how is a 'modern' person different from a 'traditional' one and how does that change take place? The work of Inkeles and Smith (1974) focused on individual modernity, what a modern individual might look like and which socialisation agencies most contribute to individual modernity. They set out the key differences as shown in Table III.

Blakemore and Cooksey (1981, pp. 169-180) added further differences: that a modern person is more individualistic as opposed to putting the family and group first; is rational (seeks scientific explanation) rather than believing in magical and religious explanations; has a need for personal achievement as opposed to emphasising habit or custom; is punctual and relies on the clock as opposed to not being regulated by precise units of time; favours urban living and working in large organisations as opposed to rural living and distrusting large organisations; sees occupation as the main determinant of status and life's purpose as opposed to traditional or religious positions being more important.

Traditional	Modern
Not receptive to new ideas	Open to new experiences
Rooted in tradition	Change oriented
Interested only in immediate things	Interested in the outside world
Denial of different opinions	Acknowledgement of different opinions
Uninterested in new information	Eager to seek out new information
Oriented towards the past	Punctual; oriented towards the present
Concerned with the short term	Values planning
Distrustful of people beyond the family	Calculability; trusts people to meet obligations
Suspicious of technology	Values technical skills
Places high value on religion and the sacred	Places high value on education and science
Traditional patron–client relationships	Respects the dignity of others
Particularistic	Universalistic
Fatalistic	Optimistic

Table III. Key differences between a traditional and a modern individual.
Source: Inkeles & Smith (1974).

The key organisational form that embodies the emphasis on rationalism in modernisation (Peet and Hartwick, 2009, ch. 4) is bureaucracy. For Inkeles, for example, the modern state and society is 'suffused with bureaucratic rationality' (1969, p. 1122). Indeed, the organisational model most commonly used to describe the school is that of a bureaucracy or rule by officials. Max Weber, a key exponent of rationalism in sociological thought, argued that bureaucracies had the following characteristics:

1. Staff members are personally free, observing only the impersonal duties of office.
2. There is a clear hierarchy of offices.
3. The functions of the offices are clearly specified.
4. Officials are appointed on the basis of a contract.
5. They [officials] are selected on the basis of a professional qualification, ideally substantiated by a diploma gained through examination.
6. They [officials] receive a money salary and usually pension rights. The salary is graded according to position in the hierarchy. The official can always leave the post and under certain circumstances it may also be terminated.
7. The official's post is his or her sole occupation.
8. There is a career structure and promotion is possible by either seniority or merit and according to the judgement of superiors.

9. The official may appropriate neither the post nor the resources that go with it.
10. The official is subject to a unified control and disciplinary system. (Weber, cited in Albrow, 1970, pp. 44-45

In his empirical work Inkeles found education to have the strongest relationship of all variables to the possession of modern (i.e. bureaucratic) attitudes, values and behaviour. This is partly because the pupil at school learns new skills such as reading, writing and arithmetic so that he or she will be able to 'read directions and instructions and to follow events in the newspaper' but also because of the bureaucratic nature of the hidden curriculum (what is taught and learned in school every day but doesn't actually appear on the official curriculum):

> School starts and stops at fixed times each day. Within the school day there generally is a regular sequence for ordering activities: singing, reading, writing, drawing, all have their scheduled and usually invariant times. Teachers generally work according to this plan ... Thus, principles directly embedded in the daily routine of the school teach the value of planning ahead and the importance of maintaining a regular schedule. (Inkeles & Smith, 1974, p. 141)

Toffler argued in a similar vein with a more critical perspective that:

> Mass education was the ingenious machine constructed by industrialism to produce the kind of adults it needed ... the solution was an educational system that, in its very structure, simulated this new world ... the regimentation, lack of individualisation, the rigid systems of seating, grouping, grading and marking, the authoritarian style of the teacher – are precisely those that made mass public education so effective as an instrument of adaptation for its time and place. (1970, pp. 354-355)

As we have seen, this modern, largely bureaucratic, organisational model of schooling was introduced to most developing countries through and during colonialism (Altbach & Kelly, 1978; Molteno, 2000; London, 2002). As Booth (1997, p. 433), for example, puts it, 'In post-colonial Africa, the school is the ultimate example of a transported alien institution designed to create change'.

Fuller (1991) argues in some detail that the push to expand schooling as a visible and tangible symbol of bureaucratic modernity in the postcolonial period in developing countries has helped to legitimate the relatively new and often fragile state, despite the regular failure of schools to actually deliver learning outcomes such as literacy and numeracy. Indeed, this failure to achieve learning outcomes starts to suggest another major problem with modernisation theory in relation to education. This concerns the reality of school organisation in developing countries. In practice, social organisations such as schools tend to reflect the actual values and behaviours of their surrounding society rather than perfectly match an ideal-type, imported Weberian bureaucracy. So it would be surprising if schools in developing countries were to act autonomously as 'modernising' change agents independently of their society, i.e. if the society is marked by non-modern structures and behaviours then why should schools be any different?

Education in a 'Prismatic Society'

> My friend Chimtali, age 14 ... recently entered a government boarding school to pursue her secondary studies ... While Chimtali obviously enjoyed becoming modern, she had not suspected that the secondary school would require such deep changes in daily habits. (Fuller, 1991, p. 96)

Riggs (1964) described developing countries as having 'prismatic societies'. He used the analogy of a fused white light passing through a prism and emerging diffracted as a series of different colours. Within the prism there is a point where the diffraction process starts but remains incomplete. Riggs was suggesting that developing societies contain both elements of a traditional, fused type of social organisation and elements of the more structurally differentiated or 'modern' societies. He argued that the societies of most developing countries, and the organisations that exist within them, are a synthesis – though not always a harmonious one – of traditional, long-lasting indigenous values and practices and relatively new ones imported during and after colonialism. They are neither fully modern nor fully traditional. As a result, within the form or facade of modern, bureaucratic organisation much that happens in schools will reflect older priorities and needs emanating from family and village as well as newer ones emanating from the Ministry of Education. For example, a basic tenet of modernity is regular attendance at a place of work, and punctuality. However, staff and student absenteeism and lack of punctuality are marked problems in schools in developing countries where harvests, markets and family responsibilities can take priority over schooling.

So, not only can there be cultural conflicts of expectations for schooling between the home and the school (Booth, 1997), but evidence from a range of developing countries suggests that schools themselves primarily reproduce the values and behaviours of the existing 'prismatic' society rather than acting as independent and self-contained agents of modernisation (Harber & Davies, 1997; Davies et al, 2003). The net result is that teachers and schools can exhibit what is regarded as unprofessional behaviour in a modern institutional setting. For example, in a more traditional and ethnically homogeneous setting such as a village, favouring one's own ethnic or clan group member for some sort of post of responsibility is normal, but once this is moved into a modern state setting, such as a school or education system, it becomes nepotism. In a traditional setting, giving priority to harvesting the crops at a certain time of year is fine, but in a modern setting like a school it becomes student or teacher absenteeism. A final example is that in a traditional rural/agricultural setting very precise time measurement is far less important, but move this into a modern setting like a school and this imprecision becomes student and teacher lateness.

Evidence of the prismatic ways that schools can operate in developing countries has come from two East African studies. In a study of Tanzanian schools, for example, Van Der Steen (2011, p. 162) found the following examples of practices at odds with modern bureaucratic principles:

- a teacher being physically assaulted by an education officer at the municipal office when complaining about a work-related issue;
- a teacher reportedly not being paid salary for five months as she refused to pay 'commission' to the accountant in charge;
- teachers ordered to carry out demographic surveys in their neighbourhood on behalf of the municipal office without financial compensation;
- the monthly payment of teachers' salaries rarely being on time;
- a teacher using her influence in the municipal education office not to be transferred to a school she did not want to go to;
- reporting of inaccurate information about progress such as exaggerating the provision of education to disadvantaged children and the number enrolled in schools;
- punitive action against a head teacher who refused to use school funds to provide visiting officials with meals;
- bribery in the allocation of secondary school places to primary school leavers.

The remainder of this chapter is concerned with a detailed case study of the contextual realities of how education can operate in a developing country. Oryema (2008) carried out a qualitative study of educational decentralisation in Uganda, using the idea of a prismatic society to link certain traditional cultural traits to actual behaviour that fell outside of a modern, rational-bureaucratic framework of policy-making to *explain* how and why educational practice in a developing country can differ significantly from the policy intentions of national governments and international organisations.

Case Study: educational decentralisation and prismatic society in Uganda

The study by Oryema used interviews (e.g. with civil servants, politicians, district and town council officials, school staff and pupils); observation (of school facilities, of teachers present, of supervision and inspection); documentary evidence (policy documents, national minimum standards indicators, inspection reports); and field notes/diary to gather data in an area dominated by the 'Lurabeni' ethnic group (not the real name). The study traced local realities in the process of the implementation of the government's educational decentralisation policy. The findings of the study illustrate well how certain traditional ways still continue to coexist with and influence the modern values embraced and enshrined in Uganda's educational devolution policy. Here we shall analyse the findings according to eight themes: family size and structure; blood link solidarity; superstition and witchcraft; perceptions of authority; specialisation problems; who is who; the documentation and records vacuum; and precision and the danger of proximities.

Family Size and Structure

In interviews, respondents said that they saw the traditional polygamous, extended family as a burden rather than the proper basis of social life. This was partly because of Western education, partly because of exposure to different ways of life from other parts of the world and partly because of the financial implications. However, the respondents also acknowledged the impossibility of achieving their ideal of a 'modern' nuclear family because of pressures from relatives and in-laws, which they described as the 'unavoidable burden'. Relatives and in-laws want to be supported or even accepted to live with the family and it is difficult to say 'no' because of social pressures. The resulting 'burden' takes the form of the payment of school fees for relatives, to gifts, clothing and supporting social events such as weddings and funerals – all of which have to be paid for on top of responsibilities for the immediate nuclear family.

The consequences of these pressures for educational decentralisation were in terms of both facility provision and trained teachers. In terms of facility provision, the large, extended family meant that there was a constant search for more money – 39 out of the 40 respondents interviewed said this was a key reason for corruption among politicians and civil servants. The losses incurred by contractors building schools and the theft of other building materials was also linked to supporting the extended family. Teacher training and teaching quality are also affected, for a number of reasons. First, because of extended families many teachers cannot afford even the most minimum costs of in-service training such as transport and personal effects, so they fail to take advantage of the training opportunities. Second, as the breadwinner for the family, the teacher finds it difficult to leave the children at home whilst they go and do training. Third, the family burden means that teachers have to find other sources of income as well as their teacher's salary. This compromises their school attendance and their time for preparation of lessons at home. Finally, extended family responsibilities make most teachers resistant to transfers, which makes it difficult for district education officers to be able to address quality or disciplinary problems in certain schools.

Blood Link Solidarity

Interviews suggested that who you are and where you come from continue to be more important in determining opportunities than what you are and what you offer. This shows itself in favouritism and nepotism with regard to the awarding of contracts for school buildings, opportunities for teacher training and in teacher recruitment. Respondents in the Inspectorate reported the influence of 'blood link' in the favours expected by some teachers because they were related to them. The District Inspector of Schools noted his own experience when his uncle, who was given a contract for classroom construction but did it poorly, expected him in his official capacity to defend him. The Chief Administrative Officer related similar experiences of how people from his own place of origin had been putting him under pressure to favour them in many opportunities in the district. However, on a more positive note, in terms of community participation in the construction of schools blood links had strengthened commitment.

Superstition and Witchcraft

Belief in witchcraft continues in this Ugandan society and is a form of invisible intimidation which has effects on education. For example, the incoming chair of the council suspected the outgoing one of placing 'deadly charms' in the existing office and buildings, meaning that the meagre district funds available were used to pay for a new office, new furnishings and the means of transport to get him there and back from his home every day rather than directly on educational provision. Moreover, one head teacher explained how she was frightened to take disciplinary action against teachers suspected of witchcraft because of the possible harmful consequences. It was also reported that a number of business people were involved in occult practices as they believed it would increase their business opportunities and contracts. Whether true or not, the consistent raising of such issues reflects how belief in witchcraft persists.

Perceptions of Authority

Traditionally, authority in Lurabeni society has always been highly respected and unopposed – the chief was the 'cock of the village', as some respondents called it, and no one challenged his authority or decisions. However, in a hangover from these attitudes, some local leaders see themselves not as representatives of the people but instead want their word to be final and not subject to opposition. In the case study such an authoritarian attitude led to conflict between the council chairman and the council, resulting in an expensive commission of enquiry, using funds that could have been used on education if there had been greater use of modern democratic practice. The teachers interviewed said that facilitating teachers to obtain further qualifications was not supported by those in authority in the district because they wished to remain at the top alone and did not want competition from more highly qualified teachers. Moreover, despite some councillors admitting that the leader of the council engaged in corrupt practices, there had been no attempt by the councillors to use their power to dismiss him, their reluctance to take such steps suggesting the persistence of traditional attitudes of obedience and subordination.

Specialisation Problems

Modernisation theory emphasises lack of specialisation as one the characteristics of traditional societies (Riggs, 1964; Peet & Hardwick, 2009, ch. 4). In a traditional society one person carries out different functions, which in a more modern, differentiated society are carried out independently by different people. This manifested itself in this educational district in a number of ways. For example, in the decentralised education system the provision of facilities is the responsibility of the school project committee. Without being given any kind of training, the government has entrusted this committee with the responsibility of monitoring the day-to-day construction work at the school site. In many areas this committee consists of ordinary people with no experience of modern construction. This was the situation in the two case-study schools, with the result that they were not able to see faults and problems and the result was poor construction. In terms of inspecting schools, any civil servant can be sent out into the field, irrespective of department, to inspect schools. A veterinary, agricultural or forest officer can be used to do school inspections in the decentralised system. While this might help to meet a general shortage of educational personnel, the reliance on lack of specialisation nevertheless has negative implications for efficiency and quality in the development of a modern educational system.

Clive Harber

Who is Who?

The impact of traditional gender roles is noticeable in relation to the performance of teachers at school. The traditional role of women in Lurabeni society is that of homemaker, domestic worker, babysitter and mother, with the man in authority in the household. Female teachers who were interviewed explained that they often came to school late because in the morning they first had to provide warm water for their husband to bathe in, prepare breakfast and get the children ready for school before they themselves could prepare to go to school. Interestingly, although male teachers were more punctual in coming to school as a result, the female teachers were still better prepared for their lessons. The head teachers in the two schools (both females) highlighted the difficulties they have in dealing with male teachers because they tend to ignore or underestimate them, and have difficulty in acknowledging their leadership because of traditional gender roles.

Documentation and Records Vacuum

Traditional education in Africa did not impart writing and reading skills. This made documentation and record keeping problematic and required reliance on memory and witnesses. However, despite the fact that many people now know how to read and write, in this prismatic society the culture of documentation and written record keeping is still weak. For example, the school management and/or project committee indicated that they are not in the habit of recording their observations or compiling reports about building work going on in the school but continue to rely on observation and memory. This provides room for inaccurate reporting, especially when it comes to precise figures, dates and times, which in turn means debates, denials and self-defence when quality complaints arise. While teachers were quite good at keeping written records of their schemes of work and student progress, there were nevertheless many gaps in the written records. In the head teachers' offices documentation was scanty and not very well organised, although the heads tended to blame this on previous regimes. Supervision and inspection done by the heads in their own schools was generally not reported, the assumption being that physical presence was sufficient and the problem teachers were known. In both schools the inventory of school property was not comprehensive and land documents were missing. During the research, phrases like 'Even so and so was present and can testify; if my memory serves me right' were commonly used.

Precision and the Danger of Proximities

The people of Lurabeni traditionally tended to be imprecise in many regards, for example, in measurement and time keeping. Thus, in a society where construction was traditionally done in poles, mud and grass, there was no need for measurements to be precise and estimates could be done by eye assessment rather than scientific measurement. There was evidence of this in the poor quality of building work in the schools. In relation to time, because there were no watches, people relied on the position of the sun and times of appointments were approximate, e.g. sunset or sunrise. Among teachers and the inspectorate precise time keeping was a problem and there were many instances of lateness. One teacher noted that 'When a meeting was scheduled to start at 2.00 p.m., be prepared to start at 4.00 p.m. When you expect a meeting to last for an hour, be prepared to sit for three hours'.

These traits of Lurabeni society reveal the complexity of operating in the prismatic space between two broad worlds, the traditional and the modern. In the decentralised educational setting, because the people in control are all local, and working for local people in a local context, there is a tendency to accommodate contradictions and problems rather than to solve or correct them. This attitude, if not handled carefully, can put quality in the modern educational sector in danger. 'Modern' systems such as schools will not function well without relatively 'modern' people in them but this itself requires some long-term social and cultural change.

Conclusion

Whether all developing countries are, or should be, developing in a linear fashion towards a Western model of modernity is very debatable. It is more likely that each will develop in its own way with a mixture of Western modernity and its own cultural traits and practices. The school, however, remains a 'modern', bureaucratic form of organisation stemming from the development of mass formal education at the end of the nineteenth century. This form was introduced into developing countries via colonialism and is now a widespread feature of developing societies. How it actually operates, and the lessons it teaches, depend on its interpretation by local actors and in local contexts and, as we have seen, the result is not necessarily modern but often a site of tension or conflict between the modern and the traditional.

References

Altbach, P. & Kelly, G. (1978) *Education and Colonialism*. London: Longman.

Albrow, M. (1970) *Bureaucracy*. London: Macmillan.

Blakemore, K. & Cooksey, B. (1981) *A Sociology of Education for Africa*. London: Allen & Unwin.

Booth, M.Z. (1997) Western Schooling and Traditional Society in Swaziland, *Comparative Education*, 33(3), 433-451.

Davies, L., Harber, C. & Dzimadzi, C. (2003) Educational Decentralisation in Malawi: a study of process, *Compare*, 33(2), 139-154.

Fuller, B. (1991) *Growing Up Modern*. London: Routledge.

Harber, C. & Davies, L. (1997) *School Management and School Effectiveness in Developing Countries*. London: Cassell.

Inkeles, A, (1969) Participant Citizenship in Six Developing Countries, *American Political Science Review*, 43, 1122-1133.

Inkeles, A. & Smith, D. (1974) *Becoming Modern*. London: Heinemann.

Leftwich, A. (Ed.) (1996) *Democracy and Development*. Cambridge: Polity Press.

London, N. (2002) Curriculum Convergence: an ethno-historical investigation into schooling in Trinidad and Tobago, *Comparative Education*, 38(1), 53-72.

McLelland, D. (1961) *The Achieving Society*. New York: The Free Press.

Molteno, M., Ogadhoh, K., Cain, E. & Crumpton, B. (2000) *Towards Responsive Schools: supporting better schooling for disadvantaged children*. London: Department for International Development/Save the Children.

Oryema, D. (2008) Decentralisation Policy and Education Provision in Uganda. PhD thesis, University of Birmingham.

Peet, R. & Hartwick, E. (2009) *Theories of Development*. London: Guilford Press.

Riggs, F. (1964) *Administration in Developing Countries: the theory of prismatic society*. Boston, MA: Houghton Mifflin.

Toffler, A. (1970) *Future Shock*. London: Bodley Head.

Van Der Steen, N. (2011) School Improvement in Tanzania: school culture and the management of change. PhD thesis, Institute of Education, University of London.

Further Reading

Fägerlind, I. & Saha, L. (1989) *Education and National Development: a comparative perspective*, chapter 4. Oxford: Pergamon.

Harber, C. & Davies, L. (1997) *School Management and School Effectiveness in Developing Countries*, chapters 3, 4 and 6. London: Cassell.

Inglehart, R. & Baker, W. (2000) Modernisation, Cultural Change and the Persistence of Traditional Values, *American Sociological Review,* 65(1), 19-51.

Preston, P. (1996) *Development Theory: an introduction*, chapter 9. Oxford: Blackwell.

Wu, J. (2012) Disenchantment and Participation Limits of Compulsory Education: lessons from Southwest China, *Compare,* 42(4), 621-646.

Discussion and Activities

1. If a *country* was simply described to you as (a) 'modern' and (b) 'traditional', what characteristics would come to mind?

2. If a *person* was described to you as (a) 'modern' and (b) 'traditional', what characteristics would come to mind?

3. 'The school is a singularly modern institution' – explain why this might be thought to be the case. Do you agree?

4. Do the findings of the studies from East Africa in the chapter surprise you in any way? Explain why.

CHAPTER 5

Political Development and Democratisation

A tyrannical regime might deprive the people of their freedom, but in return they are offered an easy life. A democratic regime might fail to beat poverty but the people enjoy freedom and dignity. (Al Aswany [2011] writing on Egypt at the time of the popular uprisings in early 2011)

Introduction

This chapter examines the role of education in political development and, more specifically, in the process of democratisation in developing countries. If you were to glance at a political map of the world thirty years ago, where authoritarian and totalitarian regimes (usually single-party or military) were coloured blue and democratic and semi-democratic ones were coloured red, then most of Africa, South America, Asia and the Middle East would be coloured blue. The same map thirty years later would look strikingly different, with large parts of the 'developing' world now coloured red rather than blue, but with the Middle East remaining stubbornly blue. In recent years, however, the 'Arab Spring' has also witnessed a wave of democratic protest and reform across the Middle East. Such changes are far from perfect or complete. In Africa, for example, since the end of the Cold War some form of pluralism has been introduced or reintroduced into over 30 out of the 53 countries (Gyimah-Boadi, 2004, p. 5). However, while there has been genuine progress in terms of more free elections, more political choice, greater constitutionalism, a more active civil society and greater freedom of the media in a number of countries, some countries remain authoritarian. In others, actual regime transitions to democracy have been only patchy, resulting in talk of 'partial reform syndrome' and 'semi-democracies'.

Nevertheless, there is no doubt about the general direction in which political change has occurred in developing countries and, indeed, democracy has been increasingly seen as *the* goal of political development. The United Nations Development Programme (UNDP), for example, put it that:

> People must organise for collective action to influence the circumstances and decisions affecting their lives. To advance their interests, their voices must be heard in the corridors of power ... Ending human poverty requires a democratic space in which people can articulate demands, act collectively and fight for a more equitable distribution of power ... Government that acts in the interest of poor people is easier to achieve in democratic political systems where the poor represent a significant electoral bloc. (UNDP, 1997, pp. 94, 103, 105)

There are many different definitions of democracy (Davies, 1999), but the following captures its salient features:

> Democracy embodies the ideal that decisions affecting an association as a whole would be taken by all its members and that they would each have equal rights to take part in such decisions. Democracy entails the twin principles of popular control over collective decision-making and equality of rights in the exercise of that control. (Beetham & Boyle, 1995, p. 1)

What most definitions seem to have in common is a concern with:

- human rights: a set of entitlements which are protected and common to all individuals;
- participation: the free involvement of individuals in the decision-making process;
- equity: fair and equal treatment of individuals and groups;
- informed choice: the tools to make decisions which are based on relevant information and reason (Davies et al, 2002, pp. 4-9).

In terms of a political system, democracy is exercised through democratic institutions and processes such as regular elections that are free and fair, a free media, the rule of laws that are equally applicable to everyone, freedom of association and the exercise of free speech. A democratic *society or culture*, on the other hand, implies much greater levels of democracy and equality in daily interactions, relationships and behaviours in the workplace and in social and domestic activities. This involves a conscious attempt to remove prejudice and discrimination on the basis of, for example, race, class, gender, sexual orientation, religion, disability and age. A citizen in such a democracy would celebrate social and political diversity, work for and practise mutual respect between individuals and groups, regard all people as having equal social and political rights as human beings, respect evidence in forming their own opinions and respect the opinions of others based on evidence, be open to changing one's mind in the light of new evidence and possess a critical and analytical stance towards information. The democratic citizen would possess a proclivity to reason, open-mindedness and fairness and the practice of cooperation, bargaining, compromise and accommodation.

The British statesman and former Prime Minister Winston Churchill once put it that democracy was the worst form of government – apart from all the others. Here he was acknowledging that democracy in practice is often far from perfect in living up to the ideals set out above, but, however flawed and imperfect in reality, it still remains preferable to any authoritarian alternatives.

Political Development Theory and Democracy

Democracy has had an ambivalent relationship with modern political development theory. The chapter on political development in an earlier textbook on education and development, published as the Cold War was coming to an end with the approaching collapse of communism, only very briefly refers to democracy in passing, and the word isn't in the index at the end of the book (Fägerlind & Saha, 1989). The most influential post-war academic writers on political development came from a group of American political scientists associated with the Social Science Research Council's (SSRC) Committee on Comparative Politics, who published a series of books from the late 1950s to the early 1970s (Higgot, 1983, p. 17). O'Brien (1972) indicates how these early writers showed a strong commitment to representative democracy as a political goal. A key figure in this emphasis on democracy was the American political scientist Gabriel Almond. While genuinely democratic processes cannot be achieved overnight or in the immediate future, 'in the new and modernising nations of Asia, Africa and Latin America, the processes of enlightenment and democratisation will have their inevitable way' (Almond, 1970, p. 232).

A corollary of this aim of democratic political development was the emphasis given to the importance of political culture and political socialisation. Political culture is the pattern of values and attitudes about politics held by a population which influences the ways in which a society's political institutions operate. Political socialisation is the process by which these values and attitudes are learned from various agencies such as the family, the mass media and the school. For writers such as Almond, therefore, key issues were the nature of the political culture that would be supportive of democracy and how and where those values might be learned.

However, O'Brien (1972) further argues that in the second half of the 1960s, in the light of a pattern of civil wars and military coups d'état in postcolonial countries, the earlier optimistic emphasis on democracy gave way to a new, more pessimistic emphasis on the importance of stability and order. From the perspective of an America embroiled in an escalating war in Vietnam, order and stability appeared preferable to the disorder and instability in which their communist archenemy could thrive. Better a pro-American authoritarian regime than the risk of an unstable democratic one. As one commentator has noted, 'The interest in order of those at the top is given a logical precedence over the interest in social justice at the bottom' (Sandbrook, 1976, pp. 180-181).

Since the early 1970s, and particularly since 1989, however, the emphasis in debates about political development has returned strongly to democracy and democratisation. Huntingdon (1991) has termed this the 'third wave' of democratisation, which began with the overthrow of the Portuguese dictatorship in 1974 and accelerated with the collapse of Soviet communism and the Warsaw Pact in 1989. The end of Soviet communism not only removed one, authoritarian, model of development but also meant that Western governments were less likely to support dictatorships simply because they were pro-Western and anti-communist. Western aid increasingly came with pro-democracy terms and conditions attached. Moreover, inside developing countries there was rising dissatisfaction with the failure of elites to provide human rights and freedoms and to deliver social and economic progress (Harber, 2002).

Capability Theory

Most recently and influentially, the development economist Amartya Sen has argued that democracy is *in itself* an important form of human development. In *Development as Freedom* (1999) he argued that democracy *is* development for two reasons:

1. *The evaluative reason*: assessment of progress has to be done primarily in terms of whether the freedoms that people have are enhanced;
2. *The effectiveness reason*: achievement of development is thoroughly dependent on the free agency of people. (p. 4)

Sen is arguing both that the achievement of democratic government and human rights in a country is a form of development in its own right and that it is also necessary for, and certainly not a barrier to, the effective achievement of other forms of development such as poverty reduction, economic growth and social provision. As Sen puts it:

the general enhancement of political and civil freedoms is central to the process of development itself. The relevant freedoms include the liberty of acting as citizens who matter and whose voices count, rather than living as well-fed, well-clothed and well-entertained vassals. The instrumental role of democracy and human rights, important as it undoubtedly is,

has to be distinguished from its constitutive importance.
(1999, p. 288)

Sen's theory is that the purpose of development is to improve human lives by expanding the range of things that a person can be and do, such as being healthy and well nourished, knowledgeable and an active citizen. So, development is about removing obstacles to what a person values and can do in life, obstacles such as illiteracy, bad health, lack of access to resources or lack of civil and political freedoms. In Sen's words it is about increasing human capabilities and removing barriers to these capabilities. Crucial to Sen's theory is the notion of freedom – from social and political oppression and from severe inequality of opportunity that restricts human participation and freedom to exercise autonomy in making decisions about one's life. Human development is about enlarging active agency and genuine choice for people from all sectors of society. Sen is therefore a strong supporter of the promotion of human rights and democratic forms of government as providing the only suitable context for the development of capabilities, and democracy is therefore a form of development in its own right regardless of any possible social and economic benefits or spin-offs (e.g. Sen, 1999, pp. 15-17). This freedom to make choices and to function in a capable way based on what is valued in a democratic setting *is* development.

Education, Political Development Theory and Democracy

Concern with the relationship between education and politics goes back at least two thousand five hundred years. In *The Politics* Aristotle wrote:

> But of all the safeguards that we hear spoken of as helping to maintain constitutional continuity the most important, but most neglected today, is education, that is educating citizens for the way of living that belongs to the constitution in each case. It is useless to have the most beneficial rules of society fully agreed upon by all who are members of the politeia, if individuals are not going to be trained and have their habits formed for that politeia, that is to live democratically if the laws of the society are democratic, oligarchically if they are oligarchic. (Aristotle, 1962, pp. 215-216)

This tension between democratic and authoritarian alternatives continues in debates about the role of education in political democratisation. Leftwich (1996, p. 18), for example, argues that unless certain socio-economic and political preconditions exist which are associated with development towards a 'modern' society, such as an ethic of science and rationality, industrialisation, urbanisation, bureaucratisation, differentiation and specialisation of social structures, the principles of individualism, and political stability, then democracy will not take root and succeed (1996, pp. 6-11). Without an existing, relatively modern social and economic infrastructure and accompanying values and behaviours, then attempts at political democratisation will fail as they will not have the required social foundations to build on.

It was as a contribution to the development of modern, bureaucratic norms and behaviours that early writers on political development theory saw the role of education. The book in the SSRC series explicitly concerned with education and political development (Coleman, 1965, pp. 15, 20) avoided the question about the ultimate direction of political development (democratic or authoritarian) by defining a 'modern' state as neither democratic nor non-democratic. For Coleman a modern state is a participatory state but this can either be participation in the coerced, centrally directed and monolithic fashion of an authoritarian state, or equally be free and voluntary association in a democratic state. The contribution of education to political development in this case would be the mass inculcation of bureaucratic skills:

> Formal education has a cardinal role to play in producing the bureaucratic, managerial, technical and professional cadres required for modernisation. Moreover, literacy helps a government with penetration i.e. the population will be sufficiently literate to understand what the government wants them to do. (1965, p. 17)

However, if formal education potentially contributes to democracy mainly indirectly through providing the basic, modern, bureaucratic and organisational skills, attitudes and behaviours (and only potentially – see chapter 4) upon which more explicitly democratic values might then be built, then its role is necessary but not sufficient. On to a modern, efficient, bureaucratic, institutional base must be added knowledge and experience of explicitly democratic values and practices in order to contribute to a democratic political culture as well as a bureaucratic, modern one, for, as Diamond (1993, p. 1) has argued:

> Prominent theories of democracy, both classical and modern, have asserted that democracy requires a distinctive set of political values and orientations from its citizens: moderation, tolerance, civility, efficacy, knowledge, participation.

The renewed interest in democracy and democratisation as political development in the 1990s following the collapse of communism brought with it both a renewed interest in the role of political culture and development in political science and a greater appreciation of a 'developmental' theory of democracy, where democracy everywhere is seen as a work in progress, developing at different rates, in different ways and forms, in different countries (Diamond, 1999). In terms of the role of education in helping to shape a mass political culture which is or isn't supportive of democracy, it is important to distinguish three different contexts for political learning more clearly – indoctrination, socialisation and education. We can define political *indoctrination* as an attempt to intentionally inculcate values and beliefs as facts or truths. The process may involve deliberately falsifying or ignoring evidence, as well as presenting it in a biased way. Historically, this process has been associated with totalitarian states such as Nazi Germany and Soviet Russia where individuals have little access to alternative viewpoints. Political *socialisation* is defined here as the learning of preferences and predispositions towards political values and attitudes, though often in contexts where other viewpoints are available. It is just that some ideas and values are taken more seriously than others. The ethos of schools in a particular country, for example, might sometimes provide cooperative experiences for children or even teach about the benefits of cooperation. Nevertheless, at the same time and overwhelmingly, daily emphasis and priority is given to examinations, class rankings, prizes and competitive sports. Children experience and learn that competition is far more important in life than cooperation. Both indoctrination and socialisation assume a 'correct' answer to social and political questions that young people must learn to accept as correct and the only right answer – the answer provided by those with power and authority.

Schools can, and do, attempt to socialise or indoctrinate a whole series of messages about, for example, nationalism and national identity, attitudes towards other nations, gender, race and ethnicity, religion, economic systems, equality and inequality, war and peace, political participation and leadership. They can do this through the selection of subjects taught on the curriculum, through the content and interpretation of each subject, through the values in textbooks, through the talk and behaviour of teachers, through teaching methods, through the organisational structure and processes of the school, through the symbols displayed in the school (flags, posters, pictures), through the content of assemblies and the nature of extra-curricular activities (for numerous further detailed examples of how political socialisation takes place in schools in developing countries see Dawson et al, 1977; Fägerlind & Saha, 1989, ch. 5; Harber 1989, 2004; Bush & Saltarelli, 2000).

Unlike political indoctrination and socialisation, a genuine political *education for* democracy is not a form of social and political control. It does not aim for the inculcation of a right answer or a particular viewpoint. It is an attempt to create critical awareness of political phenomena by open, balanced discussion of a range of evidence and opinions. It encourages individuals to make up their own minds about issues after considering the arguments and evidence. Education for democracy is not neutral – no education is neutral – but it does not, either deliberately or by default, transmit one-sided views of substantive values (e.g. in relation to controversial issues such as privatisation, the environment, nuclear weapons or abortion) as 'true'. Its values are procedural and concerned with how issues are discussed and how people relate to each other, and it operates the cultural values of democratic citizenship set out in the introduction to this chapter.

Liberation Theory and Paulo Freire

How can education contribute to development away from authoritarian relationships and towards more democratic ones? This issue has been confronted at length in liberation theory (Kruijer, 1987) and in particular in the writings of Paulo Freire. Freire, a Brazilian educationalist concerned with adult literacy, who was both imprisoned and exiled by the military regime in Brazil in the 1960s, was one of the most influential writers in and on education in developing countries and elsewhere. He is perhaps best known for his book *Pedagogy of the Oppressed* (1972), which is a significant critique of existing forms of education. Freire begins his book by arguing that the world is marked by dehumanisation; that is, many people are thwarted by injustice, exploitation, oppression, alienation and violence of the oppressors, though many yearn to recover their lost humanity by overcoming oppression. However, it is crucial that the oppressed 'must not, in seeking to regain their humanity ... become in turn the oppressors of the oppressors, but rather restorers of the humanity of both', i.e. that one orthodoxy doesn't simply replace another. In order to overcome oppression and realise a fuller sense of consciousness, it is important for people to critically recognise their oppression, its causes and the possibilities for transformation both of themselves and the world around them. This can only take place through a pedagogy of the oppressed based on critical dialogue and with a proclivity to action which is forged with, and not for, the learners, recognising that the teacher is also a learner and that the learner knows many things that the teacher does not know. Freire recognises that all education is inherently political and that any education offered as part of the existing system in an oppressive state and society will simply reproduce the ideas and interests of the oppressors. So, he prefers educational projects that work with the oppressed to official, systemic education which can only be changed by political power. However, in such projects reflective participation (rather than monologues, slogans and communiqués) is crucial.

Freire regards the usual teacher–student relationships as having a narrative character – the teacher speaks and the objects (students) listen:

> The teacher talks about reality as if it were motionless, static,
> compartmentalised and predictable ... Their task is to 'fill' the
> students with the contents of his narration – contents which
> are detached from reality ... Words that are emptied of their

concreteness and become a hollow, alienated and alienating verbosity. (1972, p. 53)

So, the abstract subject matter in education is often irrelevant to the learner, who memorises it for no apparent reason, turning the learner into a container or receptacle to be filled by the teacher so that 'The more completely she fills the receptacles, the better a teacher she is. The more meekly the receptacles permit themselves to be filled, the better students they are' (Freire, 1972, p. 53).

Education of this type is therefore an act of 'depositing' and Freire refers to it as the 'banking' concept of education. He summarises the oppressive nature of banking education as follows:

(a) the teacher teaches and the students are taught;
(b) the teacher knows everything and the students know nothing;
(c) the teacher thinks and the students are thought about;
(d) the teacher talks and the students listen – meekly;
(e) the teacher disciplines and the students are disciplined;
(f) the teacher chooses and enforces his choice, and the students comply;
(g) the teacher acts and the students have the illusion of acting through the action of the teacher;
(h) the teacher chooses the programme content, and the students (who were not consulted) adapt to it;
(i) the teacher confuses the authority of knowledge with his or her own professional authority, which she or he sets in opposition to the freedom of the students;
(j) the teacher is the subject of the learning process, while the pupils are mere objects.

So, the more students work away at storing the deposited knowledge, the less they develop critical consciousness about the world around them and the more they accept their place in society and adapt to the world as it is, thereby posing little threat to the established, oppressive order. In this way education attempts to control thinking and action. Freire further describes this as 'Education as the exercise of domination' (1972, p. 59).

This needs to be replaced by problem-posing education where issues are approached through dialogue, reflection and mutual learning. Teachers and students become jointly responsible for a process in which they all grow and this Freire regards as 'Education as the practice of freedom'. In problem-posing education, people begin to perceive critically the way they exist in the world, not as a static reality but in a process of transformation. For Freire, genuine dialogue involving critical thinking must take place in an atmosphere of humility, trust, hope and cooperation and be rooted in the historical and concrete reality of the participants. The themes that will be co-investigated as a result of dialogue will therefore be meaningful and significant to the learners.

Thus, as Torres puts it, more than thirty years after Freire's main books were published, the concept of dialogical education appears as a

> democratic tool for dealing with complex cultural conflicts in the context of unequal and combined development of Latin American education; its applicability in advanced industrial societies is well documented; and his message of a political democratic utopia in education is a political challenge to the educational establishment. (1998, p. 164)

Education and Capability Theory

Most recently, while Amartya Sen (discussed earlier) seems to have a firm belief in the potential of schooling to enhance democratic capabilities (1999; see, for example, pp. 216, 218; Walker & Unterhalter, 2007, p. 14), he does not really investigate what the implications of capability theory might be for the current, dominant model of formal education. However, this has been explored in some detail by Walker and Unterhalter (2007). They make the point that an education which contributes to 'un-freedoms', such as one that tolerates prejudice, exclusion, marginalisation or harassment or which limits access to critical and confident participation, would not be compatible with a capability approach, and they cite Martha Nussbaum, another key writer on the capability approach, on the importance of children being taught to learn capabilities of critical thinking by debating complex and controversial social and moral issues (2007, pp. 14-15).

Capability theory also has implications for decision making and the distribution of power in schools. If a capability is a person's ability to do what they consider valuable, then this contrasts with other ideas about how we decide what is just or fair in the distribution of resources. Walker and Unterhalter argue that:

> some ideas about distribution rest on what an outsider
> determines is best to create maximum opportunities to achieve
> appropriate outcomes for, say, different kinds of schools or
> students. The problem is often phrased in terms of what forms
> of curriculum, teaching, school management and learning
> resources will yield the educational achievements, such as
> examination results or skill sets, that an economy needs.
> Sometimes the question is posed in terms of how learners can
> acquire appropriate knowledge of history or religion to act as
> full members of a particular group which they are deemed to
> belong to. In both these instances the emphasis is on what
> kind of inputs (ideas, teachers, learning materials) will shape
> particular opportunities to achieve desired outcomes
> (economic growth or social solidarity) ... The capability

approach critiques this way of posing and solving questions of evaluation. Its central tenet is that in evaluation one must look at each person not as a means to economic growth or social stability but as an end. We must evaluate freedoms for people to be able to make decisions they value and work to remove obstacles to those freedoms, that is expand people's capabilities. (2007, p. 2)

As the statement in the UN Convention on the Rights of the Child puts it:

State Parties shall assure to the child who is capable of forming his or her own views the right to express those views freely in all matters affecting the child, the views of the child being given due weight in accordance with the age and maturity of the child. (Article 12, UN Convention on the Rights of the Child, signed by every country in the world except the USA and Somalia)

Bates (2007) further discusses a range of contemporary theoretical literature on education which emphasises the importance of learning democratic capabilities by actually experiencing them at school, and which

advocates an educational program quite consistent with the capability approach outlined by Sen and Nussbaum. It is, of course, a theoretical tradition that goes back to Dewey and his insistence that knowing comes about through doing, through active participation in production and active involvement in democratic social processes ... (p. 153)

and that educational leadership should be based on

a conception of the learning society that took the development of capabilities centred around ideas of human development, agency, well-being and freedom as central, thus claiming that the development of a truly democratic and free society should be the purpose behind human activity, one to which the economic development of such societies should be directed. (p. 155)

Educational Realities

A review of empirical evidence examining possible links between education and democracy (Harber & Mncube, 2012, pp. 43-46) concluded that the weight of the evidence seemed to point generally in a positive direction between more education and more stated support for democracy and to a positive relationship between higher levels of educational provision and a greater chance of the existence and maintenance of a democratic system of government. However, these studies largely left unclear exactly *how* education contributes to democracy. What macro cross-national studies carried out by economists and political scientists tend to exclude is consideration of what goes on inside education. Crucial here is the *type* of education experienced and of particular importance in this regard is the relationship between the internal micro-political structures, processes and cultures of formal education and the type of people and citizens that result.

What might these structures, processes and cultures look like? A democratic school might have the following characteristics. It would make clear and explicit its commitment to the values of education for democracy in its published documents – its prospectus, mission statement, etc. These would stress procedural values of democracy set out at the end of the introduction to this chapter, including the regular, free, but polite exchange of views and opinions. Its structures and practices would then involve a significant sharing of power over decision making between key groups – staff, pupils and parents. In practice, in most schools in most countries this would mean a significant shifting of power away from senior management and staff to others, and particularly to pupils. At the whole-school level this might well necessitate some form of freely elected school council where, depending on the size of the school, pupils and staff were represented, and some form of school governing body where staff, pupils and parents were represented. Such bodies would have some power of decision-making and rule-making over meaningful educational areas of concern such as budgets, staffing, curriculum, pupil and staff discipline/codes of conduct and the use of premises, and not just more minor matters like social events or the school tuck shop. The operation of such bodies in terms of language used and scope of decision-making might well vary according to the age of the pupils involved, but age is not necessarily a reason for excluding pupils from decision-making.

A democratic school culture or ethos would also be characterised by democratic relationships built on trust and mutual respect, and therefore corporal punishment would be absent, as would other forms of physical punishment and all forms of bullying, whether staff to pupil, pupil to pupil or pupil to staff. More peaceful forms of discipline such as peer mediation and restorative justice would tend to prevail instead.

At classroom level pupils would have a say in making class rules for classroom behaviour – a learning contract – and they would have some say about curriculum content (what should be learned and when), which classroom teaching methods should be used and which methods of assessment should be used. As a result, more democratic schools tend to be characterised by more classroom variety and engagement. Also, in the classroom teaching and learning would not shy away from controversial issues, but there would be a clear understanding of the ways they were to be discussed and debated by both staff and pupils. As well as experiencing more democratic relationships in the classroom as a result of the above, knowledge of how wider democracy works would also form part of the curriculum.

For all this to work, both staff and students and parent governors would need to be explicitly trained in democratic skills or capabilities, such as speaking skills and putting a case, listening skills, chairing skills, organising and planning skills, assertiveness and conflict resolution skills (Davies 1995; Davies & Kirkpatrick, 2000; Davies et al, 2002, 2005; Trafford, 2003).

There are quite a number of examples of schools in developing countries that have been and are organised along democratic lines (Harber & Mncube, 2012, ch. 3). However, evidence on educational realities also consistently suggests that for the majority of students the experience is very different. Not only are there problems with schools actually providing the modern, bureaucratic skills and attitudes required as a foundation for democracy, as we saw in chapter 4, but a review of evidence that included Africa, Asia, the Middle East and South and Central America and the Caribbean concluded that:

> In terms of schooling, the dominant or hegemonic model globally ... is authoritarian rather than democratic. Education for and in democracy, human rights and critical awareness is not a primary characteristic of the majority of schooling. While the degree of harshness and despotism within authoritarian schools varies from context to context and from institution to institution, in the majority of schools power over what is taught and learned, how it is taught and learned, where it is taught and learned, when it is taught and learned and what the general learning environment is like is not in the hands of pupils. It is predominantly government officials, headteachers and teachers who decide, not learners. Most schools are essentially authoritarian institutions, however benevolent or benign that authoritarianism is and whatever beneficial aspects of learning are imparted. (Harber, 2004, p. 24)

A further detailed review of evidence of schools in developing countries in terms of whole-school ethos and culture, school discipline and corporal punishment, classroom methods and assessment, teacher education and politics, resources and culture also suggests that there remain formidable obstacles to the introduction and maintenance of more democratic forms of schooling (Harber & Mncube, 2012, ch. 4). Some of these are further discussed in chapter 6. However, an additional issue that must be noted here is that the language of instruction can also be a serious obstacle. For example, Brock-Utne (2003) describes how when the teaching of the subject of political education in Tanzania changed from Kiswahili to English in the early 1990s this caused problems for both teachers and students who lacked sufficient fluency, so that students became more passive and those with better English started to dominate discussions. (Language and literacy will be further discussed in chapter 17.)

Hawkins (2007) argues that the traditional, non-democratic model of schooling persists, is dominant and is taken for granted. In discussing what he terms 'The Intractable Dominant Educational Paradigm', he recounts a research project in Ethiopia where he was regularly reminded by Ethiopians that they were one of the only African nations never to be colonised by the West and that therefore they did not suffer from many of the postcolonial legacies found in other African and developing countries. Yet visits to schools and colleges revealed little that was truly Ethiopian – indeed, they were like schools anywhere in the world, only poorer: 'When pressed as to the rationale of models from the West (or global north), the answer almost invariably was "so we can develop like them"' (2007, p. 137).

Hawkins argues that the features of this dominant paradigm, which exists almost everywhere despite the political nature of the regime, are that:

- an authoritarian relationship often lies at the core of the teacher–learner interaction;
- teachers are generally insecure because of a lack of training and poor remuneration;
- teaching methods do not generally benefit from knowledge of cognitive psychology and child development;
- teachers generally discourage discussion and questioning, and adhere to textbooks;
- a principal function of schooling is to select entrants to the next educational level;
- the selection is through a highly competitive examination system which requires the reproduction of rote learning rather than critical thought;
- the main activities of the formal school system are directed towards preparing pupils for these examinations; and
- students and parents are preoccupied with certificate-status rather than with the essence of what is taught (Hawkins, 2007, pp. 150-151).

The problem, according to Hawkins, is that this model of schooling has come, almost universally, to be regarded as the only possibility, the only model of a 'real' school.

Conclusion

In this chapter we have seen how democracy has increasingly come to be seen by many as *the* goal of political development. A sustainable democratic political culture is seen as requiring the learning of democratic knowledge, skills and values, as democracy is not genetic, it is learned behaviour. While schools may (or may not, as discussed in chapter 4) play a role in the learning of modern, bureaucratic norms and behaviours to provide an organisational basis for the operation of democracy, the theories and ideas discussed in this chapter suggest that they need to go beyond this to educate for democracy through experience. However, many (probably the majority) of schools in developing countries do not at present provide a democratic experience for their students and there are many barriers and obstacles to overcome if formal education is to play a significant part in exposing the majority of young people to education for democracy.

References

Al Aswany, A. (2011) Police Alone Can't Keep the Rulers in Power. Egypt's Battle Is On, *The Guardian,* 28 January.

Almond, G. (1970) *Political Development: essays in heuristic theory.* Boston, MA: Little Brown.

Aristotle (1962) *The Politics.* Harmondsworth: Penguin.

Bates, R. (2007) Developing Capabilities and the Management of Trust, in M. Walker & E. Unterhalter (2007) *Amartya Sen's Capability Approach and Social Justice in Education.* Basingstoke: Palgrave Macmillan.

Beetham, J. & Boyle, K. (1995) *Introducing Democracy: 80 questions and answers.* London: Polity Press/UNESCO.

Brock-Utne, B. (2003) The Language Question in Africa in the Light of Globalisation, Social Justice and Democracy, *International Journal of Peace Studies,* 8(1), 1-16.

Bush, K. & Saltarelli, D. (Eds) (2000) *The Two Faces of Education in Ethnic Conflict.* Florence: UNICEF.

Coleman, J. (1965) *Education and Political Development.* Princeton: University of Princeton Press.

Davies, L. (1995) International Indicators of Democratic Schools, in C. Harber (Ed.) *Developing Democratic Education.* Ticknall: Education Now.

Davies, L. (1999) Comparing Definitions of Democracy in Education, *Compare* 29(2), 127-140.

Davies, L., Harber, C. & Schweisfurth, M. (2002) *Democracy through Teacher Education.* Birmingham: Centre for International Education and Research/ Centre for British Teachers.

Davies, L., Harber, C. & Schweisfurth, M. (2005) *Democratic Professional Development*. Birmingham: Centre for International Education and Research/ Centre for British Teachers.

Davies, L. & Kirkpatrick, G. (2000) *The EURIDEM Project: a review of pupil democracy in Europe*. London: Children's Rights Alliance.

Dawson, R., Prewitt, K. & Dawson, K. (1977) *Political Socialisation*. Boston, MA: Little, Brown.

Diamond, L. (1993) *Political Culture and Democracy in in Developing Countries*. Boulder: Lynne Rienner.

Diamond, L. (1999) *Developing Democracy: towards consolidation*. Baltimore: Johns Hopkins University Press.

Fägerlind, I. & Saha, L. (1989) *Education and National Development: a comparative perspective*. Oxford: Pergamon.

Freire, P. (1972) *Pedagogy of the Oppressed*. London: Sheed & Ward.

Gyimah-Boadi, E. (Ed.) (2004) *Democratic Reform in Africa*. London: Lynne Rienner.

Harber, C. (1989) *Politics in African Education*. London: Macmillan.

Harber, C. (2002) Education, Democracy and Poverty Reduction in Africa, *Comparative Education,* 38(3), 267-276.

Harber, C. (2004) *Schooling as Violence: how schools harm pupils and societies*. London: RoutledgeFalmer.

Harber, C. & Mncube, V. (2012) *Education, Democracy and Development: does education contribute to democratisation in developing countries?* Oxford: Symposium Books.

Hawkins, J. (2007) The Intractable Dominant Educational Paradigm, in M. Mason, P. Hershock & J. Hawkins (Eds) *Changing Education: leadership, innovation and development in a globalizing Asia Pacific*. Hong Kong: Comparative Education Research Centre, University of Hong Kong.

Higgott, R. (1983) *Political Development Theory*. London: Croom Helm.

Huntingdon, S. (1991) *The Third Wave: democratisation in the late twentieth century*. Norman: University of Oklahoma Press.

Kruijer, G. (1987) *Development through Liberation*. London: Macmillan.

Leftwich, A. (Ed.) (1996) *Democracy and Development*. Cambridge: Polity Press.

O'Brien, D. (1972) 'Modernisation, Order and the Erosion of the Democratic Ideal': American political science 1960-70, *Journal of Development Studies,* 8, 351-378.

Sandbrook, R. (1976) The Crisis in Political Development Theory, *Journal of Development Studies,* 12, 165-185.

Sen, A. (1999) *Development as Freedom*. Oxford: Oxford University Press.

Torres, C.A. (1998) *Democracy, Education and Multiculturalism: dilemmas of citizenship in a global world*. Lanham: Rowman & Littlefield.

Trafford, B. (2003) *School Councils, School Democracy and School Improvement*. Leicester: Secondary Heads Association.

United Nations Convention on the Rights of the Child (1989). New York: United Nations.

United Nations Development Programme (UNDP) (1997) *Human Development Report.* Oxford: Oxford University Press.

Walker, M. & Unterhalter, E. (2007) *Amartya Sen's Capability Approach and Social Justice in Education.* Basingstoke: Palgrave Macmillan.

Further Reading

Cox, S., Dyer, C., Robinson-Pant, A. & Schweisfurth, M. (Eds) (2010) *Children as Decision-Makers.* London: Continuum.

Harber, C. & Mncube, V. (2012) *Education, Democracy and Development: does education contribute to democratisation in developing countries?* Oxford: Symposium Books.

Nagata, Y. (2007) *Alternative Education: global perspectives relevant to the Asia-Pacific region.* Amsterdam: Springer.

Schweisfurth, M. (2011) Learner-centred Education in Developing Country Contexts: from solution to problem?, *International Journal of Educational Development*, 31(5), 425-432.

Tabulawa, R. (2003) International Aid Agencies: learner-centred pedagogy and political democratisation: a critique, *Comparative Education,* 39(1), 7-26.

Discussion and Activities

1. What factors do you think have led to the growth in democratic political systems (and attempts at them) over the last two to three decades?
2. Do you think that for most young people, including those in developing countries, schooling is a democratic experience or not?
3. Do you think politically controversial issues should be taught in schools? If no, why not? If yes, how should they be taught?
4. What are the implications of (a) the ideas of Paulo Freire and (b) capability theory for schooling?
5. Find out more about (a) peer mediation and (b) restorative justice. Do you think these approaches would be useful in schools?

CHAPTER 6

Education as Harmful to Development?

Introduction

In this section of the book, on theories of education and development, we have so far primarily examined positive theories about how education may help or promote development and whether it actually does so, or not. However, it is important to stress that education is in fact a paradoxical social institution in that under the general rubric of 'education' many good things take place but many bad things (as well as many indifferent things) take place too. Despite the global emphasis on access to education described in chapter 2, there is nothing inherently good about education, schooling or learning. Learning can either be very good or very bad, depending on what is learnt, how it is learnt and what it is designed to do. This quotation from a teacher captures this dual potential well:

> I have come to a frightening conclusion: I am the decisive element in the classroom. It is my personal approach that creates the climate. It is my daily mood that makes the weather. As a teacher I possess tremendous power to make a child's life miserable or joyous. I can be a tool of torture or an instrument of inspiration. I can humiliate, humour, hurt or heal. In all situations it is my response that decides whether a crisis will be escalated or de-escalated, and a child humanised or dehumanised. (Ginott, 1972, pp. 15-16)

In the Rwandan genocide of 1994, for example, teachers from a Hutu ethnic background commonly denounced their pupils from a Tutsi ethnic background to the militia or even killed them directly themselves. Indeed, the role of schooling in this genocide poses some very serious and important questions about why and how we educate in all societies. As two commentators on the Rwandan genocide put it:

> The role of well-educated persons in the conception, planning and execution of the genocide requires explanation; any attempt at explanation must consider how it was possible that

their education did not render genocide unthinkable. The active involvement of children and young people in carrying out the violence, sometimes against their teachers and fellow pupils, raises further questions about the kind of education they received. (Retamal & Aedo-Richmond, 1998, p. 16)

In this final chapter of the section we therefore examine whether education can also be harmful to development, both in its effects on individuals and on the wider society. We do so by exploring how and why education can both reproduce and perpetrate violence.

Violence

Here violence is understood in the direct manner of the Gulbenkian Foundation's Commission on Children and Violence: 'Violence is defined as behaviour by people against people liable to cause physical or psychological harm' (1995, p. 4). The World Health Organisation (WHO) further defines violence as:

> The intentional use of physical force or power, threatened or actual, against oneself, another person, or against a group or community, that either results in or has a high likelihood of resulting in injury, death, psychological harm, maldevelopment or deprivation. (WHO, 2002, p. 5)

The causes of violence are understood to be primarily social in nature. Indeed, the authoritative 1986 Seville Statement on violence signed by 20 scientists from such fields as animal behaviour, psychology, sociology, neurophysiology, genetics and biochemistry – adopted by UNESCO in 1989 – rejected a biological basis to human violence and war altogether. They argued that biological explanations had been misused to justify violence; for example, that the theory of evolution had been used to justify not only war but also genocide, colonialism and suppression of the weak. They stated their position in the form of five propositions (which are further elaborated in the original):

- It is scientifically incorrect to say that we have inherited a tendency to make war from our animal ancestors;
- It is scientifically incorrect to say that war or any other violent behaviour is genetically programmed into our human nature;
- It is scientifically incorrect to say that in the course of human evolution there has been a selection for aggressive behaviour more than other kinds of behaviour;
- It is scientifically incorrect to say that humans have a 'violent brain';
- It is scientifically incorrect to say that war is caused by 'instinct' or any single motivation.

They concluded that 'biology does not condemn humanity to war ... just as "wars begin in the minds of men", peace also begins in our minds' (UNESCO, 1989).

Salmi (1999) has provided a useful categorisation of four types of violence that can also be applied to schools:

1. His first category is *direct violence* – deliberate injury to the integrity of human life. This includes murder, massacre, genocide, torture, rape, maltreatment, forced resettlement, kidnapping, forced labour and slavery.

2. *Indirect violence* is the indirect violation of the right to survival. This is violence by omission or lack of protection against poverty, hunger, disease, accidents, or natural catastrophes, or is mediated violence though harmful modifications to the environment.

3. *Repressive violence* is the deprivation of fundamental human rights such as freedom of thought, freedom of religion, freedom of speech, the right to a fair trial, equality before the law, freedom of movement and the freedom to vote.

4. *Alienating violence* or the deprivation of higher rights consists of alienating working conditions, racism (and presumably sexism), social ostracism, cultural repression and living in fear.

While all four types of violence can be found in formal schooling, a further important distinction in this chapter is the difference between the role of schools in *reproducing* violence and that of actively *perpetrating* it. For example, if pupils are involved in bullying or sexual harassment in school, which is also common in the surrounding society, but schools do nothing to attempt to stop it then they are guilty of reproducing violence by omission. If, on the other hand, corporal punishment or sexual harassment is not common in the local community or not used in individual families but is carried out by teachers, then this is a form of the perpetration of violence by schools. Indeed, certain types of violence, such as the physical and psychological harm that can be done by a heavy emphasis on testing and examinations or the official and organised learning of techniques of killing and violence by young people through the militarisation of schooling, may be specific to schooling (Harber, 2004, ch. 9; 2009, pp. 136-139).

Violence in Schools

Violence and war are both generally seen as bad for development. Yet, violence is widespread in schools internationally and schools can and do play a part in fostering both peace and violence (Bush & Salterelli, 2000; Harber, 2004; Pinheiro, 2006; PLAN, 2008). Indeed, as UNESCO put it:

> Education may not cause armed conflict in a direct sense, but education systems are critical in shaping the views that render

societies more or less prone to violence. It is only a slight exaggeration to say that a country's future will be as peaceful, prosperous and cohesive as its education system allows. If the citizens of the future receive an education that promotes tolerance, respect for others and appreciation of the complex identities that make up multi-ethic societies, appeals to violence based on bigotry, chauvinism and distrust of the 'other' will have less resonance. That is why education should be seen as a key element in the peace building agenda.
(UNESCO, 2011, p. 222)

In this part of the chapter we examine four types and examples of violence found in schools globally, though with particular reference to developing countries, before examining theories as to why violence happens in schools.

Bullying

Bullying in schools can take many forms – physical violence, threats, name-calling, sarcasm, spreading rumours, persistent teasing, exclusion from a group, tormenting, ridicule, humiliation and abusive comments. One study of 13-year-olds in 27 countries found that the majority had been engaged in bullying at least some of the time (WHO, 2002, pp. 29-30).

A summary of research on bullying in developing countries between 2003 and 2005 found that between one-fifth and two-thirds of children reported being bullied in the previous 30 days (PLAN, 2008). The report on the research went on to summarise research findings from Africa, Latin America and the Caribbean and Asia, all with high levels of bullying in schools. The report points out that reducing or eliminating bullying is made more difficult because many teachers and parents view bullying as an inevitable part of school life and growing up, though this isn't necessarily the case. The report also details the consequences of bullying – loss of self-esteem, shame, anxiety, truancy, concentration problems, reactive aggression, stress and serious psychological problems and even suicide. The bullies themselves also suffer from anxiety and depression and are at a higher risk of suicide and self-harm as well as of getting involved in criminal activity (PLAN, 2008, pp. 36-41).

Pupils certainly seem to be afraid of bullying. A study of fear of becoming a victim of school violence based on the percentage of pupils across 33 countries who thought another student might hurt them at least once during the previous month, found that on average 25.8% thought they might do so. There was no country where almost all pupils felt safe to learn at school (Akiba, 2008).

While most of the bullying referred to above is pupil-to-pupil bullying, teachers can also bully pupils. For example, a study of violence in schools in one province of South Africa found that the sample of 800 teachers reported that 43% of educators in their school had threatened one or more learners over the period of a year, whereas 17% had attacked or assaulted one or more learners in their school during the same period (De Wet 2007). A further study across six provinces in South Africa also found that verbal and physical abuse of pupils by teachers was widespread (Harber & Mncube, 2012a).

Sexual Harassment and Violence

We noted the problem of sexual violence against girls in schools in chapter 2. As the 2008 report by Amnesty International argued, acknowledging that there is a problem and that it is causing harm is the first step towards dealing with the problem. Yet the Global AIDS Alliance (2007) reviewed the Educational Sector Plans of 10 African countries that are being supported by the Education for All – Fast Track Initiative, none of which outlines a comprehensive intervention package to prevent, counter and respond to school-related violence. However, 'recent studies in Africa demonstrate that between 16 and 47 per cent of girls in primary or secondary school report sexual abuse or harassment from male teachers or classmates' (2007, p. 3). They are also critical (p. 13) of two major aid donors, the United States Agency for International Development (USAID) and the British Department for International Development (DfID), for falling short of what is needed to ensure that schools are safe learning environments for the world's children, including girls. Research for DfID in Ghana and Botswana also found bullying, sexual harassment and aggressive behaviour by boy students against girls in schools and that such behaviour is rarely punished as teachers regard such acts as normal and a 'natural' part of growing up (id21, 2005).

A Medical Research Council survey carried out in South Africa in 1998 found that among those rape victims who specified their relationship to the perpetrator, 37.7% said their schoolteacher or principal had raped them (Human Rights Watch, 2001, p. 42). Section V of the report details many actual cases of sexual abuse carried out by teachers in schools. Twenty-seven complaints of sexual misconduct against teachers were received by the South African Council of Educators between January and October 2008 and in some cases the teacher–pupil relationships took place with the consent of the children's parents based on some kind of financial agreement ('Sexual Misconduct in Schools', *Mail and Guardian Online*, 8 December 2008).

A PLAN report also pointed out that unless teachers themselves have been educated about gender and power issues, they are likely to model behaviour that reflects their own experiences and those of the wider community. They go on to note that a South African survey found that 47% of female teachers in a pilot project had suffered physical abuse at the hands of an intimate partner, and 25% of male teachers admitted that they had been physically abusive to an intimate partner (PLAN, 2008, p. 26).

The main cause of sexual harassment and violence in schools is that traditional gender stereotypes and unequal power relationships are not challenged but reproduced by the school. As the PLAN report says (2008, p. 26), 'Girls in societies where women are accorded a lower or more passive status (and where practices such as infanticide, female genital cutting and honour killings take place) are more likely to suffer sexual violence at school'.

Race, Ethnicity and the 'Other'

Schooling has always played a part, via socialisation and indoctrination, in the creation, reproduction, modification and vilification of group identities and stereotypes. Two extreme and well-known negative examples of racial indoctrination and stereotyping in schools explicitly aimed at racial inequality and violence are Nazi Germany and Apartheid South Africa. There are also many examples from the history of colonialism (see, for example, Mangan, 1993) of the nature and consequences of this type of racist education. Here we briefly discuss two examples.

Violence against lower caste people or Dalits in India is widespread (Human Rights Watch, 1999). Schooling, however, not only exacerbates prejudice against lower caste people, it also acts in a directly violent way towards them. A national report in 2002 found that many lower caste children were regularly beaten at school by teachers who regarded them as polluting the class. The caste definition of 'untouchable' was abolished in 1950 but the country's 200 million Dalits – now referred to as 'scheduled castes' or 'scheduled tribes' – still routinely suffer discrimination. The India Education Report compiled by the National Institute of Educational Planning and Administration noted that lower caste pupils were verbally and physically abused. Teachers in schools often refused to touch them and made them targets of their anger and abuse. They were punished on the slightest pretext and often humiliated. They were made to sit and eat separately. Their exercise books or writing slates were not touched by the higher caste teachers. They were made to sit on their own mats outside the classroom or at the door. In many cases they were beaten up by children from the higher castes. Many lower caste children were not allowed to walk through the village on their way to school and were denied their right to free textbooks, uniforms and a midday meal. In rural Karnataka children from the lower castes were referred to as 'kadu-jana' (forest people) by teachers who claimed that they would not learn anything unless they were given a severe beating

(Behal 2002). Padma Yedla, head of Save the Children's education programme in Orissa and Andra Pradesh, has noted that there remains ingrained prejudices against lower caste children in Indian state schools: 'Instead of finding out why a child hasn't completed their homework, or recognising that they cannot get help from an illiterate parent, the teachers resort to verbal abuse and humiliation. It's a vicious circle that only gets a bad response from the child' (Bancroft, 2006). This was further confirmed by Sayed et al's (2007) study of schools in India which found that teachers did not have any relations with Dalit pupils inside or outside the classroom, and there was no sharing of food observed across castes among teachers or pupils.

Another disturbing example was Rwanda, where in the genocide of April 1994 when between 800,000 and a million people were murdered, 'Neighbours hacked neighbours to death in their homes, and colleagues hacked colleagues to death in the workplaces. Doctors killed their patients and school teachers killed their pupils' (Gourevitch, 1998, pp. 114-115). Yet, despite all the efforts of the post-genocide government, there are still reports that 'genocide ideology' can be found in the country's schools. Research in 32 schools by a committee of Members of Parliament found that ethnic hatred is still prevalent among pupils in most of them and manifests itself in graffiti and general harassment such as putting rubbish in the beds of genocide survivors, tearing their clothes, and destroying their school books, mattresses and kitbags (*BBC News 24*, 19 February 2008).

Corporal Punishment

A form of violence institutionally sanctioned in many schools around the world is corporal punishment: 'Teachers always hold a stick. Once I argued with a teacher. I was instructed to lean against the wall and I was hit three times by a stick. I was so stressed out and I perspired heavily' (quotation from young person in Thailand, in PLAN, 2008, p. 11). Nevertheless, historically, authority and order in schools has consistently been associated with violent imposition:

> From their inception, formal schools in Western capitalist societies have been designed to discipline bodies as well as to regulate minds. A key purpose of modern state schooling has been the formation and conduct of beliefs, as well as the acquisition of prescribed knowledge. School discipline has frequently been overt and physically violent, with students most often the target of teacher-administered punishment. (Rousmaniere et al, 1997, p. 3)

In 90 countries out of 197 monitored by the Global Initiative to End All Corporal Punishment of Children, corporal punishment remains legal despite consistent and overwhelming evidence of its harmful effects and being incompatible with the United Nations Convention on the Rights of the Child. In the developed or industrialised world, it is still legal in France, South Korea and a number of Australian and US states (PLAN, 2008, pp. 12, 14). In other countries where it has been officially banned, such as South Africa (Nelson Mandela Foundation 2005) and China (PLAN, 2008, p. 12), it is still widely used, suggesting that corporal punishment in school continues to exist in at least one-third and perhaps as many as half of the countries of the world.

While there has been a drop in the number of countries officially using corporal punishment over the last twenty years, in some ways the situation is worse because the practice remains common globally despite widespread debate, all that is known about its harmful effects and the existence of many positive alternatives. Indeed, in June 2006 the United Nations (UN) Committee on the Rights of the Child adopted General Comment No. 8 on 'The right of the child to protection from corporal punishment and other cruel or degrading forms of punishment'.

So while there is no evidence that corporal punishment improves behaviour or academic achievement – quite the opposite (PLAN, 2008) – there is considerable evidence of its harmful effects, including physical harm and even death. The World Health Organisation, which explicitly includes corporal punishment in school as part of child abuse, states that

> Importantly there is now evidence that major adult forms of illness – including ischaemic heart disease, cancer, chronic lung disease, irritable bowl syndrome and fibromyalgia – are related to experiences of abuse during childhood. The apparent mechanism to explain these results is the adoption of behavioural risk factors such as smoking, alcohol abuse, poor diet and lack of exercise ... Similarly there are many studies demonstrating short-term and long-term psychological damage. Some children have a few symptoms that do not reach clinical levels of concern, or else are at clinical levels but not as high as in children generally seen in clinical settings. Other survivors have serious psychiatric symptoms, such as depression, anxiety, substance abuse, aggression, shame or cognitive impairments. Finally, some children meet the full criteria for psychiatric illnesses that include post-traumatic stress disorder, major depression, anxiety disorders and sleep disorders. (WHO, 2002, PP. 69-70)

Yet corporal punishment continues to be used in schools. For example, corporal punishment was outlawed in Uganda relatively recently, in 2006, but only after one incident where five students were admitted into hospital with severe head injuries after being assaulted by their teachers. The students had failed to report a fight between two other students and so the teachers decided to punish the entire dormitory. Two weeks before this a 20-year-old female student received severe back injuries after a beating by her geography teacher for failing to complete an assignment. She was also admitted to hospital and could not walk unaided (Kigotho, 2006). In Bangladesh, where corporal punishment is common despite a 1995 government order banning it, police investigated a teacher accused of caning eight of her pupils so hard for forgetting to bring their pencils to class that they needed hospital treatment ('Bangladeshi School Caning Puts Pupils in Hospital', *The Independent*, 9 March 2010).

The authoritarianism that is prevalent in schools in Egypt is also violent, with instances of teachers beating, insulting and humiliating children on a regular basis (Herrera & Torres, 2006). In Tanzania a survey found that approximately 80% of teachers regularly resort to physical punishment to maintain discipline and to 'promote' learning (Sumra, 2004, cited in Van Der Steen (2011, p. 32). A further study of teachers and pupils in Tanzania found that corporal punishment was the most common form of punishment used is secondary schools (Feinstein & Mwahombela, 2010). In Pakistan, teachers in both private and government schools expressed complete ignorance of either the UN Charter of Human Rights or the UN Convention on the Rights of the Child and in government schools the teachers reported the use of violence and humiliation for students as punishment for being absent, late, not wearing school uniform or forgetting to bring a textbook to the class (Nazir, 2010, p. 341). In Mexico, Martin (1994) reports that between a quarter and a fifth of the pupils he interviewed said that corporal punishment contributed to pupil drop-out, and Trippett et al (2010) report a study that found that 51% of children in Peru had experienced aggression at schools from teachers. In India, Sayed et al describe physical punishment as 'a normal and daily occurrence' in most of the schools they studied (2007, p. 98). In Ghana:

> During morning assembly, the principal or a designated teacher stands in front holding a switch to be used for punishments. For example, the principal of the demonstration school caned pupils who did not bring their school fees or who forgot their cutlasses and brooms for ground keeping. At another school, the teacher on duty caned the children who arrived late for school, checking they were not wearing extra clothing to soften the blows ... one of the trainees, Koffie, worried that 'the slightest mistake the pupils make, some teachers use that as an excuse to whip pupils mercilessly, which speaks ill about democracy in the classroom'. (Dull, 2006, pp. 18-19)

Stephens (2007, p. 181) also notes that Ghanaian student teachers recollected that their worst school experience was being caned.

Not surprisingly, corporal punishment also rarely makes pupils feel enthusiastic about schooling or learning and there is considerable evidence of the harm that it does in terms of pupil attitudes towards school (Parkes, 2009). In Nepal corporal punishment is an important reason for school drop-out (Teeka-Bhattarai, 2006) while in Botswana

> The more obvious effects of corporal punishment included increased student anxiety, fear or resentment in class. Girls, in particular, remained silent, and were mistakenly dubbed as 'lazy' or 'shy' by some teachers, and so did some boys. Other boys absconded or refused to cooperate in female teachers' classes ... Other studies have also found that excessive physical punishment, generally of boys, can prompt truancy. (Humphreys, 2006)

A major factor in the global spread of corporal punishment in schools was colonialism, particularly British colonialism. In Africa, for example, it has been argued that although corporal punishment is now sometimes justified on the grounds that it is 'part of African culture', evidence on pre-colonial education systems suggests that this is unlikely. As Tafa argues in relation to pre-colonial Botswana, where corporal punishment is still widely used in schools, 'There is no evidence to suggest that children were flogged every step of the way' (2002, p. 23). He notes that when neighbouring Zambia banned caning in 2000 it was described as 'a brutal relic of British rule'. He argues that

> Caning became ingrained in the popular minds as critical to school discipline hence the common refrain that its abolition equals classroom disorder and failure. The result is a cycle of caning transmitted from one generation to another and justified on the basis of experience and sentiment ... In a class of 35-40 authoritarianism is a means of orchestrating 'mob control'. Instant punishment and military style parades typical of Botswana schools are all about social control. Teachers are saddled with systemic constraints of large and mixed class sizes for which no extra resources were made available. (Tafa, 2002, p. 23)

Sometimes even the teachers themselves are caned. The Tanzania Teachers' Union took legal action when 19 primary school teachers were caned by a police officer after poor examination results and staff lateness at three schools. The teachers were, understandably, angry at their treatment and 'ashamed to meet my pupils now' but there was no mention of whether they themselves meted out similar treatment to the pupils in their schools (news.bbc.co.uk/2/hi/Africa/7889141.stm).

Why Do Schools Reproduce and Perpetrate Violence?

When children are trained, they learn how to train others in turn. Children who are lectured to, learn how to lecture; if they are admonished, they learn how to admonish; if scolded, they learn how to scold; if ridiculed, they learn how to ridicule; if humiliated, they learn how to humiliate; if their psyche is killed, they will learn how to kill. (Miller, 1987, p. 98)

It was suggested in chapter 5 that schools are often authoritarian institutions, with pupils having little power over what is learned, when, where and how. Here we examine a number of theoretical explanations of why and how schools are involved in the reproduction and perpetration of violence.

Role Modelling and Obedience in an Authoritarian Context

We begin with two closely interconnected social/psychological explanations of the causes of violent behaviour in relation to the socialisation of young people which are relevant to the authoritarian role of schooling in reproducing and perpetrating violence. The first is the idea of role modelling; that is, if those adults whom young people are expected by society to admire, respect and imitate are consistently authoritarian towards them they will come to accept this as the normal way of relating to others – giving orders or taking orders. Similarly, if those in authority over them are physically violent and abusive towards them, then this becomes normal for them and they will reproduce this violence in their own relationships with others. In other words, they become socialised through imitation into authoritarianism, repression and violent means to achieve ends. The psychoanalyst Alice Miller (1987) has written about the authoritarian roots of violence in child-rearing, driven partly by her need to understand how leading Nazis could have behaved in the way that they did. She states that she was unable to find a single figure amongst the leading Nazis who did not have a strict, rigid and authoritarian upbringing. Miller analyses what she terms the 'poisonous pedagogy' of doing harm to children while using a language that purports to be doing them good. Miller argues that the poisonous pedagogy of the role models of parents and teachers imparts to the child from the beginning beliefs about behaviour and relationships that have been passed on from generation to generation even though they are false. Some of these, as outlined by Miller, are:

- children are undeserving of respect simply because they are children;
- obedience makes a child strong;
- a high degree of self-esteem is harmful;

- a low degree of self-esteem makes a person altruistic;
- tenderness is harmful;
- severity and coldness (including corporal punishment) are a good preparation for life (Miller,1987, pp. 59-60).

The second, related idea is that authoritarianism and its emphasis on automatic obedience to orders is very dangerous as it conditions individuals and permits them to carry out violent acts by providing a justification or legitimation for such acts – 'I was only obeying orders'. Many individual acts of violence have been carried out and justified in the name of the duty to obey. Milgram's (1971) experiments using ordinary people to carry out what they thought were acts of violence against others simply because the authority said that it was necessary indicated that behaviour similar to that of officials in Nazi Germany could be replicated in American citizens. The experiment involved two people: an actor playing the part of a student trying to remember different words and the other – the real subject – playing the role of the teacher. The subject was told to give the student an electric shock every time he missed a word and increase the voltage as he got more answers wrong. The subject had no idea that the shouting and writhing of the 'students' were not real because the shocks did not actually take place but in many cases went on to administer the 'shocks' to dangerous levels when pressed by their instructor. Before the experiments it was predicted that about 1% would obey the order to use violence whereas incidences between 33% and 50% were recorded (Milgram, 1971).

Many of the aspects of these two explanations for the causes of violence discussed above have been, and still can be, found in the organisation, values and practices of formal schooling. Moreover, in an authoritarian setting, such as the school often is, with an expectation of obedience, with low levels of concern for social justice and with no other ways of dealing with dissent or difference, then individuals or groups who reject what is happening to them may well resort to physical violence because there is no other way to respond or because they have learned that this is the normal way to behave and respond.

Social and Political Control

Of course, a key question is why are schools so often authoritarian? Why are the key international formal institutions of learning socially constructed in this way? Here we refer back to chapter 3 where we set out the idea that schools were as much socially and economically reproductive as a source of opportunity based on merit. Part of this reproduction was as a mechanism of social control of populations. Historically, this was to help to control sections of the population that threatened both the state and the status quo – the working class in Europe and indigenous populations in colonised territories. Post-colonial governments in developing countries have been prepared to use schooling for the purposes of social and political control of populations (Harber & Mncube, 2012b, p. 33).

In reflecting on his detailed empirical five-nation study of culture and pedagogy Alexander (2000) was struck by the pervasive sense of control in all five schooling systems. The mechanisms, he argues, are universal – structure, curriculum, assessment, inspection, qualifications, school organisation and teaching. The controlling function is exercised at different levels:

> At national level ...governments devise policies and
> structures, allocate budgets, determine goals, define curricula
> and institute mechanisms for assessing and policing what goes
> on at the system's lower levels. At regional and local levels
> such systems may be replicated or, depending on the balance
> of control over what goes on in the classrooms, they may
> simply be implemented. At school level, heads exercise
> varying degrees of influence or direct control over what goes
> on in classrooms; and at the end of the line, in classrooms,
> children are every day subjected to the pedagogic controls of
> teaching and curriculum. These controls extend into the
> furthest recesses of task, activity and interaction, and are
> mediated through routine, rule and ritual. Comparative
> macro–micro analysis illuminates the way these stack up and
> cumulatively impact on the child. (Alexander, 2000, p. 562)

A useful theoretical framework for understanding schools as systems of control that help to maintain existing power relationships was provided by Michel Foucault (1977). Foucault questioned whether historical development was taking a linear path towards rationality, enlightenment and progress. He believed that, on the contrary, modern society had developed into a more limiting and inherently 'violent' form of rationality. He argued that the regulatory practices of contemporary institutions – including schools – are even more oppressive because they are more subtle and hidden. Schools, like other forms of modern institution, control through their bureaucratic, routinised authoritarianism – constantly measuring, categorising, ordering and regulating so that control becomes accepted by the majority as normal and natural. The desired result is increased docility and obedience – the bells, timetables, rules, hierarchies and punishments that form part of daily reality in most schools internationally.

Masculinity

Another important aspect of explaining violence, however, is gender based. Violent crime, including sexual violence, overwhelmingly is carried out by males, and particularly young males. This, including the role of education in shaping social constructions of masculinity, is discussed in more detail in chapter 10 of this book.

Conclusion

In this chapter we have examined whether formal education is always good for development, as is often assumed to be the case. We have taken the role of schooling in both reproducing and perpetrating violence as a focus for exploring ways in which schooling can actually be harmful to individuals and societies as well as beneficial. This is an important perspective on education and development which can sometimes be overlooked. However, the evidence suggests that schooling can indeed play a negative as well as a positive role in development and it thus becomes necessary to try to explain why this is the case. The chapter therefore examined theoretical perspectives about the social bases of learning violent behaviour and the role of schooling in social and political control to explore why schools can play a part in adding to violence in developing societies.

References

Akiba, M. (2008) Predictors of Student Fear of School Violence: a comparative study of eighth graders in 33 countries, *School Effectiveness and School Improvement*, 19(1), 51-72.

Alexander, R. (2000) *Culture and Pedagogy: international comparisons in primary education.* Oxford: Blackwell.

Amnesty International (2008) *Safe Schools: every girl's right.* London: Amnesty International Publications.

Bancroft, S. (2006) As Row Over Caste Quota Rages, India's Real Scandal is Ignored, *Times Educational Supplement*, 2 June.

Behal, S. (2002) Caste Cruelty Makes School a Nightmare, *Times Educational Supplement*, 26 April.

Bush, K. & Saltarelli, D. (Eds) (2000) *The Two Faces of Education in Ethnic Conflict.* Florence: UNICEF.

De Wet, N.C. (2007) Free State educators' perceptions and observations of learner-on-learner and educator-on-learner school violence, *Education As Change*, 11(1), 59-85.

Dull, L. (2006) *Disciplined Development: teachers and reform in Ghana.* Oxford: Lexington Books.

Feinstein, S. & Mwahombela, L. (2010) Corporal Punishment in Tanzania's Schools, *International Review of Education*, 56(4), 399-410.

Foucault, M. (1977) *Discipline and Punish.* London: Penguin.

Ginott, H. (1972) *Teacher and Child.* New York: Macmillan.

Global AIDS Alliance (GAA) (2007) *Violence Free Zone: end school related violence, prevent HIV/AIDS.* Washington: GAA.

Gourevitch, P. (1998) *We Wish to Inform you That Tomorrow We Will Be Killed with Our Families.* New York: Farrar, Straus & Giroux.

Gulbenkian Foundation (1995) *Children and Violence.* London: Calouste Gulbenkian Foundation.

Harber, C. (2004) *Schooling as Violence: how schools harm pupils and societies.* London: RoutledgeFalmer.

Harber, C. (2009) *Toxic Schooling: how schools became worse.* Nottingham: Educational Heretics Press.

Harber, C. & Mncube, V. (2012a) *The Dynamics of Violence in South African Schools.* Pretoria: Unisa.

Harber, C. & Mncube, V. (2012b) *Education, Democracy and Development: does education contribute to democratisation in developing countries?* Oxford: Symposium Books.

Herrera, L. & Torres, C.A. (Eds) (2006) *Cultures of Arab Schooling.* New York: State University of New York Press.

Human Rights Watch (1999) *Broken People: caste violence against India's 'Untouchables'.* New York: Human Rights Watch.

Human Rights Watch (2001) *Scared at School: sexual violence against girls in South African schools.* New York: Human Rights Watch.

Humphreys, S. (2006) Corporal Punishment as Gendered Practice, in F. Leach & C. Mitchell (Eds) *Combating Gender Violence in and around Schools.* Stoke-on-Trent: Trentham Books.

Id21 (2005) Making the Difference: how schools influence gender identity, *Research Highlight*, 25 January.

Kigotho, W. (2006) Brutal Beatings End Use of Cane, *Times Educational Supplement*, 1 September.

Mangan, J.A. (Ed.) (1993) *The Imperial Curriculum: racial images and education in the British Colonial experience.* London: Routledge.

Martin, C. (1994) *Schooling in Mexico.* Aldershot: Avebury.

Milgram, S. (1971) *Obedience to Authority.* London: Tavistock.

Miller, A. (1987) *For Your Own Good.* London: Virago.

Nazir, M. (2010) Democracy and Education in Pakistan, *Educational Review*, 62(3), 329-342.

Nelson Mandela Foundation (2005) *Emerging Voices.* Cape Town: HSRC Press.

Parkes, J. (2009) Perspectives on Children and Violence, in R. Cowen & A. Kazamias (Eds) *International Handbook of Comparative Education.* Dordrecht: Springer.

Pinheiro, P. (2006) *World Report on Violence against Children.* Geneva: United Nations.

PLAN (2008) *The Global Campaign to End Violence in Schools.* Woking: PLAN.

Retamal, G. & Aedo-Richmond, R. (Eds) (1998) *Education as a Humanitarian Response*. London: Cassell.

Rousmaniere, K., Dehli, K. & de Coninck-Smith, N. (1997) *Discipline, Moral Regulation, and Schooling*. New York: Garland.

Salmi, J. (1999) Violence, Democracy and Education: an analytic framework. Paper delivered to the Oxford International Conference on Education and Development, September.

Sayed, Y., Subrahmanian, R., Soudien, C., et al (2007) *Education and Exclusion: policy and implementation in South Africa and India*. London: Department for International Development.

Stephens, D. (2007) *Culture and Education in Development*. Oxford: Symposium Books.

Tafa, E. (2002) Corporal Punishment: the brutal face of Botswana's authoritarian schools, *Educational Review*, 54(1), 17-26.

Teeka-Bhattarai, S. (2006) Corporal Punishment in Schools: issues, efforts and experiences with children's clubs in Nepal. Paper delivered at Economic and Social Research Council Seminar on Children as Decision-Makers, University of East Anglia.

Trippett, L. with Banez-Ockelford, J., Mamaliga, D. Saksena, P. & Vigil, L. (2010) EveryChild: NGO experiences with children as decision-makers in Peru, India and Moldova, in S. Cox, A. Robinson-Pant, C. Dyer & M. Schweisfurth (Eds) *Children as Decision Makers in Education*. London: Continuum.

UNESCO (1989) *Seville Statement on Violence*. www.unesco.org/human_rights/hrfv.htm

UNESCO (2011) *The Hidden Crisis: armed conflict and education*. EFA Global Monitoring Report. Paris: UNESCO.

World Health Organisation (WHO) (2002) *World Report on Violence and Health*. Geneva: WHO.

Van Der Steen, N. (2011) School Improvement in Tanzania: school culture and the management of change. PhD thesis, Institute of Education, University of London.

Further Reading

Some good places to begin a more detailed study of the topic are the references to Harber (2004, 2009), Pinheiro (2006) and PLAN (2008) cited above. Some useful further reading is:

Davies, L. (2003) *Education and Conflict: the edge of chaos*. London: RoutledgeFalmer.

Smith, A. & Vaux, T. (2003) *Education, Conflict and International Development*. London: DfID.

Discussion and Activities

1. Taking Salmi's fourfold classification of violence set out in this chapter, can you think of an example of each type that can be found in schools?

2. One other way schools have been seen as being involved in reproducing and perpetrating violence is through their 'militarisation' (e.g. Harber 2004, 2009). Can you think of ways in which schools, directly or indirectly, inculcate military values and practices?

3. Choose one developing country in Africa, Asia and South/Central America and find out whether corporal punishment is still practised in schools there. Is it still legal? If it was made illegal, when was it banned and why? A good place to begin the search is the website of the Global Initiative to End All Corporal Punishment of Children.

CHAPTER 7

Education, Capitalism and Socialism

Introduction

The previous section of the book examined a number of theories purporting to explain the relationship between education and development. In this section we explore how ideology can provide the overall goal and context for development and education's role within it. We begin with a chapter on capitalist and socialist forms of development and their implications for education. This is followed by chapters on the increasing concern with ecological sustainability as the overarching goal of education and the role that religious values play in education and development.

Theories of economic growth, and in particular modernisation and human capital theories, were strongly influenced by the historical development of Western, industrialised and capitalist countries from the seventeenth and eighteenth centuries onwards. As a result they implicitly tended to assume that the goal of development and the means of achieving it within developing countries would be based on similar experience and therefore capitalism would be the economic context for education. Dependency and correspondence theories, on the other hand, stress capitalism as the cause of underdevelopment and therefore have leaned towards alternative, socialist models of development as a preferable way of combining economic growth with greater justice and equity. In this chapter, capitalist and socialist models of development are examined in relation to their implications for education.

Capitalism

Capitalism is based on the idea that each person is the best judge of his or her own interests and that the free pursuit of economic self-interest will result in higher productivity and in greater economic benefits all round. Thus the free market should be allowed to decide the level of supply and demand in an economy, with profits going to the most efficient and productive entrepreneurs. Profit maximisation is assumed to be the most important motivating force in economic life. Entrepreneurs should be free to accumulate profit in the free market and

119

this will provide the capital to finance further economic enterprises aimed at making profit. Social and economic inequality is important and an integral feature of capitalism because there must be greater rewards for those who merit it by working harder and being more productive, enterprising and efficient.

However, it is important to note that, while we have described a generalised model of capitalism, there are various types of capitalism, including, for example, the more neoliberal Anglo-Saxon model discussed in more detail below, the more social democratic Scandinavian model, the Asian model and the central European model (Amable, 2004). It is also important to remember that the degree to which a country can be classified as capitalist or socialist will depend to some extent on how democratic or authoritarian it is as well. The more democratic it is, and therefore the more a particular party in power can be challenged and possibly removed, the less extreme might be the version of capitalism or socialism. For example, Chile under the military rule of General Pinochet in the 1970s and 1980s was both capitalist and authoritarian. Tanzania under Julius Nyerere from the 1960s to the 1980s was a one-party state, and was socialist but authoritarian. India is both a predominantly capitalist and politically democratic country and Venezuela has had a democratically elected socialist government since 1998.

While some developing countries have historically chosen a form of capitalist development – for example, Kenya, Brazil and Thailand – this has often become more marked under the influence of global, but Western-dominated, institutions like the World Bank and the International Monetary Fund (IMF). Indeed, some previously socialist regimes, such as Tanzania, have become more capitalist under such pressure. We begin the chapter with an examination of the way in which capitalism, in the form of neoliberal economics, came to overtly set the policy context for education in many developing countries.

Neoliberal Economics and Structural Adjustment Programmes

Based on the free market ideas of economists such as Friedrich von Hayek and Milton Friedman (often known as the 'Chicago School' as they were based at the University of Chicago), neoliberal economic theory began to be taken more and more seriously during the 1970s and 1980s. Neoliberalism became so dominant in economic policy circles that it became known as the 'Washington Consensus' and set the agenda for loans to developing countries by the World Bank and the International Monetary Fund. Among its main free-market, capitalist characteristics were that national budgets should be balanced in terms of income from taxation and public expenditure; that when public expenditure had to be cut in order to balance the budget this should be done by cutting expenditure on the military, the civil service and subsidies to state enterprises rather than primary education, primary health care or public infrastructure investment; tax collection should be improved and taxes should be cut to improve incentives in the economy; interest rates should be market-determined rather than state-determined; exchange rates should be competitive to encourage exports, making the economy more outward-oriented; trade should be liberalised and import tariffs reduced to allow for freer trade; foreign investment should be encouraged and domestic and foreign companies should be allowed to compete on equal terms; state enterprises should be privatised as private industry is more efficient; there should be deregulation of the economy by the state, allowing businesses more freedom to operate. Basically, the policy was that the role of the state was to decrease significantly in economic terms; the market and self-interest would discipline the economy; currencies would be devalued to encourage exports; restrictions to capital movements into and out of countries would be removed, thereby joining economies together through economic globalisation; the role of trade unions would be reduced; state subsidies on food would be reduced and then eliminated; and taxes would be reduced, particularly for the better off, to be paid for by reduced public spending (Peet & Hardwick, 2009, pp. 85-86).

By the end of the 1970s many developing countries (particularly in South America and Africa) had serious debt problems stemming from borrowing to finance development projects, and balance of payments deficits worsened by the rapid increase in the price of oil. Indeed, some were in the position of borrowing more just to pay off the interest on previous loans. When the IMF and the World Bank intervened they imposed 'structural adjustment' conditions on the economies of the borrowing countries involving the application of the neoliberal policies set out above. By the mid 1980s three-quarters of South American and two-thirds of African countries were under IMF or World Bank supervision.

Developing countries with structural adjustment programmes typically underwent the following educational experiences as a result: cuts in the education budget; a shift from public finance of education to greater private financing, including more fees and other payments by parents; a sharp increase in private schooling; a decline in the value of teachers' salaries; stagnation and reduction in teacher employment; a slowdown in progress towards education for all; an increase in the student–teacher ratio; a reduction in spending on teaching materials such as textbooks; a decline in access to education for the poor and a reduction in the power of teacher unions (Graham-Brown, 1991; Samoff, 1994; Rosskam, 2009). In 2002 a four-year research project entitled 'Structural Adjustment Participatory Review Initiative' across nine developing countries on four continents found that education funding had generally decreased or 'in the best of cases' had not increased enough and that servicing the debt had been given priority over spending for social provision; that cost recovery programmes (i.e. user fees paid by parents) acted as a deterrent to poorer people getting access to education and increased drop-out, particularly among girls; that educational quality was deteriorating in many countries; and that staff salaries decreased while student–teacher ratios increased (Robertson et al, 2007, pp. 43-44).

By the early 2000s, however, the Washington Consensus was increasingly criticised for failure to achieve economic growth and for actually adding to economic and social problems rather than helping to alleviate them, especially by its failure to alleviate poverty and reduce inequality. Indeed, while it has been argued that in South America, 'in most countries of the region, neoliberalism has increased both prior inequalities in income distribution and the external debt' (Davidson-Harden & Schugurensky, 2009, p.13), countries with high sustained growth rates during the 1990s and early 2000s, like China and India, were exactly those not using Washington Consensus policies. This ushered in a new period which placed more emphasis on debt relief and which recognised that the state still had a role to play in intervening to rectify imperfections in the market, particularly in achieving the Millennium Development Goals, which included the achievement of universal primary education for all and the elimination of gender disparity in secondary education. However, the terms or conditions of debt relief have also been criticised as a continuation of neoliberal economics dressed up in the guise of liberation from poverty (Peet & Hardwick, 2009, pp. 91-98).

Capitalism Within Schooling

While neoliberal, capitalist economics may have dominated educational policy-making in many developing countries during the 1980s and 1990s, and continued to have a perhaps less overt influence in the 2000s, the question arises whether schools themselves transmit capitalist values. Fägerlind and Saha (1989, p. 238), for example, have described some of the educational differences typically found under capitalist and socialist systems in developing countries. Under capitalist systems, for example, there is an emphasis on individual achievement, and a hidden ideology supportive of capitalism is learned through the 'hidden curriculum' of competition within and between schools. However, before we consider the nature of schooling under capitalism in developing countries, it is important to note that, as we saw in the previous section of the book, the school *as an institution* is in many ways the product of late-nineteenth-century capitalism in western Europe and North America. So, the global model of 'the school' is historically in many ways also 'the capitalist school', and it is schools in socialist countries that have attempted to deviate from this historical norm in various ways, as discussed below.

Perhaps the main explanatory theory of how capitalism is manifested in schools is 'correspondence' theory. Correspondence theory focuses entirely on education in attempting to explain how socio-economic groups within countries reproduce their stratified positions in society. While this theory was originally based on an analysis of the USA (Bowles & Gintis, 1976), it can be applied to developing countries as well. It is called correspondence theory because, it is argued, the social relations of school mirror, or correspond to, the social relations of production in the capitalist workplace. It is largely through the hidden curriculum of these social relationships in schools, rather than overt indoctrination, that capitalist values are transmitted as 'normal'.

How do social relations in school correspond to those of the capitalist workplace? First, is the overwhelming emphasis on competition, success and failure. Schools globally are characterised by competition in the form of tests, examinations, grades, marks, prizes, badges, rankings within a class, competition for the teacher's attention and approval, rankings of schools in tables, competitive sports, competitions between school houses, inter-school competitions. Competition permeates the school and the workplace, with 'a close association ... between the personality and behavioural traits associated with getting good grades in school and the traits associated with garnering high supervisor rankings at work' (Bowles & Gintis, 2002, p. 13).

In South Korea, for example, historically the school curriculum and teaching methods have been dominated by examinations. The existence of fierce competition, especially for college entrance, has meant that educators are under pressure to feed their students only the knowledge and skills needed for the tests. For the majority of students and teachers schooling has been nothing more than the cramming of knowledge into the heads of students. There is little or no room to respond to the diversity of interests and capabilities among students. To deal with the pressure of examinations, schools have set up programmes of autonomous (self) study and supplementary classes. In some schools this is compulsory and done under the supervision of a teacher, either an hour before school begins or after school, sometimes until 9.00 or midnight. Thus, teachers often work up to 12 hours a day. Ko and Apple note that 'This situation has been extremely difficult for teachers and students' (1999, p. 67). Kang (2002, p. 322) writes that in South Korea:

> Students at all levels are forced to compete against each other.
> Universities are ranked according to their social prestige and
> are very difficult to get into. Many students attend expensive
> schools after regular school hours to give them a competitive

123

edge. All children are thus subject to severe pressure. One's success means another's defeat.

But there are other ways in which the social relations of school might correspond to those of the workplace. For example, those with authority (the teaching staff/bosses) dress one way while subordinates (students/workers) dress another; those with authority are physically separated from others (e.g. school staff rooms, managers' offices, separate eating areas); those with authority give orders, those without take orders; buildings (school buildings/offices/factories) are designed for mass production (of students or goods); there is quality control of workers' products (marking in schools/inspection of goods and outcomes in place of work); punctuality and an ordered time regime exist in both schools and places of work.

In these ways schooling, it is argued, corresponds to the capitalist workplace and school is a preparatory form of socialisation for the world of work. However, pupils from different social backgrounds are provided with a different education to fit the future role they will play in the workforce. The children of elite groups go to elite schools whose buildings and resources are superior and whose hidden curriculum emphasises leadership, superiority, separateness, independent thought, confidence and the giving of orders. The children of the working class or poor, on the other hand, go to schools which teach routine and a passive role based on subservience and the taking of orders, summed up in the phrase 'Learning to Labour' (Willis, 1977).

There are other ways in which schools might socialise their pupils into capitalist values as well. For example, school textbooks can stress the importance of values of enterprise, initiative and individual achievement and that failure can only be blamed on the self (Harber, 1989, p. 47 on Kenya). State schools can also be sponsored by private or multinational companies – it is quite common to see the Coca Cola logo or that of other major companies on signs outside schools in Africa, for example. Tabulawa (2003) argues that more child-centred forms of learning have also been used to promote capitalist values in developing countries. He argues that since the fall of the Berlin Wall in 1989 Western aid agencies have promoted more democratic forms of education because they have seen liberal democracy as inherently bound up with the free-market economy and neoliberal competitive capitalism. According to aid agencies, one cannot happen without the other. Therefore by promoting more democratic forms of pedagogy, aid agencies have been also been promoting neoliberalism:

> learner-centred pedagogy is a political artefact ... the interests
> of aid agencies in the pedagogy is part of a wider design on the
> part of aid institutions to facilitate the penetration of capitalist
> ideology in periphery states, this being done under the guise of

democratisation ... This process is being accelerated by the
current wave of globalisation which is a carrier of neo-liberal
ideology. (Tabulawa, 2003, p. 10)

Socialism

In contrast to capitalism, the one-party socialist state model that
dominated Eastern Europe from 1945 to 1989 and had its variants in
some developing countries such as Cuba, China, Tanzania, Mozambique,
Ethiopia and Vietnam is based on a belief that the maximisation of
production and the rational distribution of resources requires a central
production plan determined by the government. This is possible because
ownership of the means of production and distribution of goods is in the
hands of the state. There is a belief in the importance of the collectivity
over the individual and hence industrial and agricultural production is
removed from private ownership. The state extracts the profits from
state-owned enterprises for reinvestment in the economy. There is an
emphasis on social equity over economic growth. In practice some
inequality is tolerated, though usually less than in a capitalist state.

A first step for a developing country is detachment from
dependency on the world capitalist system. This means expropriation of
foreign-owned holdings and control over consumption which prevents
capital outflow from the economy as a result of the importation of foreign
goods. Additional economic independence is maintained by restrictions
on the flow of capital, whether in the form of purchases of goods or
travel to, and investment in, other countries. During the last decade of
the twentieth century many single-party (Communist) systems in Eastern
Europe and elsewhere gave way to more capitalist-oriented systems in
the search for greater economic productivity as well as the demand for
more human rights. This left only Vietnam, China, North Korea and Cuba
representing this model, though increasingly both Vietnam and China,
and to a certain extent Cuba, have also become more capitalist in their
quest for greater economic efficiency. However, in the first decade of the
twenty-first century there has been something of a 'pink', if not red,
revolution in South America where, for example, Venezuela, Bolivia and
Ecuador have repeatedly returned socialist governments which lean to
more state control of the economy, a rejection of neoliberalism and
'imperialist' American involvement, higher taxation of the rich and an
overall emphasis on wealth redistribution and greater equality.

There are a number of key features of socialist education systems.
One is an emphasis on state-provided and controlled education to
provide more equal education access and experience for all (Carnoy &
Samoff, 1990, ch. 3). The emphasis is on the collective uplifting of
society through access for all. This includes basic literacy, from which
women and rural populations benefit disproportionately (see Muller

[2007] on Vietnam, Nicaragua 1979-90 and Eritrea, and Breidlid [2007] on Cuba). However, since the 1980s emphasis on economic liberalisation for economic efficiency in both Vietnam and China has led to more private investment and the development of a market in education and to less social equity (Muller [2007] on Vietnam and Mok et al [2009] on China). Venezuela, with its government based on the 'Bolivarian revolution' and 'socialism for the twenty-first century' since 1998, has put a major effort into educational expansion. Venezuela was declared illiteracy free in 2005; the state has taken responsibility for pre-school education, which was previously in the private sector, and there was a 288% increase in the state education budget between 2001 and 2005. Fees were abolished in public schools, meals provided for school students and improved public transport provided to get pupils to and from school. As a result enrolment rates have improved at all levels of education. In Venezuela in 2005 the average 15-year-old received 8.89 years of education compared with 8.22 in 1999 and the country is now, unusually, introducing higher education for all (Muhr & Verger, 2009; Griffiths, 2010).

A second key feature of socialist education systems in developing countries such as Cuba, Mozambique, China and Tanzania has been an emphasis on bridging the gap between manual and mental work. Schools have tended to have some form of manual labour as part of the curriculum – for example, working on the school farm or vegetable garden. In Tanzania, for example, from 1967, and in contrast to neighbouring capitalist Kenya, there was a rejection of education based on competition and individualism and the phenomenon whereby educated Africans became estranged from the problems of their society by their wish to obtain the comforts and privileges of salaried employment. Instead, each school would possess a farm or other productive enterprise so that pupils did not become divorced from the agricultural production of the surrounding society and retained a respect for manual labour. In this way education would help to create self-reliant citizens and a self-reliant state (Harber, 1989, ch. 4; Harber & Mncube, 2012, ch. 2). In Cuba:

> manual, agricultural work as part of the school curriculum ...
> and a de-emphasis on university education all formed part of
> the Cuban attempt to 'de-marketise' the economy and the
> school and to form a new, collective Cuban citizen-worker.
> (Carnoy & Samoff, 1990, p. 86)

A third feature, however, is a more overt form of political indoctrination/socialisation (though often called political education) in a subject on the school curriculum, which primarily serves as a vehicle to learn about the world-view and priorities of the ruling party in an attempt to mould the new, socialist citizen. In Tanzania, in order to help achieve the change in attitudes required, political education (*'siasa'*) in the values of African socialism became compulsory throughout education (Harber, 1989, ch. 4). In China 'Ideological indoctrination is explicit and pervasive ... with the school curriculum used to mould the spirit and character of adolescents, fulfilling ideological and political purposes' (Kwan-Choi Tse, 2011, p. 161). Breidlid (2007, p. 618) puts it in relation to Cuba that 'The Cuban education system is well known for its focus on inclusion and equality of opportunity, but also for its focus on political and ideological conformity'.

In Venezuela:

> the educational reforms have explicitly identified a key
> political function of mass public education as the socialisation
> and preparation of citizens to actively participate in the
> development of the Bolivarian socialist political project. This
> involves an overt call on schools and teachers to socialise
> citizens for the envisaged transformation of society, including
> the promotion of socialist values in students. (Griffiths, 2010,
> p. 615)

As previously in education for self-reliance in Tanzania (Harber, 1989, ch. 4), in Venezuela there is currently a tension in the school between attempts to increase democratic participation in schools as preparation for democratic participation in the wider society (Griffiths, 2010) and the existence of a dominant official political ideology. Such 'democratic' debate in schools runs the risk of being confined to alternatives within the dominant philosophy rather than outside it.

Moreover, such political socialisation doesn't immediately disappear with a transition to capitalism. In Mozambique during the period of socialist government, pupils who went on a student exchange to the former German Democratic Republic retained their socialism even after Mozambique underwent structural adjustment and became more capitalist (Muller, 2012). In Ethiopia, where there has been a transition to democracy and capitalism since 1991, the Marxist-Leninist perspective of the former regime still influences school textbooks in the subject of Civic and Ethical Education (Yamada, 2010).

While there are differences between education systems in capitalist and socialist countries as described above, there are also striking similarities in practice. Schools in both capitalist and socialist countries tend to continue to operate as authoritarian bureaucracies with varying degrees of efficiency, depending on local context. Schools in capitalist Nigeria, South Korea and Brazil operate in the same routine-oriented, teacher-centred, inflexible and non-participatory manner as schools in socialist Cuba or China (Harber & Davies, 1997, pp. 48-52, 89-91, 159-60; Carnoy & Samoff, 1990, pp. 92-96). This may have less to do with the surrounding contemporary political and economic system and more to do with the historical origins of the school as a type of organisation at the end of the nineteenth century in Europe which has become adopted, with certain exceptions (Harber & Mncube 2012), in systems of mass education globally. This important aspect of schooling may be more associated with the historical legacy of (essentially capitalist) modernisation as discussed in chapter 4 than contemporary political regimes, capitalist or socialist.

Conclusion

Education is shaped and influenced by its economic and political environment. While capitalism has become ever more widespread and influential globally, we have seen how certain countries continue, in part at least, to resist this trend and how other countries have become more socialist through the ballot box. In this chapter we have also examined how capitalism and socialism have affected both educational provision and the content and processes of schooling, but how education also has certain characteristics that remain the same under both systems.

References

Amable, B. (2004) *The Diversity of Modern Capitalism.* Oxford: Oxford University Press.

Bowles, S. & Gintis, H (1976) *Schooling in Capitalist America.* New York: Basic Books.

Bowles, S. & Gintis, H. (2002) Schooling in Capitalist America Revisited, *Sociology of Education*, 75, 11-18.

Breidlid, A. (2007) Education in Cuba – an alternative discourse: lessons to be learned?, *Compare*, 37(5), 617-634.

Carnoy, M. & Samoff, J. (1990) *Education and Social Transition in the Third World.* Princeton, NJ: Princeton University Press.

Davidson-Harden, A. & Schugurensky, D. (2009) Neoliberalism and Education in Latin America, in D. Hill & E. Rosskam (Eds) *The Developing World and State Education: neoliberal depredation and egalitarian alternatives.* London: Routledge.

Fägerlind, I. & Saha, L. (1989) *Education and National Development: a comparative perspective.* Oxford: Pergamon.

Graham-Brown, S. (1991) *Education in the Developing World: conflict and crisis.* Harlow: Longman.

Griffiths, T. (2010) Schooling for Twenty-first-century Socialism: Venezuela's Bolivarian project, *Compare*, 40(5), 607-622.

Harber, C. (1989) *Politics in African Education.* London: Macmillan.

Harber, C. & Davies, L. (1997) *School Management and School Effectiveness in Developing Countries.* London: Cassell.

Harber, C. & Mncube, V. (2012) *Education, Democracy and Development: does education contribute to democratisation in developing countries?* Oxford: Symposium Books.

Kang, S-W. (2002) Democracy and Human Rights Education in South Korea, *Comparative Education*, 38(3), 315-326.

Ko, J-H. & Apple, M. (1999) Teachers, Politics and Democracy: the Korean teachers and educational workers union and the struggle for independence, *Education and Social Justice*, 2(1), 67-73.

Kwan-Choi Tse, T. (2011) Creating Good Citizens in China: comparing grade 7-9 school textbooks, 1997-2005, *Journal of Moral Education*, 40(2), 161-180.

Mok, K.H., Wong, Y.C. & Zhang, X. (2009) When Marketization and Privatisation Clash with Socialist Ideals: educational inequality in urban China, *International Journal of Educational Development*, 29(5), 505-512.

Muhr, T. & Verger, A. (2009) Higher Education, Neoliberalism and Socialism, in D. Hill & E. Rosskam (Eds) *The Developing World and State Education: neoliberal depredation and egalitarian alternatives.* London: Routledge.

Muller, T. (2007) Education and Gender in Revolutionary Societies: insights from Vietnam, Nicaragua and Eritrea, *Compare*, 37(5), 635-650.

Muller, T. (2012) The 'German Children' of Mozambique: long-term legacies of a socialist educational experiment, *Comparative Education*, 48(1), 57-70.

Peet, R. & Hardwick, E. (2009) *Theories of Development*, 2nd edn. New York: Guilford Press.

Robertson, S., Novelli, M., Dale, R., et al (2007) *Globalisation, Education and Development: ideas, actors and dynamics.* London: Department for International Development.

Rosskam, E. (2009) Introduction, in D. Hill & E. Rosskam (Eds) *The Developing World and State Education: neoliberal depredation and egalitarian alternatives.* London: Routledge.

Samoff, J. (1994) *Coping with Crisis.* London: Cassell.

Tabulawa, R. (2003) International Aid Agencies: learner-centred pedagogy and political democratisation: a critique, *Comparative Education*, 39(1), 7-26.

Willis, P. (1977) *Learning to Labour.* Farnborough: Saxon House.

Yamada, S. (2010) Equilibrium on Diversity and Fragility: civic and ethical education textbooks in democratising Ethiopia, *Journal of International Cooperation in Education*, 14(2), 97-113.

Further Reading

Heyneman, S. (2003) The History and Problems in the Making of Education Policy at the World Bank 1960-2000, *International Journal of Educational Development*, 23, 315-337.

International Journal of Educational Development, 29(5), Education and Development in Contemporary China

Hill, D. & Rosskam, E. (Eds) (2009) *The Developing World and State Education: neoliberal depredation and egalitarian alternatives.* London: Routledge.

Mok, K. (2005) Riding over Socialism and Global Capitalism: changing education governance and social policy paradigms in post-Mao China, *Comparative Education*, 41(2), 217-242.

Discussion and Activities

1. Draw a horizontal line with socialism at one end and capitalism at the other. Now draw a second, vertical line through the middle of the first one with authoritarianism at the top and democracy at the bottom. You now have four sections to your diagram – authoritarian socialist, authoritarian capitalist, democratic socialist and democratic capitalist. Where would place the following countries in relation to each other and why? – China, USA, Venezuela, Norway, the United Kingdom, Cuba, South Africa and Saudi Arabia.

2. Take one capitalist and one socialist country and read about their education systems. How different are they in terms of (a) policy and (b) practice?

3. Discuss the idea that socialisation of political values via schooling takes place in both capitalist and socialist countries.

CHAPTER 8

Education and Green or Sustainable Development

Introduction

Both capitalist and socialist models of development are concerned with economic growth, though, as we saw in chapter 7, capitalism has tended to become the more dominant of the two world economic models. However, not everybody thinks this emphasis on economic growth is entirely desirable in development. There are those who argue that unchecked capitalist growth would be disastrous for the planet. 'Green' or 'sustainable development' writers fear that the self-interest, greed and ever-expanding consumption at the heart of capitalist markets will eventually destroy the planet by over-exploiting resources such as water, soil and minerals, by polluting the environment and by adding to the problem of climate change. For example, what good, it is argued, is the freedom to buy a car if the city is choked with traffic and nobody can move or breathe? Yet unregulated, free-market policies have led to this situation in a number of cities in developing countries. And what happens when the oil eventually runs out?

Hart (1997, p. 6) draws on the work of Korten (1990) to compare the growth-centred vision of development with a green or 'people-centred' vision. The former assumes that the earth's physical resources are, for all practical purposes, inexhaustible or, if not, that science will provide a substitute. Growth theories also assume that the environment has an infinite ability to absorb waste. On the other hand, people-centred development assumes that the earth's physical resources are finite and that there is a limit to the productive and recycling capacity of ecological systems. There is a preference for national investment in small, locally based and ecologically sustainable forms of production over mass production for export.

These debates on economic growth versus global sustainability have led to an increasing emphasis on sustainability in debates about development. In 1987 the Brundtland Commission defined sustainable development as 'development that meets the need of the present without compromising the ability of future generations to meet their own needs' (World Commission on Environment and Development [WCED], 1987,

p. 8). The aim of sustainable development was endorsed at the United Nations Conference on Environment and Development in Rio de Janeiro in 1992, which agreed on Agenda 2, a global action plan for sustainable development. At the subsequent conference in Johannesburg in 2002 the emphasis was on implementation as part of the United Nations Millennium Development Goals. Agenda 21 laid stress on:

- reducing the use of resources and production of waste; increasing resource efficiency; reusing; recycling;
- conserving fragile ecosystems;
- greater social equity between and within countries and across generations;
- the quality of life – a broader interpretation that just the standard of living;
- respect for traditional knowledge, ways of life, diversity (UNCED 1992).

Conceptually the United Nations (UN) now, for example, includes sustainability as one of its four essential components of development: 'Access to opportunities must be ensured not only for the present generations but also for future generations as well. All forms of capital – physical, human, environmental – should be replenished' (United Nations Development Programme [UNDP], 1995, p. 12). In its 2011 report on human development the UNDP noted that the environment had been a central concern of its annual reports since 1990 and talked of the 'pernicious link between environmental degradation and economic growth that has tainted much of the development experience of at least the past half-century and threatens future progress'. It also noted the emphasis on sustainability in its overall definition of human development:

> Human development is the expansion of people's freedoms to
> live long, healthy and creative lives; to advance other goals
> they have reason to value; and to engage actively in shaping
> development *equitably and sustainably on a shared planet.*
> (UNDP, 2011, pp. 13-14, original emphasis)

Moreover, green indicators are increasingly being used to monitor damage to the world's resources. The World Wide Fund for Nature, for example, produces the living Planet Index which contains data on biodiversity in terms of vertebrate populations from over 150 countries (http: //wwf.panda.org). The UNDP in its annual Human Development Report uses indicators such as ecological footprint, environmental performance index, percentages of fossil fuels used as opposed to renewable forms of energy, green house gas emissions per capita, urban pollution, natural resource depletion, fresh water withdrawals, forest area and change in forest area, and endangered species in ranking countries according to environmental sustainability (UNDP, 2011, pp. 146-149).

Green Education or Education for Sustainable Development

The role of education in sustainable development and global environmental debates has long been established. A particularly important case for the role of education in sustainable development was made at the United Nations Conference on Environment and Development (UNCED) in 1992. This noted that

> Education is critical for promoting sustainable development and improving the capacity of people to address environment and development issues … It is critical for achieving environmental and ethical awareness, values and attitudes, skills and behaviour consistent with sustainable development and for effective participation in decision-making. (Cited in Manteaw, 2012, p. 377)

Most international organisations and national governments now recognise that green, environmental or ecological issues of sustainability are an important element in any model of national development. They also recognise that education needs to play some sort of role and, indeed, this book is being written towards the end of the United Nations Decade of Education for Sustainable Development, which runs from 2005 to 2014).

However, while outlining the nature, priorities and purposes of education for sustainable development is possible in a general manner, greater precision is more difficult because use of the concept is often imprecise, contested and indeed confusing (Blüm, 2008, p. 349; Manteaw, 2012, pp. 378-379). Iyengar and Bajaj (2011, pp. 426, 428) note this problem of clear definition but nevertheless suggest that most definitions of environmental education have a cognitive component (knowledge, awareness), an affective component (attitude, behaviour), an action-oriented behaviour (skills) and an impact component (sustainability, equity) and argue that its main objective is 'the creation of culturally and socially aware citizens who are respectful of human rights and participate in the promotion of a well-balanced environment'.

The nature of green education or education for sustainable development in schools depends on whether it is seen as a total approach to, and goal for, education or is simply a subject on the curriculum – or somewhere on a continuum in between. Certainly, UNESCO, for example, would seem to favour more basic and complete change. According to some commentators UNESCO supports a 'fundamental change of mind in every individual citizen, small adjustments will not do', citing UNESCO's aim for education for

133

sustainable development as being 'to integrate the principles, values and practices of sustainable development into all aspects of education and learning' (de Haan et al, 2010, p. 201).

Some see green education as requiring a more comprehensive and indeed transformative approach involving a major change in schooling:

> The educational formal system, in general, is based on
> competitive principles, on instrumental rationality,
> reproducing unsustainable values. In order to introduce a
> culture of sustainability at school systems we need to re-
> educate the systems themselves. They are part of the problem,
> not just part of the solution. (Gadotti, 2010, p. 225)

Others have specifically argued for a more 'holistic' approach to education and a move away from 'fragmentationalist' thinking in schools and higher education. Greig et al (1989, p. 45), for example, define a fragmentationalist world-view as one where humanity is seen as separate and divorced from nature and can therefore exploit the environment. Nature is seen as being made up of a series of isolated building blocks. Individuals are encouraged to compete in the marketplace as free agents. Associated with this is a 'transmission' model of curriculum and instruction where education is a one-way, top-down movement of knowledge skills and values. Its focus is on the traditional school subjects taught in the traditional way. The student is seen as a passive recipient of conveniently packaged and programmed blocks of teaching labelled 'maths', 'science' or 'history'.

A 'holistic' world-view, on the other hand, sees all life on the planet as interconnected and interdependent. Meaning is derived from understanding relationships and connections. Individuals cannot act in isolation as the actions of any one impact on the system. Associated with this world-view is a 'transformational' model of curriculum and assessment where education is a process of personal and social development which focuses on the aesthetic, moral, physical, emotional and spiritual development of a student as well as on cognitive attainment – the student is seen as a whole person and an integral part of the natural environment.

Particular stress is also laid on the need to move away from hierarchical and authoritarian forms of educational organisation to ones that stress participation and education for democracy. Hart (1997), for example, argues for education to involve young people in environmental action projects in their local communities:

> children now need to be investigating their own communities
> in ways that will heighten their awareness of the need for a
> people-centred approach to development. At the same time,
> through their community research and action, children will
> develop a sense of shared responsibility and skills that will

enable them to continue to participate as adults and to
recognise the importance of their participation in local,
national and even global environmental decisions. This
fundamental democratisation of children is the most important
aspect of their participation in the environment of their
communities, more than the particular impact of any of their
projects. (Hart 1997, p. 8)

So for such green educationalists, the world would be studied
thematically and holistically using an integration of perspectives from
the natural sciences, the social sciences, the arts and humanities and
practical forms of activity. There would also be a preference for small,
'human-scale' local schools over large, impersonal ones and schools
would practise what they preach in terms of environmentally auditing
school policies (such as a recycling programme for paper, cans and
bottles or purchasing environmentally friendly products only).

A more common, and more limited, approach is the inclusion of
education for sustainable development, or environmental education, as a
subject on the curriculum or a theme to be studied, often in conjunction
with some of the sort of green practices around the school as outlined in
the paragraph above. This approach is discussed more fully in the three
case studies of education for sustainable development in developing
countries set out below.

Green Education and Prescription

Green education or education for sustainable development is included in
this section of the book partly because there is inevitably a large element
of ideology, prescription and 'ought' in advocating that this should be
the overarching goal for education under which other goals should be
subsumed and existing goals and practices rejected or changed to fit into
a green agenda. Like capitalism and socialism, there is a danger that
there can be a broadly defined outcome or predetermined set of answers
for education – the green citizen and the green society as defined by
those who favour these outcomes. An education for democracy, on the
other hand, does not have a predetermined outcome but encourages
debate and a choice between alternatives or combinations of alternatives,
including environmental ones. Indeed, Wals and Jickling argue for
education for sustainable development to be within this latter, more
democratic framework:

Environmental education, and sustainability education that is
focused on human development, rather than human
behaviour, contributes to the formation of a new lens which
allows us to critically examine lifestyles, power relationships,
inequities, our connections to Earth, and our connection to

other human and non-human beings. Such a focus may facilitate a cessation of unsustainable routine and patterns and propagate alternative pathways for living. Education, in the tradition of pedagogues such as John Dewey in North America and Paulo Freire in Latin America, is viewed as a means to become critical, self-actualised members of society who are looking for meaning, developing their own potential and jointly creating solutions. In this view, a sustainable world cannot be created without the full and democratic involvement of all, including young members of society: a sustainable world without participation and democracy is unthinkable. (2009, p. 78)

Indeed, even if education for sustainable development is not advocated as a complete, holistic alternative to conventional schooling and is merely seen as a new curriculum subject or cross-curricular theme, then there can still remain the potential problem that it can be criticised as an instrument to achieve predetermined, green goals, i.e. there are clear 'factual' or 'right' and 'wrong' answers about issues such as climate change, pollution or resource depletion. As Jickling (2005, p. 252) puts it in a critique of education for sustainable development, 'it is anathema to think that education should serve predetermined ends'. Perhaps an important distinction is that between education *for* sustainable development, which can be interpreted as suggesting that there is an already agreed set of problems and solutions, and education *about* sustainable development, which recognises that there are indeed important environmental issues but which seeks to explore a range of evidence, arguments and ideas about them without preconceived answers. The approach recommended by Oakley (2008), for example, recognises the importance of ecological issues in education but treats environmental issues as contentious and subject to discussion and debate.

In the next section of this chapter we examine what kind of impact debates on sustainable development have had on schools in some developing countries in terms of curriculum provision.

Education and Sustainable Development in Developing Countries

UNESCO reports that 'The number of countries including sustainable development as an aim of education tripled between the 1980s and the 2000s, albeit from a low base. The trend is particularly prominent in developing countries' (UNESCO, 2005, p. 148). The number of countries overall requiring study of environmental science/ecology from grades 1 to 9 increased from between 72 and 85 in the 1980s to between 93 and 127 in the 2000s (UNESCO, 2005, p. 151).

A questionnaire survey of UNESCO's Associated Schools Project across 91 countries found that activities to promote a sustainable environment such as tree planting, cleaning beaches and picking up litter were claimed as common (Davies et al, 2003, p. 15). However, some caution needs to be exercised about how widespread innovations in education for sustainable development really are. In Africa, for example, 'it has become clear that verbal commitments are easier to make than to be supported with concrete actions and policies. At best, current policies can be described as sporadic and incoherent' (Manteaw, 2012, pp. 377, 380).

Here we therefore examine three case studies of education for sustainable development in different developing countries based on studies of Costa Rica by Blum (2008), India by Iyengar and Bajaj (2011) and Madagascar by Stephens et al (2008) and Stephens (2012).

Costa Rica

Costa Rica has for some time taken a lead in sustainable development, environmental management and ecotourism, bringing with it a reputation as the 'green republic', and there is much media attention to environmental issues, including environmental education. In 1995 a study concluded, for example, that there were more conservation projects going on in tiny Costa Rica than in the whole of Brazil. This emphasis has been reflected in a 'deep faith in the transformative possibilities' of education in regard to sustainable development (Blum 2008, p. 350). In 1993 an Office of Environmental Education was established as a separate division of the Ministry of Education and the national curriculum now requires environmental learning. Also, both international and domestic non-governmental organisations (NGOs) and for-profit business interests are involved in environmental education. A major emphasis has been put on teacher education as 'teachers often commented that they felt unprepared to meet national curriculum requirements for environmental education in their classrooms' (p. 351). This has included the publication of self-training guides for teachers. The Ministry of Education has also promoted the study of 'transversal themes' that cut across subject areas through integrated classroom activities, one of which is environmentalism and sustainable development. For example, one teacher asks students on a music course to listen to 'natural music' (birds, wind, sea) and then engages them in a discussion about what would happen if forests are cut down or animals become extinct. In addition, older students in some state schools can opt to receive more specialist training in environmental topics, including ecotourism.

However, there remain problems with environmental education in Costa Rica. A general problem is a lack of resources and training and the heavy demands of the national curriculum and assessment system. Indeed, environmental education, as with the other transversal themes, is not examined by a separate national examination and so is often neglected by teachers. As a result, 'many students receive little or no environmental education in practice and schools may rely on outside organisations such as conservation areas or NGOs where they are available' (p. 356).

Another, connected, problem is the tendency in many schools to rely on rote learning and memorisation:

> Classroom teaching methods, for example, frequently centre around teachers writing information on a chalkboard and requiring students to copy it into notebooks for later memorisation; alternatively, they may read aloud and ask students to repeat the recitation. Student boredom with such teaching methods is often cited as a reason for misbehaviour and a general lack of interest in studying, particularly within adolescent age groups. Educators with an interest in promoting social values through environmental education see this kind of pedagogical orientation as particularly troubling, and in some cases even counter to the central goals of programmes. (p. 355)

There are also, as elsewhere, tensions and disagreements about the extent to which environmental education should be based on the natural sciences, such as biology, or whether it should be taught in relation to critical enquiry about social issues and values, such as human rights, peace, poverty and gender inequality.

India

Iyengar and Bajaj (2011, p. 433) note that environmental education has deep roots in India's education system as ancient Hindu texts address environmental protection, restraint in consumption of natural resources, living in harmony with the natural environment and the promotion of sustainable development of 'Mother Earth'. Moreover, in more recent times, the basic education movement of Mahatma Ghandi included an emphasis on respect for nature, and environment education still features in contemporary syllabi. The 2005 national framework for environmental education stresses the importance of both science and social science and the need for an active approach to environmental education that goes beyond the classroom (Iyengar & Bajaj, 2011, p. 436).

However, in this study Iyengar and Bajaj focus on environmental education in the Indian state of Madhya Pradesh, the capital of which is Bhopal where a gas leak from a Union Carbide pesticide factory in 1984 killed an estimated 2000 people, with over 300,000 injured and up to 20,000 dying in the aftermath. They examined state syllabi in environmental education and then compared them with the National Board syllabi of the rest of India. Overall, they found that educational materials largely focus on the natural sciences and exclude most social science dimensions of environmental education:

> Thus, environmental education becomes a medium to make children knowledgeable about scientific facts rather than providing a holistic approach toward the environment, sustainable development and the adverse impacts of natural, and human-caused disasters. Our findings indicate that the national and state syllabi have made little or no effort to contextualise environmental education by using the Bhopal gas tragedy as a learning experience. (p. 425)

Iyengar and Bajaj conclude that education for sustainable development in India faces a lack of a holistic approach and a connection to real-life socio-economic and environmental problems and that the science-based emphasis 'undermines the essence of education for sustainable development which seeks to integrate the cultural, social, political and economic aspects of humans and their environments' (p. 453). Also, unlike other subjects in which students take examinations and obtain marks, in environmental education they receive a letter grade at the end of the school year which does not count for promotion or admission to higher studies.

Madagascar

Madagascar has been described as a 'living laboratory of evolution' with a unique concentration of biodiversity, yet it faces many environmental problems, such as deforestation and habitat destruction, bush fires, erosion and soil degradation, over-exploitation of living resources and the introduction of alien species. Stephens et al (2008) and Stephens (2012) discuss and review the ProVert or Green Education programme in Madagascar, initiated by the Malagasy Lutheran Church in partnership with the government. ProVert is a holistic programme for green education that combines theoretical learning with practical life skills and which tries to reconcile economic development with sustainable use of natural resources and protection of the environment. The programme has significant social goals which include the promotion of gender equality, human rights, including the rights of young people within education, and democracy. Its overall aims are set out in Figure 1.

In a mid-term review of the ProVert programme, Stephens et al (2008, pp. 24-25) concluded that the programme was now well established and noted that

> All schools have established a school garden, and several had introduced a variety of techniques concerning reduction of

energy consumption, soil improvement, tree planting etc. Several of the institutions also address or mobilize the local population. Within the Bara region, for example, the establishment of ProVert schools involves specific contracts with the local community concerning the protection of the local environment. Also the agricultural school Fihaonana engages in activities involving the local population (offering training in agricultural techniques, reduction of energy consumption, nutrition etc.).

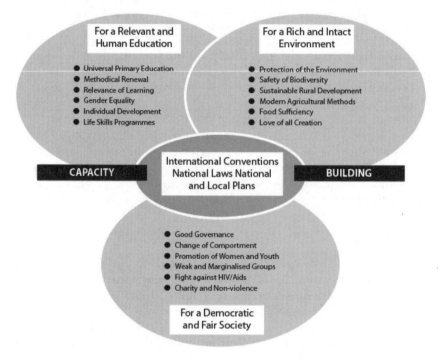

Figure 1. Green Education Programme in the Malagasy Lutheran Church. *Source*: Stephens (2012, p. 102).

They provided the following useful example of a successful ProVert school:

> The primary school in Vohiposa is a good example of the *ProVert* strategy of making 'models of good practice'. The school is well-run and was doing well in terms of exam result already before it was selected for *ProVert*. The school was established in 1945, but closed in the late eighties, and was reopened again in 1998. Together with the secondary school situated in the same compound, there are in total 335 pupils

and 11 teachers. The staff at the primary school consists of the principal and three students from the teacher training college SFM. Since 2000, about 100% of the pupils at the primary school have managed to pass the CEPE exam. While both boys and girls pass the exam, more boys than girls have to repeat classes. Committed and competent leadership seems to be an important explanation of the success. The teachers offer extra teaching on Wednesday (normally day off) in order to follow up areas where pupils have particular problems. Each Sunday afternoon the teachers organize sport activities. The school formally enrolled within the *ProVert* program the autumn 2008, but started integration of green activities and new pedagogical methods last term. The school has now a school garden.

Every week has a particular *ProVert* theme – hygiene the week when the Team visited. The *ProVert* themes are integrated in the school program as a whole. The principal highlighted relevance as the main reward of *ProVert* and new teaching methods: As she said: 'The children do not only learn "traditional school knowledge" but they learn how to use the knowledge and acquire much to carry back into their lives.' The school has a 'friendship-relation' with a school in England which has supplied them with books, videos, a TV/video-player and a generator.

The staff at Vohiposa has managed, with simple means, to produce an assortment of didactic materials. We asked the principal if they had any particular needs, problems or challenges. She answered, like most did when they got this question, 'we need equipment, for the green activities as well as pedagogical materials.' She also talked about social differentiation; the big differences in terms of wealth between the pupils which create a lot of problems. Some pupils do not get enough food, parents struggle to manage school fees and otherwise support the school. The school relies on parental support; parents have recently financed and constructed a new building in order to increase the classroom capacity. Though they have no multigrade classes, the classes are big, and the principal dreams about classes with no more than forty pupils. Access to water is also on her list of wants, and a library. (Stephens et al, 2008, pp. 21-22)

However, for green education or education for sustainable development to succeed in Madagascar, as with any other educational innovation in Africa, it has to overcome the serious quality problems facing African schools that are discussed in chapter 2 of this book. Stephens argues in this regard that

Good education for sustainable development has to address the endemic quality issues that have bedevilled the education system of sub-Saharan Africa for decades: relevance, efficiency and effectiveness ... effective means of pupils' assessment and teacher evaluation; and strong school–community links ... good teacher education and effective high quality classroom learning require less of a focus upon content and more attention to be paid to pedagogy. (2012, p. 107)

Conclusion

Green issues are now central to debates about international development. Correspondingly, education in developing countries has witnessed an increasing concern with the environment and sustainable development over the last two to three decades. Approaches to education for sustainable development vary between calls for a fundamental change in the nature and purposes of education and the addition or inclusion of environmental subjects or themes in the existing school curriculum. Approaches to education for sustainable development also differ according in the extent to which they do or do not combine natural sciences with social sciences and the extent to which they provide learners with environmental 'correct answers' or provide opportunities for critical enquiry of environmental issues. However, the actual nature of provision of education for sustainable development depends on the realities of the educational context into which it is introduced and we have described three such contexts and the issues that they raise for education for sustainable development in developing countries.

References

Blum, N. (2008) Environmental Education in Costa Rica: building a framework for sustainable development?, *International Journal of Educational Development*, 28(3), 348-358.

Davies, L., Harber, C. & Schweisfurth, M. (2003) *Report on the Global Review of the UNESCO Associated Schools Project*. Birmingham: Centre for International Education and Research.

Gadotti, M. (2010) ESD and Education for All: synergies and potential conflicts, *International Review of Education*, 56, 221-234.

Greig, S., Pike, G. & Selby, D. (1989) *Earthrights*. London: Kogan Page.

Hart, R. (1997) *Children's Participation*. London: Earthscan.

Haan, G. de, Bormann, I. & Leicht, A. (2010) Introduction: The Midway Point of the UN Decade of Education for Sustainable Development: current research and practice in ESD, *International Review of Education*, 56, 199-206.

Iyengar, R. & Bajaj, M. (2011) After the Smoke Clears: Toward education for sustainable development in Bhopal, India, *Comparative Education Review*, 55(3), 424-456.

Jickling, B. (2005) Sustainable Development in a Globalising World: a few cautions, *Policy Futures in Education*, 3(3), 251-259.

Manteaw, O. (2012) Education for Sustainable Development in Africa: the search for pedagogical logic, *International Journal of Educational Development*, 32(3), 376-383.

Oakley, D. (2008) Schools for the Future: sustainability in schools, in C. Harber & J. Serf (Eds) *Comparative Education and Quality Global Learning: engaging with controversial issues in South Africa and the UK*. Birmingham: Teachers in Development Education.

Stephens, D. (2012) A Critical Overview of Education for Sustainable Development with Particular Focus upon the Development of Quality Teacher Education in Sub-Saharan Africa, in R. Griffin (Ed.) *Teacher Education in Sub-Saharan Africa: closer perspectives*. Oxford: Symposium Books.

Stephens, D., Nielssen, H. & Rajaonah, R. (2008) *Provert, An Integrated Green Education Programme for Madagascar: mid-term review*. Antananarivo: Norwegian Agency for Development Cooperation.

United Nations Conference on Environment and Development (UNCED) (1992) *Agenda 21*. Geneva: UNCED.

United Nations Development Programme (UNDP) (1995) *Human Development Report*. Oxford: Oxford University Press.

United Nations Development Programme (UNDP) (2011) *Human Development Report*. Basingstoke: Palgrave Macmillan.

UNESCO (2005) *The Quality Imperative*. EFA Global Monitoring Report. Paris: UNESCO.

Wals, A. & Jickling, B. (2009) A Framework for Young People's Participation in Sustainability, in P. Corcoran & P. Osano (Eds) *Young People, Education and Sustainable Development: exploring principles, perspectives and praxis*. Wageningen: Wageningen Academic.

World Commission on Environment and Development (WCED) (1987) *Our Common Future*. New York: United Nations.

Further Reading

Huckle, J. & Sterling, A. (Eds) (1996) *Education for Sustainability*. London: Earthscan.

Hutchinson, D. (1998) *Growing Up Green: education for ecological renewal*. New York: Teachers College Press.

Little, A. & Green, A. (2009) Successful Globalisation, Education and Sustainable Development, *International Journal of Educational Development*, 29(2), 166-174.

Clive Harber

Sterling, A. (2001) *Sustainable Education: re-visioning learning and change.* Totnes: Green Books for the Schumacher Society.

Discussion and Activities

1. List what you think would be the key features of a truly 'green' school.
2. What do you think might be the key obstacles to introducing education for sustainable development in schools in developing countries?
3. How might an approach to education for sustainable development based on the natural sciences be different from one that combined the natural sciences with the social sciences?

CHAPTER 9

Education, Religion
and Development

In many developing countries religion is one of the most
powerful sources of personal identity – for good and ill.
Understanding these identities is critical to tackling conflict
and understanding politics. Equally, the role of religion in
forming attitudes and behaviour can be profoundly important
in addressing the causes and effects of poverty. (Tony Blair,
'Engage with the Faithful', *The Guardian*, 7 September 2009)

Introduction

The role of religion in development is contentious and also has its
critics. One academic report on the role of religion in development, for
example, noted that 'The record of regimes in which religion is formally
or informally integrated with politics suggests that they have a poor
record of improving governance or achieving human development
objectives' (Rakodi, 2011, p. 36). Yet, contrary to the emphasis on
secularisation in modernisation theory discussed in chapter 4, religion
continues to play an important role in the lives of people in developing
societies. Africa, for example, is one of the most devout regions in the
world, with 89% of people surveyed saying they were religious
compared to only 59% in the world at large. In Ghana the figure was
96% and in Nigeria 93%. Yet, even in Africa, religion remains
controversial and there are also humanists, atheists and secularists who
challenge these dominant religious beliefs from a development
perspective. For example, the Nigerian humanist Leo Igwe has argued
that 'With its overwhelming religiosity and adherence to superstition like
witchcraft, Africa also figured at the tail end of UN indices on
development and headed those on poverty and early death' (Evans,
2012).

However, despite its obvious prominence in many developing
societies, until relatively recently the role of religion in development has
been a neglected topic. Yet,

> Neglect is inappropriate when most people in developing countries claim to be religious, faith-based organisations are active in development and when religion motivates many supporters of development assistance and major NGOs in industrialised countries ... On the one hand, religion is implicated in conflict situations or associated with values and attitudes that are antithetical to desired social changes. On the other, religion is regarded as an important basis for ethics and morals and a source of humanitarian motivations. (Rakodi 2011, p. 3)

Indeed, some states, such as Iran, have set a clear religious 'ought' goal for development – the creation of a state based on a single religion – the Islamic Republic of Iran. Pakistan is a state based on Islam created at the time of the decolonisation of the British Indian empire in 1947. Another state based on a sole religion is Israel, with Judaism. So at the very least, those working in development, including education and development, need to be aware of and understand the cultural, economic and political significance of the religious contexts in which they are working.

Marshall (2010, pp. 274, 278) argues that faith institutions play vital roles in at least five dimensions of the global challenges facing education:

1. They can be powerful advocates for action to achieve social justice, including Education for All.
2. They run large education systems that provide a significant, if poorly measured, share of education, some of excellent quality and some of poor quality (for example, the Catholic school system is the world's largest faith-based educational network with 120,000 schools and over 1000 colleges and universities).
3. They contribute to defining what is taught in education systems about religion.
4. They train religious leaders and it is important that this involves social change-cum-development issues such as HIV/AIDS.
5. They have an important role to play in preparing young people to be informed and active global citizens, including social cohesion.

In this chapter, then, we focus on some key debates about the role of education in relation to religion and development. We will explore the role of religion in terms of access to education, its role within education and the outcomes of religion and education and the implications for wider society.

Access to Education

It is important to remember that from early times religious leaders in developing countries were teaching religious beliefs to children, whether this be in such religions as Judaism, Hinduism, Buddhism, Confucianism or Islam (Watson & Ozanne, 2010). However, formal education was initially introduced in many developing countries during colonialism through the educational activities of Christian religious missionaries. Their main purpose was to proselytise, but by so doing they introduced education for girls and among different ethnic groups ignored by the colonial administration, and promoted basic literacy so that pupils could read the Bible and memorise the catechism. However, they have also been criticised for denigrating local culture and practices through imposing the values of the type of Christian education provided (Watson, 1982). In northern Nigeria, for example, there has been resistance to imported, Western, formal schooling partly because of its early association with Christianity. Indeed, the name of the violent Islamic group Boko Haram, which operates in northern Nigeria at the time of writing, means 'Western education is sin'. Elements in the Taliban in Afghanistan and Pakistan have also rejected Western education, particularly for girls.

However, the role of Christianity and other religions in education did not end with the demise of colonialism. Religious organisations still play a significant role both in providing formal education and sometimes, particularly in the case of Islamic madrassas, in providing an addition, or an alternative to Western-style formal schooling. Religion can be manifested in schooling in a number of ways – through religiously owned schools, through schools that are state supported but have a religious denomination and ethos, and through the holding of religious assemblies and teaching of a religion or religions in schools. Indeed, it could be argued that, as with private schools and community-financed schools that are discussed in chapter 12, religious schools, or religious-supported schools, help to fill a potential gap in educational provision where governments in developing countries do not necessarily have sufficient resources to provide education for all. For example, in Burkina Faso in 2006 there were 99 private Protestant schools, and such evangelical schools play a significant role in the education of girls (Ouedraogo, 2010). Marshall (2010, p. 274) puts it that

> the Fe y Alegria and the Christo Rey systems in Christianity
> (in South America), and the Gulen movement and varying
> Islamic systems in Indonesia, Malaysia, Pakistan and India,
> illustrate the constructive roles faith institutions can play in
> meeting service delivery challenges for the poorest
> populations.

In countries where Islam is a major religion, madrassas or Islamic religious schools can offer an alternative form of educational access to Western-style schooling. However, despite concerns about their role in the formation of extremist views that can lead to terrorism, research suggests that there has not been a dramatic increase in enrolment in such schools in Pakistan and that they account for less that 1% of overall school enrolment in the country. Even in the districts that border Afghanistan, where madrassa enrolment is highest, it is less than 7.5% (Andrabi et al, 2006). This may be because state schools themselves are seen as providing a sufficiently Islamic education. Moreover, the choice of whether or not to send a child to a madrassa may have to do as much with financial decision-making as religious decision-making.

In terms of gender equality and access to education, a study of religion and development in Pakistan, India, Nigeria and Tanzania noted that

> Religious traditions are closely associated with patriarchy and religious organisations are dominated by men ... [However] In practice, disentangling views influenced by religion from those embedded in equally patriarchal cultures is difficult, if not impossible. (Rakodi, 2011, pp. 27-28)

Among Hindus in India local faith-based organisations support educational projects among poor residents, including low-caste Hindus and Buddhists. These promote gender equality and try to enable households to increase their financial security, but they find it hard to maintain girls' attendance. In the four countries concerned, Rakodi's study found that there was widespread support for education for women among Muslim teachers and leaders, but with the qualification that the purpose and content should differ from boys' education. In their view, girls needed to focus on becoming good wives and mothers, and boys needed to earn enough to support their families. Some Muslim women held relatively conservative views similar to those of men but other women had more liberal views which emphasised a more balanced curriculum. Most Muslims wanted religious education in the curriculum and schools to be single sex. Interestingly, in the more conservative north of Nigeria both Christians and Muslims favoured an education for females that focused on their household tasks, whereas in the more liberal south both Christians and Muslims saw education as a means of empowering women and achieving greater social equality (Rakodi, 2011, pp. 28-29).

Religion within Education

> In the religious violence that flared up in India in March 2002 a crowd of 10,000 Hindus dragged a Muslim M.P., his brother-in-law, his brother-in-law's wife and their two small sons into the street from their house and set them alight. The Police Commissioner for the city where it happened stated 'I hang my head in shame. The people responsible for all this come from

the better sections of society. They are not criminals. *Many of them are educated ...*' (Harding, 2002)

What was it about their education, or what was missing from their education, that still allowed them to behave in this way? Despite the role of religious organisations in facilitating access to school, the role of religion within education remains controversial. Here, it might be useful to distinguish between education *for* and *in* a religion and education *about* a religion. Education for and in a religion aims to use education to make the individual a follower of that particular religion by positive and exclusive exposure of the learner to the desired religious values, practices and beliefs at school. This can therefore be a form of religious indoctrination and has been quite common in many societies. As the Ghanaian Humanist Association have put it in relation to Africa, 'Believing in the existence of God is inculcated from childhood through family, community, church and school. Questioning the truth of religion was discouraged by ostracism and other consequences and the media were often hostile to free-thinkers' (Evans, 2012, p. 9). A more moderate form of this can be where the learner is educated in a religious school where that religion forms part of the timetables and ritual life of the school but where pupils also learn about other religions. In this context, which could be termed religious socialisation, preference and greater significance is given to the desired religious outcomes even though pupils learn about other religions.

This teaching and learning of *a* religion as *the* truth can be encountered within individual schools but is most overtly linked to development when the explicit national goals of the state are influenced by a religion, and the teaching of a faith as a single, unchallenged truth forms part of the curriculum of state schools. In the early twenty-first century, the Hindu nationalist party, the BJP, was in power in India and used its power to influence the school curriculum in a direction favoured by its interpretation of the Hindu religion (Harber, 2004, p. 92). In Iran:

> The religio-political leaders of Iran have used education as an agent of politicisation and Islamisation since they came to power in 1979. Iranian schools are openly and avowedly religious and ideological and have been assigned the task of politicising the young and transforming them into the soldiers of Islam and the revolution. (Mehran, 2003, p. 324)

Indeed, the Governor of Tehran has introduced lessons in chastity and wearing the hijab that are to begin in kindergarten ('Toddlers in Iran to be Given Lessons on Hijab and Chastity', *The Guardian*, 27 February 2013). Ahmad (2008) provides an interesting discussion of the tensions between two competing visions of the relationship between religion and the state in regard to citizenship education in Pakistan – the theocratic, according to which only an orthodox Muslim can be a good citizen, and the liberal democratic, which draws a line between the state and religion. However, Ahmad is clear that the theocratic interpretation remains dominant in Pakistan, a point reinforced by Dean (2005, pp. 40-41), who puts it that 'The nature of the aims and objectives indicates that the curriculum makes no distinction between Islamic education and citizenship education. Social studies education must produce true practicing Muslim citizens who will work to strengthen the Islamic state'.

This religious indoctrination or socialisation of a dominant religion in a society can affect both pupils that come from families of that religion as well as pupils whose background is another religion. In Egypt,

> Implicit in the upbringing component of schooling is the attempt – by planners and educators – to transmit to students, regardless of their religious affiliations, a sense of belonging to a Muslim society with a culture and history embedded in Islam. Islamic messages and symbols are formally incorporated into the daily life of schools through, among other means, rituals, religious passages in textbooks, religious signs and posters displayed throughout schools, and the emphasis, by teachers, on an 'Islamic disposition'. (Herrera, 2006, p. 27)

Writing of Christian evangelical schools in Burkina Faso, Ouedraogo (2010, p. 402) notes the strong support of the government for evangelical schools but also makes it clear that, in the words of members of the evangelical church, their role is one of indoctrination:

> There is a need to direct people to God through reading of the Bible message. The Evangelical schools are a means by which children hear the Word of God ... the goal of Evangelicals is to participate in the development of the country and the education of Burkinabe children. The aim is to share the good news of Jesus Christ. (2010, p. 397)

Of course, non-religious values or life stances can be involved in indoctrination as well. In communist North Korea, for example, atheism has been stressed as the national belief system in schools and is taught as a form of indoctrination.

Perhaps more compatible with a democratic, pluralist state is education about religion where religious and non-religious beliefs are considered private, family matters and where the role of the school is to make sure that learners are informed about a variety of religions and other belief systems – a sort of religious literacy. Though, as Marshall (2010, p. 281) notes, 'Teaching about different religious traditions is a sensitive topic, easier said than done', she nevertheless uses as a positive example of education about religion the United World College system, which draws together students from some 120 countries in 13 schools and which is inspired by a philosophy of achieving international peace and understanding (include a religious dimension) by educating future leaders together.

Malawi provides an interesting example of the clash between different approaches to religious education. In Malawi, a new subject, Religious and Moral Education, was introduced into the curriculum in 1991 to replace Bible Knowledge. The new subject took a more liberal pluralist view of religious education, of educating about a range of religions as opposed to the more 'exclusivist' position of Bible Knowledge, which was education in and for the Christian faith. However, the Christian church in Malawi (whose population is 80% Christian) has resisted the move through public campaigns, government lobbying, through continuing to teach Bible Knowledge in their own schools and through threatening to withdraw their schools from the government system. The result is that although Religious and Moral Education exists in the national curriculum, it is Bible Knowledge that continues to be taught in schools, despite there being a substantial Muslim minority in the country (Matemba, 2013).

Religion and Outcomes

Whether or not religious schools in developing countries are more effective in terms of better academic achievement seems still open to question and is difficult to disentangle from other factors which might be more important, such as the level of resource input into schools and the social and economic status of the communities that the schools serve. The examination results of private evangelical schools in Burkina Faso tend to be better than their state counterparts, though it is not clear whether this is because they were private (and therefore possibly better resourced) or because they were evangelical. Those who attended such schools put their success down their discipline and their stress on obedience. One school principal even said that it was the experience of these schools that made their graduates perform well in public office, their belief in God protecting them from temptations of corruption (Ouedraogo, 2010). A study of faith-based schools in Africa, Latin America and Asia also suggests that they can be more effective in terms of outcomes, particularly in disadvantaged areas, though not always so, and the reasons why they may be more effective are not clear (Barrera-Osorio et al, 2009).

The teaching of religion in schools, whether for, in or about religion, can impart important positive ideas about the need for common understanding and mutual respect across religions. For example, the Al-Muayyad Windan, an Islamic school in Indonesia, is a strong promoter of democracy and pluralism and has an emphasis on conflict resolution and interfaith understanding (Pohl, 2006, p. 408). Nevertheless, there are also concerns that schools can use religion for socially divisive purposes which negate social cohesion. Marshall (2010, p. 279) refers to the

> debate about whether distinct faith-run schools contribute to
> or detract from social cohesion in plural societies. An example
> is the concern that some madrassas convey messages of hate,
> or that some Christian schools entrench exclusive tendencies
> for communities to identify with their own members. Faith-
> run systems are seen in some situations as undermining state
> authority and provoking tensions among communities in
> plural societies.

Indeed, Pohl (2006, p. 389) mentions another Islamic school in the same region of Indonesia which has been mentioned repeatedly in the international press and was also implicated by an International Crisis Group report as the centre of a network of Muslim militants in Indonesia with suspected links to al-Qaeda. Davies (2008, ch. 3) argues in some detail, using evidence from both developed and developing countries, that such segregation of learning through separate religious schools does not contribute to social cohesion, and indeed can be bad for it, and that it can in some cases also contribute to the development of violent forms of political extremism. She concludes, 'Schools segregated by faith or ethnicity do not help social cohesion. At best they do little or no harm to integration; at worst they are incubators for unitary views, stereotypes of the "other" and a dishonest pretence at equity' (2008, p. 97).

However, negative stereotypes of the religious 'other' can be transmitted not only in separate religious schools but also via mainstream state schooling, and here we will discuss examples of the latter. In Mindanao in the Southern Philippines:

> The Islamization of education in Muslim Mindanao could
> reinforce Filipino Muslim bias against their Christian fellow
> citizens, while the lack of a multicultural education that
> promotes positive awareness of Islam in the rest of the country
> fails to address Filipino Christian biases against their Muslim
> fellow citizens. Again, the result could be a widening of the
> gap between the Christian majority and the Muslim minority.
> (Milligan, 2006, p. 429)

In India in 2000, the government, led by the Hindu nationalist Bharatiya Janata Party, began to rewrite state school textbooks to depict Muslims and Christians as alien villains. New textbooks were to defend the caste system and to contain a laudatory account of Hitler. One examination question in the state of Uttar Pradesh asked, 'If it takes four savaks (Hindu religious workers) to demolish one mosque, how many does it take to demolish twenty?' A social studies text in Gujarat describes the country's caste system as an ideal way of building society's social and economic structure and says of lower caste people, 'Of course, their ignorance, illiteracy and blind faith are to be blamed for lack of progress because they still fail to realise the importance of education in life'. Other textbooks in Gujarat extol the superiority of the Aryan race. A new history and civics textbook claimed, 'Aryans were the most illustrious race in history. They were a tall, fair complexioned, good looking and cultured people'. Another of the state's social studies books finds no space for describing Hitler's persecution of the Jews but claims, 'he instilled the spirit of adventure in the common people'. Though liberal educationalists have tried to challenge the government in the Supreme Court, it is perhaps not surprising that there were communal clashes in Gujarat in March 2002 which affected schools and left more than 700 dead (Harber, 2004, pp. 92-93).

Lall (2008) further shows how school textbooks in both India and Pakistan were rewritten to present antagonistic views of each other's religion and history. This disrespect or even hatred of the religious 'other' can also exist in terms of sects within the same religion. The following example is from a novel on Afghanistan:

> For years that was all I knew about the Hazaras, that they were Mogul descendants, and that they looked a little like Chinese people. School textbooks rarely mentioned them and referred to their ancestry in passing ... Then I found one of my mother's old history books ... I read that my people, the Pashtuns, had persecuted and oppressed the Hazaras ... The book said that part of the reason Pashtuns had oppressed the Hazaras was that Pashtuns were Sunni Muslims, while Hazaras were Shi'a ... The following week I showed the book to my teacher and pointed to the chapter on the Hazaras. He skimmed through a couple of pages, snickered, handed the book back. 'That's one thing Shi'a people do well', he said, picking up his papers, 'passing themselves off as martyrs'. He wrinkled his nose when he said the word Shi'a as if it were some kind of disease. (Hosseini, 2003, p. 8)

Conclusion

The role of religion in relation to education in developing countries is an area that is important but needs further research and discussion. It is important because religion plays a significant role in the lives of many people in developing countries, and formal education is both provided, and strongly influenced, by religious organisations. National governments and local and international organisations concerned with education and development have to consider in particular what their attitudes and policies are toward the role of religion in educational provision, especially of single-faith schools, and within education in

153

terms of whether religious teaching as indoctrination in schools is acceptable or whether education should rather be about religions in plural. This is because these questions have meaningful outcomes for the wider society. There is a danger that a 'we're all right and they're all wrong' approach can lead to narrow, exclusive thinking and even to extremism and violence. There are many such examples of this type of thinking in the world today and of its consequences. In plural societies – and most contemporary developing societies are plural societies at least to some extent – there is a need for more attention to, and discussion of, the place of religion in formal education.

References

Ahmad, I. (2008) The Anatomy of an Islamic Model: citizenship education in Pakistan, in D.L. Grossman (Ed.) *Citizenship Education in Asia and the Pacific*. Dordrecht: Springer.

Andrabi, T., Das, J., Khwaja, A.I. & Zajone, T. (2006) Religious School Enrolment in Pakistan, *Comparative Education Review*, 50(3), 446-477.

Barrera-Osorio, F., Patrino, H. & Wodon, Q. (2009) *Emerging Evidence on Vouchers and Faith-based Providers in Education: case studies from Africa, Latin America and Asia*. Washington: World Bank.

Davies, L. (2008) *Educating against Extremism*. Stoke-on-Trent: Trentham Books.

Dean, B. (2005) Citizenship Education in Pakistani Schools: problems and possibilities, *International Journal of Citizenship and Teacher Education*, 1(2), 35-55.

Evans, R. (2012) African Humanists Hoping to Challenge 'Destructive Forces', *The Mercury* (Durban), 16 December.

Harber, C. (2004) *Schooling as Violence: how schools harm pupils and societies*. London: RoutledgeFalmer.

Harding, L. (2002) A Vision of Hell in Indian City Gorging on Violence, *The Guardian*, 2 March.

Herrera, L. (2006) Islamization and Education: between politics, profit and pluralism, in L. Herrera & C.A. Torres (Eds) *Cultures of Arab Schooling*. New York: State University of New York.

Hosseini, J. (2003) *The Kite Runner*. London: Bloomsbury.

Lall, M. (2008) Educate to Hate: the use of education in the creation of antagonistic national identities in India and Pakistan, *Compare*, 38(1), 103-120.

Marshall, K. (2010) Education for All: where does religion come in?, *Comparative Education*, 46(3), 273-287.

Matemba, Y. (2013) Spaces of Contest for Religious Education Reform in Comparative Perspectives: Scotland and Malawi as cases, *Compare*, 43(3), 366-386.

Mehran, G. (2003) Khatami, Political Reform and Education in Iran, *Comparative Education*, 39(3), 311-329.

Milligan, J.A. (2006) The Islamization of Education in the Southern Philippines, *Comparative Education Review*, 50(3), 410-430.

Ouedraogo, P. (2010) The Legacy of Christianity in West Africa, with Special Reference to Burkina Faso, *Comparative Education*, 46(3), 391-405.

Pohl, F. (2006) Islamic Education and Civil Society: reflections on the *Pesantren* tradition in contemporary Indonesia, *Comparative Education Review*, 50(3), 389-409.

Rakodi, C. (2011) *Inspirational, Inhibiting, Institutionalised: exploring the links between religion and development*. Birmingham: International Development Department, University of Birmingham.

Watson, K. (Ed.) (1982) *Education in the Third World*. Beckenham: Croom Helm.

Watson, K. & Ozanne, W. (2010) Education, Religion and Politics: can they ever be disentangled?, *Comparative Education*, 46(3), 267-271.

Further Reading

Antal, C. (2008) Reflections on Religious Nationalism, Conflict and Schooling in Developing Democracies: India and Israel in comparative perspective, *Compare*, 38(1), 87-102.

Comparative Education, 46(3) (2010), special edition on education and religion.

Comparative Education Review, 50(3) (2006), special edition on Islamic education.

Halstead, J.M. (2004) An Islamic Concept of Education, *Comparative Education*, 40(4), 517-529.

Working Papers of the Religions and Development Research Programme (University of Birmingham/Department for International Development).

Note: Those readers interested in connections between religion, education and gender, the subject of the next chapter, should see Z. Gross, L. Davies & A.K. Diab (2013) *Gender, Religion and Education in a Chaotic Postmodern World*. Dordrecht: Springer.

Discussion and Activities

1. Should state schools in developing countries educate for/in religion or about religion?

2. Do you think that separate schools for different religions are good for development?

3. How do debates about the role of religion in education relate to debates about democracy and education in chapter 5?

4. Critically investigate the policies and practices of one religious organisation involved with education in developing countries.

CHAPTER 10

Gender, Education, Development and the Role of Masculinity

If you educate a man, you educate an individual, if you educate a woman you educate a family. (Old African proverb)

Introduction

In no society do women yet enjoy the same opportunities as men. They work longer hours, and they are paid less, both in total and pro rata. Their choices as to how they spend their time, in both work and leisure, are more constrained than they are for men. These disparities generate substantial gaps between how much women and men can contribute to society, and how much they respectively share in its benefits. In most countries, a fundamental aspect of these disparities, which is both one of their causes and one of their continuing consequences, is inequality in access to and performance in education. These inequalities are deep seated.
(UNESCO, 2003/04, p. 24)

In this section we explore a series of key issues concerned with education and development. We begin with an issue that has already arisen in earlier chapters of the book – the role of gender in education and development. The United Nations (UN) Millennium Development Goal 3 is 'promoting gender equality and empowering women'. We saw in chapter 1 how gender inequality is an important indicator of development for the United Nations; in chapter 2 how gender is related to educational access, quality, outcomes and inequality; in chapter 6 how it is related to violence in schools; and in chapter 9 how it is related to religion and education. In this chapter we look at gender in more detail as a topic in its own right and, in particular, examine ideas of masculinity in relation to gender.

Here we differentiate between the sex of people, which refers to the biological distinctions between men and women and boys and girls, and gender, which refers to the social and cultural construction of what it means to be male or female – how one is expected to behave and to do things in life, particularly in relation to the other gender. While there are dominant or hegemonic forms of gender identities across many societies, it has to be remembered that gender is interpreted and acted out within societies in many different ways, particularly in terms of other cross-cutting forms of social identity such as race, class and religion.

Aikman et al (2011) differentiate between four different but overlapping approaches to gender and education but here the main distinction is between two broad approaches. The first is a traditional Women in Development (WID) approach which is mainly concerned with equal access, retention and opportunities for girls and which sees gender equality foremost as a girls' and women's issue. The second sees inequality based on gender identities rooted in unequal power structures and relationships between males and females and asks what can be done to change these to provide greater capabilities for both genders. We begin with more of an emphasis on the first by examining the current situation for both boys and girls in terms of access and outcomes before looking in more detail at how gendered relationships play out in schooling, and in particular by looking at the role of masculinity.

Gender Equality and Education

In 2003-04 UNESCO devoted its annual Global Monitoring Report on Education for All to gender inequality in education. It made the following case for the importance of gender equality in education and development:

> There is also a powerful development case for achieving gender equality. It is clearly in the private and social interest to eliminate gender inequalities in education wherever they exist. The personal and social benefits are immense. Livelihoods are improved, families are healthier and better nourished, education is valued, and civic responsibility is enhanced. It is an affordable investment with high pay-offs. (UNESCO, 2003/04, p. 17)

It defined gender equality in education in the following way:

> Full gender equality in education would imply that girls and boys are offered the same chances to go to school and enjoy teaching methods, curricula and academic orientation unaffected by gender bias. And more broadly, equal learning achievement and subsequent life opportunities for similar qualifications and experience. (UNESCO, 2003/04, p. 17)

So, what is the current situation with regard to gender parity in education? In UNESCO's recent assessment of gender parity in education in terms of access and outcomes (2012a, pp. 106-121), it notes that there has been considerable success in the convergence in primary school enrolment between boys and girls, but that there are still 68 countries which have not achieved gender parity in primary education and that girls are disadvantaged in 60 of them. In low-income countries in 1999, the gender parity ratio was 0.91 girls to every 1.0 boy whereas by 2010 the figure was 0.97. In lower-middle-income countries the respective figures were 0.83 and 0.87. Despite significant progress since 1999, the Arab states and sub-Saharan Africa are yet to achieve parity. Also, the incidence of severe gender disparity had also declined so that the number of countries where fewer than nine girls were in primary school for every ten boys fell from 33 to 17 between 1999 and 2010. A key reason for fewer girls being in school is that fewer start school in the first place, but once in school their chances of progressing are similar to those of boys. Reasons cited as disadvantaging girls in terms of entering schools are distance to school, early marriage, poverty and schools which are not necessarily gender-friendly. At the secondary level, the gender parity index of 0.82 for girls to boys in sub-Saharan Africa has not changed since 1999 and girls remain at a disadvantage in the Arab states and in South and West Asia. In Latin America and the Caribbean, on the other hand, there is a reverse gender gap, with more girls enrolled than boys.

In terms of outcomes, girls perform better than boys in reading and there is evidence that the gap is increasing. Boys retain an advantage in maths, though there is some evidence that the gap may be narrowing (UNESCO, 2012a, p. 111). However, as UNESCO notes, the reasons for this are not genetic: 'There is no inherent difference in the capacities of boys or girls in reading, mathematics or science. Girls and boys can perform equally well in these subjects under the right conditions' (UNESCO, 2012a, p. 112). For more than half the 97 countries that have not achieved gender parity in secondary education, the problem is that fewer boys are enrolled in school than girls. The reason for this is a higher drop-out rate for boys than girls. A key factor in this is poverty and the need to earn an income, with boys being more likely to work outside the home than girls, and therefore less able to attend school. UNESCO uses the example of Honduras where 60% of boys aged 15-17 were engaged in economic activity compared to 21% of girls – about 82% of the boys engaged in economic activity were not in school compared with 61% of the girls (2012a, p. 116).

Gender (In)Equality within Education?

Whatever the progress of gender parity in terms of access and outcomes, in chapters 2 and 6 in particular we saw that there is considerable evidence that female pupils are not always treated fairly in relation to attitudes towards their schooling or to what happens to them inside

159

schools. To understand better the different ways in which gender inequality can occur in practice as part of daily 'normality' *within* schools, and to preface a discussion of masculinity and education later in the chapter, we next describe in some detail a study of the gender dimension of everyday life in six junior secondary schools in Botswana and six in Ghana (Dunne, 2007). In reading about this study it might be useful to think in terms of opposites – what are the male and female attitudes and behaviours that would best help to foster a more equal set of gender relationships in such schools?

In both countries there was a dominance of male teachers in senior and management positions and on the whole both female and male teachers seemed happier to work under a male head. Teaching staff attributed the male and female resistance to female leadership to cultural expectations which cast men as leaders and women as followers. It was accepted by many as 'natural' and a mirror of their domestic gender relations, and not an issue to be addressed. Male pupils, in public affirmation of their masculinity, often attempted to challenge the authority of female teachers in refusals to accept punishment from them. Some of the boys in Botswana expressed a dislike of female teachers, referring to them as 'pompous and showy' in one school and in another as moody, emotional, 'hormonal' and inconsistent. They also claimed not to take lessons taught by female teachers seriously. The boys did not respond to the male teachers in the same way. Female teachers reported an uncomfortable working environment where they were not given the same authority or respect as male teachers by the pupils or by their colleagues and school managers.

Staff rooms were gender-segregated, with minimal teacher interaction across the gender boundary. The view of most female teachers was that male teachers were more often consulted and given decision-making roles, leaving them in subordinate positions. Female teachers tended to carry out social tasks such as greeting visitors and offering seats whereas male teachers took responsibility for sports, school grounds, sanitation and tasks that required physical exertion. Male teachers also tended to deal with discipline, especially corporal punishment. Around the school high-status duties such as helping to organise assemblies and ringing the bell between lessons were carried out by boys – these duties were almost never carried out by a girl. There was also a tendency for male prefects to be responsible for male pupils and female prefects for female pupils. In terms of general school duties, in all schools in both countries girls were usually responsible for cleaning classrooms and offices and for fetching water. Boys did weeding, picking up litter, cleaning windows and tree cutting. Seldom were boys seen with brooms or mops. Whereas girls sometimes helped boys in their tasks, the reverse was not observed. In some cases teachers used pupils, especially girls, to carry out private duties for them like cleaning their house or running errands. Boys who swept or did 'female' duties were ridiculed by both other boys and girls. Rather than being passive, the girls were active in colluding with the gender order, thereby helping to sustain it.

Whenever pupil lines were formed, for example in assembly or when entering the school in the morning, they were gender segregated and this gender segregation also occurred among the teachers. In both countries the dominant pattern of seating in the classroom was for boys to sit at the back and along the sides, as if surrounding or controlling the girls, and teachers rarely intervened in the seating arrangements. A misbehaving boy would be made to sit amongst the girls as a discipline strategy. Boys dominated communication in the classroom by being most vocal, by shouting answers to teachers, by verbally harassing girls who attempted to answer questions and by ridiculing them if they gave the wrong answer. This had the effect of discouraging participation by girls. Intimidation of girls by male teachers in question and answer sessions was observed in both countries.

Corporal punishment was common in both countries and those who carried it out were male teachers and those who received it were more often male pupils. Female teachers used less demonstrative forms of violence such as pinching and verbal abuse, the latter being described by the pupils as more damaging and violating. Within the classroom and informally around the school, male teachers communicated with female pupils in a more personal, sexist and even sexually suggestive way. Gender stereotypes and sexist behaviour presented in textbooks in both countries tended to be left unchallenged by teachers. Boys engaged in routine intimidation of girls, and older boys snatched money or other property from girls. It was also common for boys to sexually harass girls by pinching or touching their breasts or buttocks. However, in all the schools negative gendered behaviour was not seen as a matter of concern as it was seen as 'natural', so that complaints from girls about sexual harassment and verbal abuse were largely ignored or trivialised, being regarded by teachers as a normal part of growing up.

It is important to note, however, that such unequal and separate gender relationships don't just begin in secondary school. Research by Bhana et al (2011) in South Africa showed that in the early years of primary school friendships were already highly gendered by the age of seven or eight. Moreover, the young girls in the study were very clear about their accounts of boys' violence, referring to verbal as well as physical accounts of violence, though sexual violence was already implicit in some of the comments of the boys. The 'masculine' identity of the boys was already forming through physical prowess and dominance over girls.

Masculinity and Education

> It is clear that, globally, men have a lot to lose from pursuing
> gender equality because men, collectively, continue to receive
> a patriarchal dividend. (Connell, cited in Arnot & Fennell,
> 2008, p. 516)

In this chapter, and in various other places in this book, we have examined evidence about gender equality and education in developing countries. In terms of access and examinations considerable progress has been made, but in terms of what goes on inside schools and what happens to females when they leave school to go home or when they finally leave school altogether, it is a different story. However, in many contexts the main obstacle to gender equality both inside and outside of education remains men and boys and the unequal power that they exercise. Greig et al (2000) argue in relation to development that men have tended not to think of themselves as gendered beings and this is one reason why policy makers and development practitioners, both men and women, often misunderstood or dismissed gender as a purely women's issue. However, as Greig et al also argue, achieving equality is not possible without changes in men's lives as well as women's. Thus, the social construction of masculinity, and how it is socialised and learnt, is of considerable importance in understanding gender inequality in education and development.

Although there are multiple forms of masculine identity within and between societies – masculinit*ies* – there are also dominant or hegemonic forms of male identity internationally which have traditionally preserved patriarchal power and privilege. Among the characteristics of this hegemonic form of masculinity are argued to be misogyny, homophobia, racism, compulsory heterosexuality, the importance of sport, a denial of emotions, competition, success, individualism, strength, toughness and the threat or use of violence to get what is wanted or, often, what it is assumed the male is entitled to and has a right to. Boys or men who deviate from this model where it dominates can be seen, labelled and treated as 'unmanly' (Salisbury & Jackson, 1996; Morrell, 1998, 2001a).

Elsanousi (2004), writing of the Yemen for example, notes the dominant position of men in Yemeni society and that women 'silently' accept this because they have no alternative. She argues that

> Boys and men are socialised within a narrow concept of
> 'masculinity'. They are supposed to be strong, dominating,
> earners and breadwinners, guardians of their female
> counterparts (mothers, sisters, wives, daughters and female
> relatives). Reflecting this image, the national costume for men
> includes a knife worn at the front, emphasising the importance
> of courage and the ability to fight. (2004, p. 164)

A workshop of both men and women in Yemen produced the following ways in which gender is socialised:

- boys are treated as superior to girls in the family;
- women in the family serve men with the best food going to men;
- boys' education is given precedence over girls' education;
- men are discouraged from performing domestic work;
- males are allowed complete freedom of movement in public and boys can come home late without being questioned;
- men are meant to be strong but not emotional; they should not weep or cry;
- men are brought up to be decision-makers and to hold power over women;
- the educational curriculum reinforces the pattern of men's and women's socialisation (for example, girls clean and cook, boys play outside);
- men are socialised to be violent (with toy guns and sticks and aggressive games);
- misinterpretations of Islam enforce men's domination;
- girls' schools do not provide sporting activities (2004, p. 164).

This dominant model of masculinity is predicated on aggressive behaviour and a proclivity towards violence and, as we have seen in chapter 6, male teacher and pupil violence against females is not uncommon in schools. However, as Salisbury and Jackson put it, 'men and boys aren't violent because they have male bodies. They are violent in order to become more masculine' (1996, p. 106). Physical violence, including sexual violence, overwhelmingly is carried out by males and particularly by young males. Nevertheless, whilst most violence is carried out by men, most men are not violent. Violent behaviour by males is not biologically determined by, for instance, high levels of testosterone. If it were, then all, or at least most, most men would be violent. The Gulbenkian Foundation made the following case against biological determinism of violence in males:

> First, one can point to the admittedly unusual societies in which the biologically normal females have shown a greater tendency to violence than the biologically normal males. Secondly, we know that boys brought up in non-violent households with parents providing good quality care and living in non-violent neighbourhoods, show levels of violence that are very little different from girls brought up in the same circumstances. Thirdly, there is evidence that the levels of testosterone in young violent males are no different from those in non-violent young males. (1995, p. 42)

Moreover, as Connell (2000, p. 22) notes, cross-cultural studies of masculinities reveal a diversity that is impossible to reconcile with a biologically fixed master pattern of masculinity.

So, what might be the role of schooling in learning dominant or hegemonic forms of masculinity? Salisbury and Jackson (1996, p. 105) argue that 'Schools, clubs and colleges are institutions where gender is actively forged. Gender isn't just reflected or expressed. They are places where a certain type of "top dog" masculinity is made, celebrated and confirmed through daily acts of violence and bullying'. Woolley (2007, p. 29) adds:

> From the earliest years of schooling, masculinity and the
> undermining of an individual's perceived masculinity, is a
> powerful socialising tool. The taunts of the playground bully
> make clear what is socially acceptable in terms of being a man
> and from that point onwards many males seek to define
> themselves in terms of the dominant hegemony.

How, then, does schooling play a part in both reproducing and forging the sort of hegemonic model of masculinity outlined above? Again, when reading this discussion it might be useful to think not only about how valid it is but also what alternative forms of masculinity there are, or might be, that would be more supportive of gender equality in development. The first and most obvious point is that, for better or for worse, teachers are role models. Male teachers act as role models for male students. A study of perceptions of teachers in South Africa, for example, saw male teachers as unbending, unfeeling, violent, egocentric, competitive, unsympathetic and rigid whereas female teachers were perceived as being prepared to abandon their formal positions of authority to create a climate of understanding and negotiation. Male teachers were seen as dogmatically wedded to their authority (Morrell, 2001b, p. 150). By being involved in sexual harassment, as described in this chapter and chapters 2 and 6, male teachers are actively encouraging their male pupils to behave in a similar manner.

Salisbury and Jackson (1996) further identify a number of ways that schools can actively perpetuate forms of masculine identity that lend themselves to violent interpretation. First, they argue that the way that schools are organised – their authority patterns and forms of discipline – reinforce key aspects of the hegemonic masculinity outlined above, which is why men have traditionally dominated school management:

> Teaching is seen to be about control and authoritarian
> certainty. It is also the visible face of material male power in
> the establishment. The characteristics of effective teaching
> become talking from the front and controlling any child's
> responses. It is also about a system of duties, patrolling
> corridors and the constant checking of students' presence. The

atmosphere of control will be underpinned by the need to impose a strong, hard, authoritarian disciplinary system ... Many male teachers maintain their authority over pupils by a 'hard-line' rule of fear. They control by threats and a loud voice to reduce students to frightened silence. From such an aggressive disciplinary style boys learn that 'this is how you get what you want'. Male teachers are also very competitive around their ability to establish firm discipline. There is ridicule of 'soft' members of staff behind their backs ... Boys learn to expect dominant authoritarian behaviour from male teachers since it provides a role model for superior power and strength. It mirrors much of the power they see exhibited by other men in their daily lives – their fathers, brothers, uncles and grandfathers. (1996, pp. 18, 22, 28)

Second, the curriculum is seen as 'academic masculinist' in that knowledge is presented as abstract, neutral and value-free:

School knowledge retains the academic form of a self-referring, abstract body of knowledge which strongly separates what is learned from the personal and social experiences of the learner. Knowledge is also organised hierarchically from the less difficult to the more difficult. This emphasises the idea of there being one path through the material which it is necessary to follow. The way knowledge is imparted is by means of transfer teaching, i.e. something the teacher knows is transferred to the mind of the student, i.e. a 'delivery' model. This still occurs by means of chalk and talk and teaching from the front so that impersonal science demands an impersonal teaching style with no attempts to link what is done with the lives of children. Links with students as people are superficial because of the way teachers know their subject and desire to impart subject knowledge. Knowledge control and what needs to be known is in the hands of men. (1996, p. 25)

Third, Salisbury and Jackson argue that closely allied to this curriculum is the way learning is organised and tested. The emphasis on individual competition is closely linked with patriarchal values. They argue that 'Competition brings up many kinds of unpleasant feelings, such as being pushy and arrogant around winning and sneakily resentful around failure' (1996, p. 31). The important point here is that examinations, league tables and competition 'activates the notion of manly values around winners and losers' and that

not to shape up properly as a boy in competition with others causes pain, resentment and anti-social behaviour in the form of truancy, disruptiveness and other attention-grabbing

devices. After all, a competitive system that fails some boys
academically and physically compels a compensatory
assertion of masculine pride, a competition in machismo to
enable male power to be demonstrated and admired. (p. 32)

A fourth way in which schools reinforce hegemonic models of
masculinity is through sport. Playing sport in a manly way means a
determination to win at all costs by gritting one's teeth and ignoring the
hurt of physical clashes:

The language of school sports for many boys is the language of
warfare – 'Hit them hard today, lads!' All the talk is of combat,
battles, seeing your opponent as the enemy and military
conquest. There is a gladiatorial type of imagery of sparring,
grappling and not deserting your post. The result of this sport-
as-welfare approach is often to normalise aggressive
competitiveness in the lives of many boys.
(Salisbury & Jackson, 1996, p. 205)

It also has to be noted that one of the ways that male violence can
manifest itself in schools that hasn't been mentioned previously is in
bullying gay and lesbian pupils and those perceived to be so. This is a
serious problem in schools internationally (PLAN, 2008, pp. 38-39) and
can manifest itself through such phenomena as 'corrective rape' in South
African schools where lesbian girls are raped to 'make them
heterosexual' (see, for example, Action Aid, 2009) and homophobic
bullying generally, which is now recognised by the UN as a major
problem (Pinheiro, 2006). A UN study, for example, stated that the
problem was global but under-researched and, amongst other evidence,
noted that a high proportion of lesbian, gay and bisexual learners report
homophobic bullying in Chile (68%), Guatemala (53%), Mexico (61%)
and Peru (66%). In Brazil, more than 40% of gay men reported that they
had been physically assaulted when they were at school (UNESCO,
2012b, p. 18).

Moreover, schools do not necessarily educate about masculinity in
order to curb more violent or unequal interpretations of it, partly because
teachers themselves have rarely confronted the idea of masculinity in
their own education. A survey of South African and English teacher
education students found that few had studied or discussed gender
issues, including the nature of masculinity, either at school or in their
teacher education (Harber & Serf, 2006). Part of the problem may be the
teaching methods used in schools and the fear of teaching controversial
issues such as gender in the classroom. However, on a more positive
note, there are many educational projects that exist in developing
countries that provide ideas and advice on working towards greater
gender equality in education and development. For example, Leach and
Mitchell (2006) include chapters on strategies for change that discuss

arts-based participatory methodologies for working with young people, reframing masculinities using films with adolescent boys in South Asia, engaging with young men in violence prevention in Latin America, working with young men and violent masculinities in South Africa, using theatre with trainee teachers in Ghana, using teacher memories to tackle gender violence in Kenya, the role of classroom assistants in refugee schools in West Africa and gender and AIDS education in Uganda. Ruxton (2004) has case studies of organisations working on gender equality education programmes with men and boys from South Africa, the Caribbean, Timor Leste, Latin America, Yemen and India and Pakistan. Chikoko et al (2011) include references on ways of teaching controversial issues in the classroom in relation to Africa and elsewhere.

In order to provide examples of how positive gender equality programmes might work in practice we now explore two case studies in more detail. Volume 55 (5-6) of the *International Review of Education* (2009) is devoted to 'undoing gender', with the introductory article entitled 'From Denouncing Gender Inequities to Undoing Gender in Education: programmes and practices towards change in the social relations of gender', and contains articles on Zambia and Iran as well as one on Honduras which forms our first case study.

Murphy-Graham (2009) discusses the Tutorial Learning System or SAT in Honduras, which is a programme for lower and upper secondary schools. The programme uses textbooks that are written in the form of a conversation with students, inviting questioning and investigation. It also has tutors to guide students in their study of the texts, to encourage reflection and to supervise projects – their role is as a guide and facilitator of reflection and discussion rather than a lecturer. Study groups of 15-25 adolescents meet weekly with their tutor and together they participate in a wide variety of educational, productive and organisational activities in their communities. At the end students receive the equivalent of a secondary school diploma. A key principle of SAT is that of gender equality, which is explicitly mainstreamed into the curriculum and which emphasises change at the individual and structural level. Students are encouraged and facilitated in questioning and discussing gender relationships with the overt aim of more equality within the family, community and society. In researching the programme among a primarily female sample, Murphy-Graham found that students who had undergone SAT did have an increased consciousness of gender equality. A comparison of women in SAT with those not in SAT suggested a higher level of consciousness among the SAT members. Data from open-ended interviews suggested that students had reflected critically on the injustice of hegemonic masculinity, including the need for a more equal sharing of domestic duties. The findings suggested that change would be slow and that change was not always automatic or sustainable – in two cases students' husbands verbally abused and physically threatened them because they did not agree with their participation in the programme. However, the research suggested that participation in SAT did provide women with the interpersonal and communication skills to use 'underground' and 'direct confrontation' strategies to negotiate new roles with partners, such as sharing textbooks with partners, open discussions and telling them that they wanted a more equal division of labour. However, as she concludes, more investigations are needed, that

> focus in particular on the process by which boys' and men's
> attitudes and actions change. Men, after all, must be equal
> partners with women in our efforts to turn relationships of
> domination into relationships of collaboration, cooperation
> and reciprocity. (2009, p. 518)

On this note, Morrell and Makhaye (2006) describe work on masculinity with young men in KwaZulu Natal, South Africa, which, importantly, has the title 'working not blaming'. They point out that there are more men who avoid violence than who resort to it, but that it is nevertheless important to develop new models of masculinity that help to prevent violence as most people involved in violence are men. In South Africa there is a particular challenge because of the HIV/AIDS pandemic and the risk that the aggressive sexual behaviour of boys towards girls spreads the disease even further.

Morrell and Makhaye examine two projects that work with young men. The first is the Shosholoza AIDS project, which aimed to raise AIDS awareness by working with young men of about 16, whereas it had previously worked with young women but with no discernible effect on reducing the spread of HIV. Part of the work examined gender roles and presented positive visions of masculinity and fatherhood as well as promoting women's rights as human rights. Traditional cultural values supported the rights of men to have many sexual partners and to dictate the terms of sexual intercourse and, in addition, poverty had limited the possibility of the young men expressing their masculinity in healthy ways. The second is the Inkusi Isematholeni project, which focused on boys of 11-15 and which aimed to support the development of boys into good fathers and sexually responsible partners. All the boys in the project were at school. Apart from the content of sex education, there was an emphasis on participation and encouraging the boys to think for themselves. Caring behaviour was fostered by establishing vegetable gardens at the schools to provide food for the younger children and by planting indigenous trees which the boys were also responsible for. The idea was to introduce the participants to caring for and supporting others.

The boys discussed violence, including sexual and domestic violence, and gradually began to identify the failings of men rather than just focusing on female weaknesses. They referred to problems such as a lack of communication and understanding within relationships, to infidelity, alcohol abuse and unemployment. Men who had no income from employment failed to meet family expectations of providing and responded by exerting their power over women or by becoming jealous of their successful partners. As a result of these discussions and activities, the boys expressed contrition for their past actions and identified positive courses of action for the future. In both projects there was evidence of increased awareness of women's rights and a commitment to the equal distribution of domestic work between boys and girls. By the end of the workshops most felt that they had no right to force a girl to have sex and had become much more confident about talking about difficult emotional and relational issues. The authors conclude that the two projects succeeded because

> they involve young men in activities that improve their self-
> knowledge and analytical skills. They develop confidence in
> themselves and trust in the facilitators. They are given a
> supportive environment in which to express difficult
> emotions. They are not interpolated as oppressors of women or
> perpetrators of violence ... They also come to realise that they
> can have healthier relationships with other people and lead
> happier lives by developing new models of masculine
> behaviour which do not include any recourse to violence.
> (p. 160)

Conclusion

Gender equality is a significant social issue and a concern for education globally. However, it is particularly important for international development for reasons set out at the beginning of this chapter. Considerable progress has been made in relation to equal access to and outcomes from education, though there is still much to do. Within debates about gender equality the need to end gender violence and sexual harassment in schools is a priority and it is here that the role of masculinities is so important. There are now many projects concerned with reducing notions of masculinity based on violence and aggression. However, while many of these take place with young people of school age and within schools, they are often not part of mainstream schooling and not therefore necessarily sustainable. At the moment both schools and teacher education do not seem to be providing sufficient opportunities for the examination and discussion of gender and masculinity, and an institutional culture that is more conducive to gender equality, even though knowledge and resources on how to do so exist.

References

Action Aid (2009) *Hate Crimes: the rise of 'corrective' rape in South Africa.* London: Action Aid.

Aikman, S., Halai, A. & Rubagiza, J. (2011) Conceptualising Gender Equality in Research on Education Quality, *Comparative Education*, 47(1), 45-60.

Arnot, M. & Fennell, S. (2008) Gendered Education and National Development: critical perspectives and new research, *Compare*, 38(5), 515-524.

Bhana, D., Nzimakwe, T. & Nzimakwe, P. (2011) Gender in the Early Years: boys and girls in an African working class school, *International Journal of Educational Development*, 31(5), 443-448.

Chikoko, V., Gilmour, J., Harber, C. & Serf, J. (2011) Teaching Controversial Issues in England and South Africa, *Journal of Education for Teaching*, 37(1), 5-19.

Connell, R. (2000) Arms and the Man: using the new research on masculinity to understand violence and promote peace in the contemporary world, in I. Breines, R. Connell & I. Eide (Eds) *Male Roles, Masculinities and Violence.* Paris: UNESCO.

Dunne, M. (2007) Gender, Sexuality and Schooling: everyday life in junior secondary schools in Botswana and Ghana, *International Journal of Educational Development*, 27(5), 499-511.

Elsanousi, M.M. (2004) Strategies and Approaches to Enhance the Role of Men and Boys in Gender Equality: a case study from Yemen, in S. Ruxton (Ed.) *Gender Equality and Men: learning from practice.* Oxford: Oxfam.

Greig, A., Kimmel, M. & Lang, J. (2000) *Men, Masculinities and Development.* UNDP Monograph 10. http://un.by/pdf/UNDP_Men_and_Masculinities-26557.pdf

Gulbenkian Foundation (1995) *Children and Violence.* London: Calouste Gulbenkian Foundation.

Harber, C. & Serf, J. (2006) Teacher Education for a Democratic Society in England and South Africa, *Teaching and Teacher Education*, 22(8), 986-997.

Leach, F. & Mitchell, C. (2006) *Combating Gender Violence in and around Schools.* Stoke-on-Trent: Trentham Books.

Morrell, R. (1998) Gender and Education: the place of masculinity in South African schools, *South African Journal of Education*, 18, 218-225.

Morrell, R. (2001a) The Time of Change: men and masculinity in South Africa, in R. Morrell (Ed.) *Changing Men in South Africa.* Pietermaritzburg: University of Natal Press and Zed Books.

Morrell, R. (2001b) Corporal Punishment and Masculinity in South African Schools, *Men and Masculinity*, 4(2), 140-157.

Morrell, R. & Makhaye, G. (2006) Working not Blaming: masculinity work with young African men in KwaZulu-Natal, in F. Leach & C. Mitchell (Eds) *Combating Gender Violence in and around Schools.* Stoke-on-Trent: Trentham Books.

Murphy-Graham, E. (2009) Constructing a New Vision: undoing gender through secondary education in Honduras, *International Review of Education*, 55(5-6), 503-521.

Pinheiro, P. (2006) *World Report on Violence Against Children*. Geneva: United Nations.

PLAN (2008) *The Global Campaign to End Violence in Schools*. Woking: PLAN.

Ruxton, S. (Ed.) (2004) *Gender Equality and Men: learning from practice*. Oxford: Oxfam.

Salisbury, J. & Jackson, D. (1996) *Challenging Macho Values*. London: Falmer Press.

UNESCO (2003/04) *Gender and Education for All: the leap to equality*. EFA Global Monitoring Report. Paris: UNESCO.

UNESCO (2012a) *Youth and Skills, Putting Education to Work*. EFA Global Monitoring Report. Paris: UNESCO.

UNESCO (2012b) *Education Sector Responses to Homophobic Bullying*. Paris: UNESCO.

Woolley, R. (2007) What Makes Men? Masculinity, Violence and Identity, in C. Harber & J. Serf (Eds) *Comparative Education and Quality Global Learning*. Birmingham: Teachers in Development Education.

Further Reading

Bhania, D. (2012) 'Girls are not free' – in and out of the South African school, *International Journal of Educational Development*, 32(2), 352-358.

Chisamaya, G., DeJaeghere, J., Kendall, N. & Khan, M. (2012) Gender and Education for All: progress and problems in achieving gender equity, *International Journal of Educational Development*, 32(6), 743-755.

Creighton, M. & Park, H. (2010) Closing the Gender Gap: six decades of reform in Mexican education, *Comparative Education Review*, 54(4), 513-537.

Compare, 43(3) (2013), has a number of articles on gender and education; 40(2) (2010), Special Issue on Gender Mainstreaming in Education, and 38(5) (2008), Special Issue on Gendered Education and National Development.

Dunne, M. (2008) Gender, Sexuality and Development: education and society in sub-Saharan Africa. Rotterdam: Sense Publishers.

Unterhalter, E. & North, A. (2011) Responding to the Gender and Education Millennium Development Goals in South Africa and Kenya, Compare 41(4), 495-512.

Note: Those readers interested in connections between gender, education and religion, the subject of the previous chapter, should see Z. Gross, L. Davies and A.K. Diab (2013) Gender, Religion and Education in a Chaotic Postmodern World. Dordrecht: Springer.

Discussion and Activities

1. Have you ever considered gender or, more specifically, masculinity in your own education up to this point? If yes, what approach was taken? If no, why do you think this was omitted?

2. From your own experience, to what extent would you say that the analysis of schooling as often transmitting a particular set of masculine values of the sort described by Salisbury and Jackson (1996) above is valid?

3. From what you have read about gender, education and development in the book so far, what do you think are the key issues facing schools in developing countries in this respect and what still needs to be done?

4. Reading through the two case studies at the end of the chapter, what obstacles might there be to teachers using these approaches as part of mainstream schooling in developing countries based on what you have read in the book so far?

CHAPTER 11

Education in Emergencies

Introduction

Education in emergencies is something of an umbrella term for education during and in the aftermath of a crisis such as a severe flood or drought, a tsunami, an earthquake or widespread violent conflict. The United Nations (UN) has defined an 'emergency' as:

> 'Emergencies' are any crisis situation due to natural causes such as earthquake, tsunami, flood or hurricane, or armed conflict, which may be international (including military occupation) or internal, as defined in international humanitarian law, or post-conflict situations, which impair or violate the right to education, impede its development or hold back its realization. (United Nations Report on Right to Education in Emergency Situations, 2008, cited in Davies et al, 2009, p. 4)

Such emergencies are a development issue because they tend to have more impact on poorer people, the majority of whom live in developing countries. The housing of poorer people, for example, may well be less able to withstand an earthquake or flood, and their financial circumstances, and more direct reliance on agriculture, may mean that an emergency has a rapid impact on their lives and livelihood.

Education in Emergencies

Education is now increasingly seen as a priority in helping populations during and after an emergency along with other priorities such as food and water, shelter and healthcare. Indeed, Machel (1996) called it the 'fourth pillar' of humanitarian response. This is because education allows for the immediate dissemination of important messages such as landmine awareness and HIV/AIDS sensitisation, provides a sense of normality during a context of instability, reduces the risk of children dropping out of school permanently and can provide physical protection from the dangers of a crisis environment. 'When a child is in a safe learning environment he or she is less likely to be sexually exploited or exposed to other risks, such as voluntary recruitment into an armed group' (Karpinska, 2012, p. 17). It can also be a way of helping to prevent or minimise such emergencies in the medium- and longer-term future.

Help for education in a crisis context, whether provided locally or with international aid, is aimed at restoring educational provision as rapidly as possible, but the phrase that is often used is to 'build back better'; that is, to provide a better educational experience for learners than that which existed before the emergency. The idea is to 'construct a more orderly transition out of protracted and devastating crises into phases of recovery and development' (Barakat et al, 2013, p. 126). This requires support for building and maintaining schools; the transport of learning and construction materials; the ensuring of good-quality teaching and learning in a safe space; data collection, collation and analysis; community mobilisation; management training of educational staff; and often negotiation between parties in a conflict (Karpinska, 2012, pp. 15-16). Depending on the nature of the emergency, it may also require relevant curriculum innovation for a longer-term impact, such as peace education, vocational education or even a greater emphasis on being able to swim. It can also provide psychosocial counselling for young people and others to help to reduce trauma resulting from the emergency.

In 2000 the Inter-Agency Network for Education in Emergencies (INEE) was established to provide support for professionals working in the field of education in emergencies. The aim was to raise the profile and improve the quality of such work, leading to the Minimum Standards for Education in Emergencies, Chronic Crises and Early Reconstruction in 2004. As Barakat et al (2013, p. 125) put it:

> The INEE Minimum Standards now constitute the normative
> framework for humanitarian response in the education sector
> and are increasingly becoming points of reference for
> government ministries of education, as they systematically
> address their responsibilities in response to conflict and
> natural hazards and those affected by such events.

The Minimum Standards focus on five areas of education – community participation, access and the learning environment, teaching and learning, teachers and other education personnel, and education policy and coordination – and have been used in contexts such as the 2005 earthquake in Pakistan and the conflicts in Darfur and northern Uganda. Such global standards in emergency education have arisen and are possible, according to Bromley and Andina (2010), for two reasons: first, because education is now seen as a fundamental human right, even for those experiencing a major emergency, and second, because of the increasingly interconnected and globalised world culture, as discussed in chapter one.

Education and Violent Conflict

One particular type of emergency that has seriously affected developing countries, and which has attracted a good deal of academic and professional attention, is war and violent conflict. Indeed, many, if not most, violent conflicts in recent decades have occurred in 'developing' countries. Much conflict has taken place in what are often referred to as 'fragile states', i.e. where the state and government are not seen as providing the functions and services that would be expected of a 'normal' or more secure or developed state (Bengtsson, 2011). The 2011 Education for All Global Monitoring Report was entitled 'The Hidden Crisis: armed conflict and education' (UNESCO, 2011) and specifically looked at the issue, both in terms of the impact of war on education and education's role in either helping to increase or decrease the chances of violent conflict.

In terms of the impact on education, from 1998 to 2008 thirty-five countries experienced armed conflict, of which thirty were low- and middle-income countries. Some 42% of out-of-school children live in conflict-affected, low-income countries. The average duration of violent conflicts in these countries is 12 years, the entire primary and secondary school cycle. Only 79% of young people are literate in conflict-affected poor countries compared to 93% in other poor countries. Schools and schoolchildren are often seen by combatants as legitimate targets, in clear violation of international law. Over 43 million people have been displaced by armed conflict, and refugees and internally displaced people face major barriers to education. In 2008 only 69% of primary-school-age refugee children in UNHCR (UN High Commissioner for Refugees) camps were attending primary school (UNESCO, 2011, p. 2). On the other hand (and as discussed in chapter 6), education can fuel violent conflict:

> Education has the potential to act as a force for peace – but too
> often schools are used to reinforce the social divisions,
> intolerance and prejudices that lead to war. No country can
> hope to live in peace and prosperity unless it builds mutual
> trust between its citizens, starting in the classroom ... Schools
> should be seen first and foremost as places for imparting the
> most vital of skills: tolerance, mutual respect and the ability to
> live peacefully with others. (2011, p. 3)

However, as Rappleye (2011) points out, the role of education in either catalysing conflict or contributing to peace cannot be viewed independently of a wider conception of the relationship between violent conflict and development and a hypothesis about causality: what causes what? He provides an interesting summary of the different views of the relationship between development, conflict and education, which is set out in Table IV.

View of 'development' and conflict	Theorists and representative texts	Dominant assumptions and hypothesis about causality	Prescribed intervention	Education implications
(Neo) Classic Development	Schultz (1971) Rostow (1960) Chicago School (1970s)	• Centering of economic factors, democracy to correct market • Conflict as result of poverty, economic growth reduces likelihood of conflict (Collier et al, 2003) • 'Development' as unequivocally positive; more 'development' reduces the likelihood of conflict; conflict as 'development in reverse' (WB, 2003)	• More 'development' for greater *economic* growth, market-based solutions • 'structural adjustment', despite short-term 'pain', inequalities • Conflict resolution indirectly through economic growth; few direct interventions	• Education for economic growth, linking education to the needs of the economy: labor markets, etc. • Greater internal and external efficiency for educational system, usually through market solutions: private schools, school choice (increased enrolments viewed as gains in human capital)
Moderated Classic Development	Sen (1985,1997) UNICEF (1997) UNDP HDI	• Parity of non-economic factors • Conflict equally the result of human factors such as relative economic inequality; non-parity of religion, gender, ethnicity; ideology, etc. • 'Development' as unequivocally positive; *right kind* of 'development' reduces likelihood of conflict	• More 'development', but one adjusted to focus on human factors: horizontal inequality, human rights, democracy, inclusion • Direct conflict resolution, targeting of pockets/ populations of inequality or oppression	• Education for wider political and social 'development'; education that combats economic inequality • Decentralization for democratization, focus on marginalized communities, curricula and delivery that responds to diverse groups • Aid to *Peacebuilding Education*

Failed Development	Stiglitz (2002) Browne (2006)	• Centering of 'development' itself in the analysis, focus on its distortion of local economy, society, and culture; aid exacerbates divisions/inequality • External donors bear responsibility for failure to develop; aid never sheer altruism but linked to ideological and geopolitical agendas	• Not tinkering, but a major overhaul of modus operandi of aid • Much more context sensitivity in delivery • Consideration of the way that interventions exacerbate conflict	• 'Educational 'development' considered holistically as part of a major rethink of dominant aid paradigms, total impact of 'development' and overall donor–recipient relationship • Few prescriptions, education cannot be uncoupled from 'dev'
Conflict as Development Success	Freire (1970) Archer (1990)	• Oppression/marginalization fuels a latent pool of angst and indignation • 'Development' helps spark collective action by oppressed groups • If power structures do not accommodate demands for equity then conflict may emerge *but* conflict a lesser evil than the perpetuation of a cycle of oppression and passivity	• 'Development' for conscientization, local empowerment, and catalysing collective action • Focus on adults and oppressed/marginalized populations	• More educational intervention focusing on 'conscientization' and ownership of 'development' and 'education' • More of the same for NGOs and other organizations working at grass-roots levels making local populations aware of oppression ?
'Development' as Cause of Conflict	Escobar (1995) Ferguson (2005) Pigg (1993)	• The narrative 'development' a powerful myth that structures reality failing to approximate conditions on the ground; perpetuates 'underdevelopment', fabricates 'abnormalities', 'Third World' • The 50+ year failure of 'development' caused the idea of 'development stairways' to break down, replaced by belief in 'exclusionary walls' where the only way around is *exit or violence*	• End of 'development'; critical re-evaluation of most fundamental truths of development • Wider global inequalities • Refusal to specify solutions, preferring to see what emerges once contexts are unburdened of 'development'	

Table IV. Five different perspectives on conflict, development, and education.
Source: Rappleye (2011, pp. 88-89).

177

Rappleye argues that the overwhelming ideological consensus within current academic work and within international aid agencies and international organisations is on the first two types of development (which he calls 'neo-classical development' and 'moderated classical development') and which, he thinks, thus crowds out the other three, more critical, positions. Indeed, the reasons for, and contexts of, violent conflict differ considerably and it may well be that some of the above theories, or combinations of them, apply more to one conflict context than another.

There is now a burgeoning literature on education and violent conflict and its causes and contexts. This literature describes various interventions to both mitigate the effects of violent conflict on education and to try to reduce it in the future. These include, for example, the immediate tasks of rebuilding schools, providing teaching and learning materials, reintegrating child soldiers into education, creating 'zones of peace' around educational establishments, providing psycho-social support for children and teachers and getting refugees back into education, as well as the longer-term tasks of peace and human rights education to help to create a less violent society in the future. These longer-term goals are part of 'building back better', i.e. that schools should actually become safer, more tolerant and generally more democratic and inclusive institutions.

Two major issues relating to education in conflict and post-conflict contexts are the degree to which educational reform is actually possible and what impact such change may have on creating more peaceful attitudes and behaviour in the longer term. The remainder of this section of the chapter therefore reviews recent literature on the important question of educational change and its impact in post-conflict, developing contexts. For example, a recent study of UNICEF's Education in Emergencies and Post-Crisis Transition Programme in Nepal, South Sudan and Kenya (Barakat et al, 2013), though optimistic in tone, found that in each case very little monitoring data had been collected so it was difficult to make firm judgements about the efficacy or impact of the programme. Pagen (2011) presents a case study of a country that has experienced considerable levels of violent conflict – South Sudan. Interestingly, the study examines empirical evidence on where Sudanese citizens actually learn about democracy and human rights. Schooling comes a poor fourth behind political leaders, relatives and friends, and churches. Matsumoto's (2011) study of post-conflict Sierra Leone asks whether education is making a positive contribution to development there. Matsumoto is critical of pre-war schooling for contributing indirectly towards the war because of its divisive and elitist nature and because of the gap between the expectations created and the realities of the labour market. He describes the post-war educational changes that have taken place, including an attempt at greater vocationalism, but is doubtful whether they will work because of the prevalence of 'Sababu' or social connections in getting employment – who you know is more important than what you know. However, at one point he touches on a significant internal aspect of schooling in Sierra Leone that has resonance elsewhere. Good students – those with a 'blessing' – are perceived to be those that obey teachers, the principal and others. Elsewhere Wright (1997) is very critical of the pre-war education system in Sierra Leone for having an over-emphasis on conformity and sycophancy which has helped to facilitate a population that is too docile in the face of dictatorial leaders, even noting that the very violent Revolutionary Front had 'an unusually high proportion of ex-teachers and ex-students in its ranks' (1997, p. 25).

The final three chapters of Paulson's edited book on education, conflict and development (2011a) all focus on northern Uganda, dealing with sexual violence during the conflict as a – continuing – barrier to female participation in schools, and both teachers' and young people's perspectives of the devastating impact of the war on education in the region. The section makes clear the enormous demands made on teachers in simply coping with and trying to help traumatised children when the teachers themselves have not been well trained in such areas and lack motivation and morale. The discussions also pose fundamental questions about whether the present, predominantly authoritarian schools in northern Uganda are contributing, or could contribute, to peacebuilding in the sense of developing a more peaceful society in the medium and longer terms. The continued use of corporal punishment doesn't help. Indeed, a separate study of an explicit peace education programme in northern Uganda (Najjuma, 2011) found only limited impact largely because of incompatibilities between the values and practices of peace education and the 'normalities' of formal schooling – interestingly, also a serious problem in the United Kingdom (Harber & Sakade, 2009).

A volume also edited by Paulson (2011b) contains a number of studies on education and reconciliation. Noting that forgiveness is central to reconciliation, it states in the introduction, 'that education contributes towards reconciliation is one of the "foundational assumptions" that informs international work around education in emergencies' (p. 3). However, as the editor herself admits (p. 6), the book only offers 'glimpses' of reconciliation in action. The first chapter by Hart (2011) notes the paucity of evaluations of peace education in conflict contexts but that where they do exist they show the difficulty of achieving measurable, let alone sustained, change. As discussed above, he attributes this (pp. 25-26) to incompatibilities between the goals and practices of peace education and formal schooling. Certainly, in the context of ongoing violent conflict (such as Israel–Palestine, which he focuses on), reconciliation through formal education would be near to impossible. Talking of a Palestinian young person undergoing occupation, he writes, 'it is doubtful that her feelings would be assuaged by fine-sounding messages delivered in the classroom, no matter how expertly designed and delivered, when her daily experiences of occupation remain unchanged' (p. 19).

Paulson's own chapter in the book (2011c) looks at the 20-year violent conflict between governments and Shining Path guerrillas in Peru where there was a Truth and Reconciliation Commission following the end of the fighting. Shining Path had a great deal of support membership among teachers and 'It helped that Shining Path indoctrination mirrored the authoritarian, didactic and unquestionable pedagogic style that had long characterised teaching and learning in Peru's state schools' (p. 130). The Truth and Reconciliation Commission in Peru recommended a move away from such authoritarian practices to greater democratisation in school in its final report in 2003 but nothing much has happened subsequently – 'a real contribution to reconciliation via education reform is not evident in Peru' (p. 145).

Kearney's chapter in the same book (Kearney, 2011) examines the Ingando Peace and Solidarity Camp in Rwanda which exists to strengthen Rwandan identity as opposed to ethnic ties. The argument of the chapter is that the top-down, authoritarian and unequivocal approach of the camp is more a method of establishing unity and social cohesion through a single view of history rather than an attempt at reconciliation through discussion and open debate. Moreover, this authoritarian style is reinforced by intense military training involving physical punishment.

Brannelly et al (2009) deal explicitly with the role of Western donors in trying to assist in both immediately restoring education after violence and developing it peacefully in the longer term. They note that 'Education is also increasingly perceived as a key factor in restoring normalcy and hope, a necessity that can be both life sustaining and life saving, providing physical, psychosocial and cognitive protection' (p. 33). Not only is this a very difficult task for the donor agencies in the context of, often weak, organisational and physical infrastructure but, as Brannelly et al make clear, it is also a very dangerous one for the personnel concerned, who sometimes lose their lives. A further difficulty is the key question of whether or how formal education actually does, or even can, do these things, however well intentioned and organised the donors are. As Brannelly et al state, 'Donors also have limited evidence as to the impact of their education interventions in difficult situations' (p. 51). One intriguing intervention by the IRC (International Rescue Committee), the Healing Classrooms Initiative (p. 168), focuses on teacher motivation and well-being in order to help to create supportive learning environments so that children can move forward from traumatic experience of conflict or natural disasters. However, the approach and the tools used are 'yet to be evaluated independently', so again the jury is out (p. 168).

Nicolai (2009) discusses the opportunities for positive innovation, reform and even transformation that emerge from education systems damaged or destroyed by violence, i.e. a chance to start from scratch, rethink and 'build back better'. Nicolai cites a positive evaluation of peace education in Kenya by Obura (2002) as evidence of success, though this was in schools in refugee camps and among community youth and adults rather than in mainstream formal schooling. However, the book contains very little in the way of researched examples of success of reform, even transformation, of formal education – schools – because of the catalyst of war. For example, chapter 7 is on the provision of education to girls at home or in the community in Afghanistan, because 'Emerging research indicates that government teachers use harsh and discriminatory methods, such as corporal punishment on children from particular ethnic and linguistic groups, and with assumed political affiliations' (p. 105).

In another chapter on peace education in Sri Lanka and Uganda, the section on Uganda does record some success but the programme (the Alternatives to Violence Project) is aimed at adolescents and adults, not schools. In Sri Lanka, peace education is supposed to be integrated into all subjects in formal schooling (p. 296). However, the problem is that 'the system appears to be anti-minorities, because the Sinhala nationalist ideology is persistent in some textbooks' (p. 208), and while 'trainee teachers are expected to develop the skills of empathetic listening, democratic leadership, developing children's self-esteem and conflict resolution ... these expectations might be too high, given the often poor quality of teacher training' (p. 209). Moreover, the Sri Lankan educational system continues to be organised along ethnically segregated lines, so that, as the authors note, although democratically organised schools do exist internationally, 'they are still the exception in Sri Lanka' and overall 'There has been only limited attention to the promotion of peaceful relations and democratic values and attitudes' (p. 210).

The final chapter on the teaching of history in Rwanda echoes that by Kearney mentioned above. There is only one official 'true' version of history, and challenge, debate and analysis is discouraged: 'The government-supported discourse is rarely questioned because the post-conflict climate limits open discussion about historical events. This indirectly stifles teaching and learning' (p. 223).

Mundy and Dryden-Peterson (2011) analyse both the impact of violence on education and education's role in reproducing and perpetrating violence. However, again there is little evidence of working examples of a successful restructuring of schools in a more peaceful and democratic direction. As Lynn Davies writes in chapter 3 of the book, 'we may hold assumptions that civic and human rights will build the

181

nation, but the long-term evidence is not there – or perhaps never can be. The evidence about negatives is much clearer. I therefore have focussed more on what is derived from the research than on aspirational conjectures about education's role' (Davies, 2011, p. 37).

And indeed she does provide examples of education playing a role in enhancing community security and reducing tension. However, in the literature on education and violent conflict overall there is only very limited evidence of the structures and processes of schools themselves being changed in any significantly peaceful and democratic way by, during or after the crisis of violent conflict and of this having an impact. There is much more evidence of successful attempts to return to the 'normality' of providing access to conventional schooling. The evidence tends to suggest that schools might stop doing the harm that they do and be better able to help pupils 'cope and hope' but at the moment there is little sign or evidence of them successfully educating for a more peaceful future via their organisation, pedagogy and curricular emphases. Indeed, Shah (2012), writing on post-conflict Timor-Leste, argues that the political and administrative conditions necessary for such educational change are rarely present in fragile states shortly after the end of hostilities or turmoil. It appears, then, that serious change is very difficult, and on the whole tends not to take place in formal education in and after violent conflict. Genuinely different, non-authoritarian approaches are more likely to take place outside of mainstream schooling.

Education, Emergencies and Vulnerabilities

When an emergency occurs in a developing country, the education of some children and young people is more affected and more vulnerable than others. This section presents in some detail a study of the impact of emergencies on the education of vulnerable children in South Asia (Afghanistan, Bangladesh, Bhutan, India, Maldives, Nepal, Pakistan and Sri Lanka) – and what might be done in response (Davies et al, 2009). This study identified six broad types of educational vulnerability in an emergency – gender-related disadvantage, internally displaced persons and refugees, minority groups/castes/ethnic groups, the economically disadvantaged, the invisible (those without any formal or bureaucratic identity) and the differently affected (e.g. children with disabilities, orphans, child-headed households, child soldiers, drug users, etc.). The study noted that 'Emergencies often act as a magnifier for pre-existing disadvantage or for discrimination as well as creating new vulnerable groups, such as orphans, refugees and internally displaced persons' (Davies et al, 2009, p. 3). It argued that in order to reduce educational vulnerability it was necessary to make such children visible, safe and capable and that the learning spaces needed for this would have to be (1) child-seeking, (2) child-friendly and (3) child-enabling. Below are listed examples of each category in order to illustrate the particular problems and tasks facing those engaged with education in emergencies:

1. Examples of promising practices and strategies in *child-seeking* schools would be:

- Monitoring systems, with class registers so that teachers know who should return after an emergency and so that they can visit homes (if still there) to encourage them to return.
- Monitoring systems to identify which schools are affected by an emergency, visiting children in shelters to check that they are all right, and again encouraging them to return to school. Children themselves becoming monitors and encouraging others to return (as in Sri Lanka).
- Outreach work, such as the 'street educators' and 'street schools' for street children around the world, or the itinerant teachers who follow nomadic Kurdish herders.
- 'Welcome to school' packs for girls (as is done in rural areas in Nepal).
- School feeding programmes, including 'Food for learning' (girls being given 2 litres of cooking oil for 80% attendance in Nepal).
- Scholarships for the economically disadvantaged and/or for dalit girls; 'dalit' motivators who visit homes or give extra tuition (Nepal).
- Grants for shoes, uniforms and books after the tsunami (Maldives) – a clean image of students was important to them.
- 'Back to school' project with printed T shirts saying this, that could be worn as a uniform until the 'proper' uniform could be distributed.
- Running, or working with those who run, Child Lines, who may be able to identify out-of-school children (as long as confidentiality is not compromised).
- Teachers or others working with traditional communities to encourage them not to lock females away for 4-10 days during menstruation (Nepal) or working on menstruation management (India).
- Deploying final-year teacher education students as temporary teachers, making it possible to reopen schools as soon as possible after emergency (Maldives).
- An open school programme (Sri Lanka), including two schools in prisons. This has no age limit and serves children in remote areas and in war and disaster affected areas. Teachers are mobile and reach children where they are, during different seasons.
- Early Learning Centres and mobile crèches.

- Catch-up programmes with a condensed curriculum and with less time needed. This is particularly important for returning child soldiers or for the 'lost generation' who have missed out in times of conflict.
- Home–school modules and booklets for children in conflict zones who cannot come to school every day (Sri Lanka).
- Transportation for students (and teachers), for example, by providing bicycles; children helping disabled children to get to school, perhaps using wheelbarrows.
- At checkpoints, teachers or other adults to help children get through and get to school.
- Staff visiting sites where street children often congregate, to encourage them to go to school, or running transitional schools to enable catch-up.
- Training and provision of female teachers for some ethnic communities.
- Equivalency programmes which ensure that student accreditation can be transferred between state and non-state education providers, as in Thailand.
- Building links between schools in peace-time or 'normal' time might improve parent resolve to send children to unfamiliar schools or increase tolerance in schools receiving new children (e.g. Maldives).

2. Examples of *child-friendly* practice would be:

- Physically safe schools able to survive in natural disaster (schools on boats, schools on stilts, schools that can be dismantled which are held together with nuts and bolts, etc.). Physically safe schools are also those built to good standards, where they are not more likely to collapse because of lack of attention to earthquake safety or because of corruption.
- Psychological safety: psycho-social care for those with trauma; for example, discussion at school in the aftermath of a tsunami, and lessons about it, to share experiences. One-to-one, or community-level approaches using theatre and singing to talk about issues.
- Non-violence: absence of bullying, sexual harassment and corporal punishment, and developing alternative methods of 'discipline'.
- Sanitary facilities for girls. Separate toilets with locks. Safety and the location of toilets is an issue. Provision for hand washing, with clean water and soap, and health education to stress this. Provision of sanitary pads at the school, for female students and teachers.
- Active learning methodologies based on participation, expression and investigation, which help in the aftermath of a disaster.
- Flexibility: flexibility in the school day to accommodate working children of all categories (home, domestic labour in other homes,

child labourers, the 'tidal workers' in fishing communities). Curricular programmes need to be flexible during and after emergencies, as, for example, children may be moved from one region to another where there are different political motivations and their learning experiences will contrast (Nepal); abbreviated/accelerated programmes with prioritised learning skills may facilitate catch-up for children returning to school.

- Teacher compensation: flexible administration for teachers, to enable them to receive their salary in new or temporary schools. Temporary housing for teachers and their families, if necessary.
- Community involvement: communities becoming more involved in management of the schools (India).
- Physical safety: children developing and documenting their safety plans, or School Emergency Response plans for each school, displayed on the wall so that teachers and students can familiarise themselves with them (India, Sri Lanka).
- 'Sanctuary' – a safe space to play, make friends, do sports, interact with trusted adults, which is available at all relevant times.

3. *Child-enabling* strategies would include the following examples:

Examples relating to rights, including participation rights, would be:

- Children's clubs (India, Sri Lanka, Nepal) which do Disaster Risk Response (DRR) activities, or which monitor teachers' behaviour.
- Child rights forum, where children talk about their rights and how to protect themselves, setting codes of conduct for the school and discussing issues such as child marriage (Nepal).
- Children participating in decisions: various forms of student councils and representation; children's committees.
- Children's declaration for protection of their rights during the Constituent Assembly.

Examples relating to emergency preparedness would be:

- Swimming lessons (particularly for girls and disabled children in the school), acknowledging challenges for female traditions of modest dress.
- Hazard awareness education (earthquakes, tsunami, cyclone, floods), including health messages, to minimise loss of life. This would include child-led DRR, where children conduct assessments and engage in awareness campaigns. They identify problems and draw up 'our suggestions to those in authority'. DRR also includes practical skills such as making portable clay ovens for shelters, building bamboo bridges to help evacuate the most vulnerable, bamboo shelves for high storage etc.
- Emergency plans in the school.

- Discussion of when an emergency can override cultural and religious restrictions and norms, such as dress.
- Health education: this may involve child-to-child work to educate families as well as direct teaching and learning in school. Agencies such as UNICEF will work with host families for displaced children to make sure that children benefit from immunisation campaigns, vitamin A supplementation, etc.

Examples relating to future preparedness for economic and other survival would be:

- Life skills: schools for domestic workers in Kathmandu, teaching exam curriculum but also about religious sites and tourism, so that children could act as guides.
- Research skills: children involved in data collection on needs after emergencies (after earthquake in Pakistan, rapid assessments during flood in India, consultation sessions in Bangladesh, and identifying child led indicators for use in monitoring and evaluation (Nepal, Sri Lanka and India).
- Training by specialists, e.g. lawyers and police (children's rights), health educators (reproductive health), military (mine and munitions awareness), employers (job opportunities, 'careers guidance').

Cutting across these three domains would be certain principles:

- There should be neutral spaces for learning (an 'educational Red Cross'). This does not mean that the content of learning cannot be 'political', for example, in citizenship education, but that schools should not be taken over by political parties, security forces, or even cultural events not linked to the school. This was the original impetus for 'Schools as Zones of Peace' in Nepal.
- Children as participants in decisions and actions (taking part in seeking others, taking part in governance, child-to-child learning).
- Flexibility of schools, to enable working children to attend, to incorporate different religious backgrounds and needs, to enable joining of school at any time of the year, to accommodate learning experiences of returnees or internally displaced persons.
- Value added: schools need to be viewed by children and parents as worthwhile places to go, which would justify the opportunity costs, especially after emergency. In camps, children need something to do, and may not need an incentive; but elsewhere, there are crucial choices to make. This is particularly true at the margins: in extreme food insecurity it does not matter how enticing the school is, children will be taken out in order to work; yet in less critical times, participants can be persuaded of the value of education in the long

term. Children can see going to school as worthwhile, if only as beneficial places for friendship with other children or teachers.

However, while there were examples of good and promising practice, as set out above and in more detail in the report itself, the study also found that there was much that could still be done. There were some serious remaining issues and problems in terms of educating for resilience, survival and a better-quality education and way of life for the most vulnerable in and after an emergency. For example, lack of records and information affected many of the countries in the study, making emergency education interventions much more difficult. In Bangladesh physical punishment of pupils in schools is common, providing a disincentive for attendance, and there is still a gender bias in school textbooks and a need to educate men and boys about gender relations and masculinity. In India teacher education does not interrogate prejudices against vulnerable groups; pedagogy does not allow questioning of the authority of teacher and text. Teacher attitude was widely cited as a problem in relation to vulnerable groups. Corporal punishment is widespread and Dalits are much more likely to be victims of it. The National Council for Teacher Education was singled out by respondents for its corrupt practices in giving affiliations to inappropriate institutions. In Nepal there is still violence and corporal punishment in schools and there is no programme to enable children in terms of the knowledge and skills of how to deal with real situations (natural disasters, child labour, epidemics, HIV/AIDS, drugs, etc.). The school enrolment of children with special needs is very low in Sri Lanka. Schools can refuse children with special needs due to the 'lack of resources'. Although schools have a policy of inclusion, it was reported that parents with special needs children fear that their child will be bullied once they have been to school. The lack of training for teachers in mainstream schools to work with these children is also apparent. Children with special needs are an 'invisible' group in Sri Lanka.

Conclusion

Education is now seen as something that needs attention in the event of an emergency in a developing country and elsewhere, both during and in the immediate aftermath of an emergency and in the medium to longer term to help to minimise the chances of similar emergencies and their effects in the future. When restoring an education system in the context of an emergency, however, the idea is to not just to replace it as it was but to replace it with something better and to make sure that those groups of children that are particularly vulnerable in an emergency are fully included. Education in emergencies is a relatively new field of international development, both in a practical and academic sense, and a lot of progress has been made over the last two decades. However, there are now plenty of ideas about what this better form of schooling might or ought to look like and there are some useful examples of how schools might be more 'child-friendly' and 'child-enabling' in the future. Nevertheless, the evidence, particularly in relation to education and violent conflict, suggests that serious change in these directions is both very difficult – the traditional model of the school is very resilient – and that we still need to know more about the impact of such projects where they do exist.

References

Barakat, S., Connolly, D., Hardman, F. & Sundaram, V. (2013) The Role of Basic Education in Post-conflict Recovery, *Comparative Education*, 49(2), 124-142.

Bengtsson, S. (2011) Fragile States, Fragile Concepts: a critical reflection on the terminology in the field of education in emergencies, in J. Paulson (Ed.) *Education, Conflict and Development*. Oxford: Symposium Books.

Brannelly, L., Ndaruhutse, S. & Rigaud, C. (2009) *Donors' Engagement: supporting education in fragile and conflict-affected states*. Paris and Reading: IIEP and CfBT.

Bromley, P. & Andina, M. (2010) Standardising Chaos: a neo-institutional analysis of the INEE Minimum Standards for Education in Emergencies, Chronic Cases and Early Reconstruction, *Compare*, 40(5), 575-589.

Davies, L. (2011) Can Education Interrupt Fragility? Towards the Resilient Citizen and the Adaptable State, in S. Mundy & S. Dryden-Peterson (Eds) *Educating Children in Conflict Zones*. New York: Teachers College Press.

Davies, L., Harber, C., Schweisfurth, M., et al (2009) *Education in Emergencies in South Asia: reducing the risks facing vulnerable children*. Kathmandu: UNICEF.

Harber, C. & Sakade, N. (2009) Schooling for Violence and Peace: how does peace education differ from 'normal' schooling?, *Journal of Peace Education*, 6(2), 171-187.

Hart, J. (2011) Young People and Conflict: the implications for education, in J. Paulson (Ed.) *Education and Reconciliation: exploring conflict and post-conflict situations*. London: Continuum.

Karpinska, Z. (2012) *Education, Aid and Aid Agencies*. London: Continuum.

Kearney, J. (2011) A Unified Rwanda? Ethnicity, History and Reconciliation in the Ingando Peace and Solidarity Camp, in J. Paulson (Ed.) *Education and Reconciliation: exploring conflict and post-conflict situations*. London: Continuum.

Machel, G. (1996) *Impact of Armed Conflict on Children*. Report of the Expert of the Secretary General of the United Nations. New York: UN and UNICEF.

Matsumoto, M. (2011) Expectations and Realities of Education in Post-conflict Sierra Leone: a reflection of society or a driver for peacebuilding?, in J. Paulson (Ed.) *Education, Conflict and Development*. Oxford: Symposium Books.

Mundy, S. & Dryden-Peterson, S. (Eds) (2011) *Educating Children in Conflict Zones*. New York: Teachers College Press.

Najjuma, R. (2011) Peace Education in the Context of Post-Conflict Formal Schooling: the effectiveness of the Revitalising Education Participation and Learning in Conflict Affected Areas Peace Education Programme in Northern Uganda. PhD thesis, University of Birmingham.

Nicolai, S. (Ed.) (2009) *Opportunities for Change: education innovation and reform after conflict.* Paris: IIEP and UNESCO.

Obura, A. (2002) *UNHR Peace Education Programme: an evaluation report.* Geneva: UNHCR.

Pagen, C. (2011) Sources of Learning about Human Rights and Democracy in Southern Sudan, in J. Paulson (Ed.) *Education, Conflict and Development.* Oxford: Symposium Books.

Paulson, J. (Ed.) (2011a) *Education, Conflict and Development.* Oxford: Symposium Books.

Paulson, J. (Ed.) (2011b) *Education and Reconciliation: exploring conflict and post-conflict situations.* London: Continuum.

Paulson, J. (2011c) Reconciliation through Educational Reform? Recommendations and Realities from Peru, in J. Paulson (Ed.) *Education and Reconciliation: exploring conflict and post-conflict situations.* London: Continuum.

Rappleye, J. (2011) Different Presumptions about Progress, Divergent Prescriptions for Peace: connections between conflict, 'development' and education in Nepal, in J. Paulson (Ed.) *Education, Conflict and Development.* Oxford: Symposium Books.

Shah, R. (2012) Goodbye Conflict, Hello Development? Curriculum Reform in Timor-Leste, *International Journal of Educational Development*, 32(1), 31-38.

UNESCO (2011) *The Hidden Crisis: armed conflict and education.* EFA Global Monitoring Report. Paris: UNESCO.

Wright, C. (1997) Reflections on Sierra Leone: a case study, in *Final Report and Case Studies of the Workshop on Educational Destruction and Reconstruction in Disrupted Societies.* Paris: UNESCO.

Further Reading

Bethke, L. & Baxter, P. (2009) *Alternative Education: filling the gap in emergency and post-conflict* situations. Paris and Reading: IIEP and CfBT.

Brock, C. (2012) Education as a Humanitarian Response as Applied to Teachers and Their Training in Sub-Saharan Africa, in R. Griffin (Ed.) *Teacher Education in Sub-Saharan Africa: closer perspectives.* Oxford: Symposium.

Compare, 35(4) (2005), Special Issue on Education in the Twenty-first Century: conflict, reconciliation and reconstruction.

Comparative Education Review, 52(4) (2008), Special Issue on Education in Conflict and Post-conflict Societies.

Clive Harber

Davies, L. (2011) Learning for State-building: capacity development, education and fragility, *Comparative Education*, 47(2), 157-180.

Harber, C. (2013) Education in and after Violent Conflict: stability and the status quo or transformation and peace?, Review Essay, *International Journal of Educational Development*, 33(2), 213-216.

International Review of Education 55 (2009), Special Issue on Education for Reconciliation and Conflict Resolution.

Obura, A. (2003) *Never Again: educational reconstruction in Rwanda*. Paris: IIEP.

Penson, J. & Tomlinson, K. (2009) *Rapid Response: programming for education needs in* emergencies. Paris and Reading: IIEP and CfBT.

Retamal, G. & Aedo-Richmond, R. (1998) *Education as a Humanitarian Response*. London: Cassell.

Sinclair, M. (2002) *Planning Education in and after Emergencies*. Paris: UNESCO/IIEP.

Sullivan-Owomoyela, J. & Brannelly, L. (2009) *Promoting Participation: community contributions to education in conflict situations*. Paris and Reading: UNESCO, IIEP and CfBT.

Discussion and Activities

1. Research one of the countries affected by an emergency that is mentioned in this chapter:

- What problems did the emergency cause?
- What educational improvements were put in place?
- Is there any evidence of their success?
- What educational problems still remain?

2. Go on to INEE website (www.ineessite.org):

- Who are its members?
- What are its key aims?
- Where does it work?
- What are its main activities?
- What are the strengths and weaknesses of the way that it works?

3. Flooding is a serious threat to life and livelihood in Bangladesh. Based on your research, which groups of young people in Bangladesh would be most vulnerable to serious flooding and why? What are the educational implications?

190

CHAPTER 12

Non-state Educational Provision

Introduction

Chapter 2 of this book discussed the issue of access to education for all in developing countries. Non-state provision is important partly because many developing states cannot afford to provide primary education for all and partly because increasing numbers of parents in developing countries are opting to send their children to non-state educational providers, often because of the poor quality of state provision. Some forms of non-state provision, such as community financing of education, have attracted attention for some time but more recently there has been considerable academic and ideological interest in 'low-fee private schools' for the poor as a supplementary way of achieving education for all. In this chapter we initially review some non-state forms of provision that are not normally considered to be 'private' education before examining forms of private provision in more detail.

Not-for-Profit Alternatives to State Provision

There is a long-standing tradition of non-state provision of education in developing countries, mainly through religious schools, such as those run by Christian missionaries, or Islamic schools, as discussed in chapter 9. However, the provision of public education for all has always been a problem for the state in developing countries as there is often insufficient money from taxes to pay for such provision. As a result, other providers have helped to fill the gap. In this section of the chapter we discuss some of those providers not primarily motivated by profit, though, as we shall see, this distinction is not necessarily a hard and fast one.

Some communities have collectively provided education themselves to fill the gap created by lack of state provision. This has been known as 'community financing of education'. The identity of such communities may, for example, rest on the possession of a 'we' feeling based on geography (e.g. a village or small town), religion or ethnicity. Such communities have organised educational provision as a self-help, stop-gap measure in the hope that the state would eventually take over running of the school when funds permitted, or at least start to make a contribution.

Typically, in order to raise the funds for the capital works needed to construct the community school buildings, communities would have fund-raising activities such as launches and rallies, fetes, carnivals, cultural shows, raffles, sponsored walks and a levy on individual households. Community members may also offer their labour to help build the school. In order to meet recurrent needs such as teachers' salaries, community-financed schools have also raised school fees, though teachers may also accept at least partial payment in food, accommodation or labour on their agricultural holdings. If a school is sponsored by a religious organisation, then collections during religious ceremonies are a source of income and they can also receive some funding from fellow religious organisations in more prosperous countries (Bray, 1996). Kenya's 'harambee' ('let's pull together') schools have been a particularly well-known and widespread example, but Bray and Lillis (1988) also provided case studies from Nigeria, Zambia, Botswana, Papua New Guinea, Burma, China and Guyana. While this may mean that children and young people get a formal education that they would not otherwise have had, the drawback is that better-off communities are more able to afford such schools and to provide better quality ones, thereby contributing to inequality in provision and broader social inequality. Moreover, ethnically or religious-based community-financed schools can help to reinforce social divisions (Bray, 1996, 1999).

Another non-state provider of schooling in developing countries is non-governmental organisations (NGOs). In her useful overview of such provision, Rose (2009) notes that NGOs are primarily involved in providing educational opportunities to children excluded from government schooling, such as children who are 'hard to reach', possibly because of where they live, their way of life (nomadic pastoralists or street children) or their status (orphans, child soldiers. child labourers, children from indigenous groups). While the motivations of such NGOs are normally seen as philanthropic and not for profit, they are often funded by national and international donors, and those working for the NGO benefit from the donor funding in the form of preferential salaries and other non-salary benefits. Rose estimates that in the four countries she examined (Bangladesh, India, Ethiopia and Ghana) NGOs provide education only to a small proportion of the primary-age population, ranging from 2.5% to 10%. Partly because of the children being provided for, NGO provision is also seen as an 'alternative' to state provision and is often referred to as 'non-formal' education, though recently the term 'complementary' has come into use to emphasise that NGO provision is part of a process of getting children into the formal system. NGO-provided education is also often perceived to be better quality and more cost-effective than government schools, though as Rose (2009, pp. 222-223) argues, the lack of systematic critical analysis based on a diversity of programmes makes it difficult to make judgements about its efficacy. However, in practice its integration into formal schooling can be a problem because of differences in learning styles, the social backgrounds of students and an insufficient supply of secondary schools.

While often more flexible and responsive to community needs than government provision, including those communities not usually provided for, NGO provision often depends on donor funding and therefore faces issues of sustainability – when the money runs out, so does the project. A study of internationally funded NGOs and locally funded TVOs (traditional voluntary organisations) in Pakistan (Bano, 2008) showed that the TVOs reached out to the poor and were sustainable but very limited in the scale of their operations. On the whole the NGOs used more child-centred teaching methods than TVOs but they had inherent limitations of sustainability once the money ran out, and there was a need to shift the focus and geographical location of their work frequently to meet the funding priorities of their donors. Also, because of fears concerning sustainability, most NGOs charged a fee to parents even during the funded period so that there would be finance available when the donor funding ran out:

> Therefore the only way the NGO model could survive was by moving to private provision once the donor funding was over ... NGOs did seem to play an important part in motivating the community to educate their children; many parents admitted that they are today more convinced of the need to send their children to school than before the start of the non-formal programme. However, given the inherent limitation of the non-formal cycle, the end result of this mobilisation was a move to the private sector. (Bano, 2008, pp. 498-480)

We now turn to the issue of 'for-profit' private education in developing countries, which has received increasing attention over the last decade. We begin by examining the phenomenon of private tutoring, which is clearly a form of for-profit, non-state educational provision, before examining the growth and role of low-fee private schools.

Supplementary Private Tutoring: a parallel education system?

It has long been the case that parents and pupils have paid for extra help outside of school hours to increase the chances of success in examinations. However, it is argued by some that the poor quality of state provision and highly competitive education systems means that this has now reached a scale where it amounts to a parallel or shadow education system. UNESCO (2012, p. 76) cites figures of 67% of parents with children at primary school using such private tutoring among richer families in Bangladesh while even 43% of those from the poorest quintile also do so. The corresponding figures for Egypt are 47% and 25%. It also notes that 'In some countries, including Cambodia and Egypt, it has been reported that teachers withhold curriculum content during the school day, forcing students to attend tutorials where the omitted area is covered' (UNESCO, 2012, p. 76).

Sobhy (2012) provides a particularly detailed study of private tutoring in secondary schools in Egypt. She argues that the growth of private tutoring was part of a deliberate policy of promoting privatisation and reducing public spending on education under the previous Mubarak regime. She notes that 80% of secondary students report year-long enrolment in private tutoring. The main motivation for middle-class parents is to obtain an acceptable level of education for their children whereas poorer families are pressured, intimidated and harassed by poorly paid and unaccountable teachers to enrol their children in order that they pass from one year to the next:

> Harassment by teachers ranges from physical beating and verbal humiliation to threats of expulsion and actual expulsion to students who had not yet enrolled. This is typically done under the pretext of non-compliant uniform, attendance, tardiness or misbehaviour. After enrolling in tutoring, this wave of teacher complaints ends and many violations are tolerated. (Sobhy, 2012, p. 59)

Sobhy argues that in Egypt parents regard the education system as of such poor quality as to be virtually non-existent, so much so that over one-third of those who complete the nine years of compulsory education remain illiterate. While aspects of the growth of private tutoring in Egypt will be further discussed in chapter 14, on corruption and education, the net results, according to Sobhy, are that

> the general school has been almost completely eliminated as a site of learning as it becomes displaced by tutoring centres and home tutoring. Private tutoring is no longer seen by individual students as a 'choice' ... This mode of privatisation has reinforced the transformation of much of formal youth schooling into private tutoring focused on exam readiness in a few 'key' subjects. It has structured the effective removal of art, music and sports components from the actual curricula of public schools, eliminating key spaces that had been intended to allow young people to develop a range of skills, abilities and experiences. (2012, p. 63)

In their comprehensive study of shadow education systems in Asia, Bray and Lykins (2012) show that shadow education has a long history in parts of the region but has greatly expanded over the last couple of decades. In South Korea nearly 90% of elementary students receive some sort of shadow education and in Hong Kong, China, about 85% of senior secondary students do so. In West Bengal, India nearly 60% of primary school students receive private supplementary tutoring and in Kazakhstan a similar proportion of students do so at the senior secondary level. Bray and Lykins argue that proportions are lower in other countries, but that throughout the region the shadow is spreading and intensifying. Bray and Lykins (2012, p. x) summarise the pros and cons of private tutoring as follows:

> Among the beneficial dimensions of private tutoring are the ways in which it can help slow learners to keep up with their peers, and can help high achievers reach new levels. The extra learning may contribute human capital for economic development, and many families consider extra lessons to be a constructive way to use the spare time of adolescents who might otherwise be at loose ends. On the negative side, private tutoring may dominate the lives of young people and their families, reducing the time available for sports and other activities, which are important for well-rounded development. Shadow education also maintains and exacerbates social inequalities. Rich families are clearly able to pay for better quality and greater quantities of tutoring than can middle-income and poor families, and disparities may threaten social cohesion. Moreover, tutoring can create inefficiencies in education systems. Particularly problematic are situations in which teachers deliberately reduce the effort that they devote to their regular classes in order to reserve energy for private tutoring.

Low-fee Private Schooling

During the last decade there has been increasing recognition of, and interest in, the rapid growth of low-fee private schooling for the poor and, in particular, the extent to which it can help to make up government shortfalls in providing education for all. This is a phenomenon that has been particularly marked in India and has been widely, though not exclusively, studied there. As we saw in chapter 3, private education is an area normally associated with the education of the rich, but low-fee private education is now increasingly being provided to the poorer sections of society in developing countries. This partly reflects the preference for private provision in the wider global context of neoliberal economic policy discussed in chapter 7. However, another important factor in the rapid growth of private education in developing countries is the poor quality of some state provision, as further discussed in chapters

2, 4 and 14. Bangay and Latham (2013, p. 246) cite Harma's research in India where she found that, although state schools had better buildings,

> The government schools had virtually no teaching activity.
> One para-teacher at one school was found to be teaching.
> While in another school an older child was instructing while
> the teachers (two were present) sat idly by. In the rest of the
> government schools there was an air of chaos and neglect, as
> the teachers simply read the newspaper or chatted with
> friends ... By way of contrast, at the low-fee private schools
> there was always an air of seriousness and discipline, with
> children sitting in orderly rows ... It was extremely common to
> observe children working diligently on their own in their
> copybooks and then bringing these to the teacher to be
> checked, while the teachers sat and waited to be approached ...
> There was an overall discipline enforced at the low-fee schools
> that was found to be absent in government schools and it was
> this and the fact that children learn basic material that parents
> seized on in their comparisons of the schools types.

Bangay and Latham go on to cite further studies suggesting that teachers at private schools are less likely to be absent and more likely to be engaged in teaching activities at any given point in time with the result that a child in a low-fee private school gets three to four times more contact time than in a government school. Research also suggests that head teachers in private schools are far more likely to fire a teacher for repeated absence than are head teachers in government schools (2013, p. 246).

Thus, it is not perhaps surprising that a study in Andra Pradesh, India, found that the uptake of such private education in the large research cohort doubled from 22% in 2002 to 44% in 2009 (Woodhead et al, 2013, p. 72). Indeed, globally, private provision is reported to have increased by 58% between 1991 and 2004 (Srivastava, 2013, p. 8) and Walford (2011, p. 401) notes that countries as diverse as India, Nigeria, Uganda, Mongolia, China and Vietnam have all seen a dramatic growth in the private sector. However, as Srivastava (2013, pp. 16-18) notes, the actual figures may be even higher because many schools are unrecognised and unaccounted for in official administrative data. Some argue that low-fee private schools are therefore making a substantial contribution to achieving education for all (Tooley & Dixon, 2006; Tooley et al, 2007) whereas others, such as Lewin (2007), think the contribution is very limited. This is also an arena of ideological debate between those who think the solution to poor quality lies with improving state education and those who think that a thriving private sector is in itself a good thing because it improves access and provides choice for parents, as well as competition with state schools, leading to the improvement of both.

While there are certainly problems of definition, a private school is one where the major source of revenue is from non-state, private sources, usually fees paid by parents, and where the state plays no part in the management and governance of the school. A low-fee private school is one where the fees are substantially lower than those paid at elite private schools. In her study in India Srivastava defined this as not exceeding one day's earnings of a daily wage labourer at primary and junior levels (up to grade 8) and two days' earnings at secondary and higher secondary levels (grades 9 to 12) (Srivastava, 2013, pp. 11-16).

One major motivation for setting up such a school might be profit, but to simply apply the term 'for profit' to all such schools would be misleading as motivations for starting and maintaining such schools may well be more complex and diverse than just profit and may include a need to secure employment, to further a religion, or may just be based on a recognition that a community is not served, or not well served, by state education. As evidence for the sometimes altruistic motive for setting up such schools their proponents note the free or subsidised places offered to poor students by the schools, though as Walford notes (2011, p. 404), this is often a case of the poor subsidising the even poorer. While the offering of free or concessionary places to children from very poor backgrounds may be at least partly philanthropically motivated, it is also the case that this is also useful for marketing, it helps to keep enrolments up and there is a hope that they will pay in the future (Srivastava, 2013, p. 20). Phillipson (2008, p. 16) lists the following reasons for the existence and expansion of low-fee private schools:

- the hidden costs of government schooling (e.g. uniform, books and sometimes fees); the poor quality of state provision (e.g. teacher absenteeism is often cited as a problem in India);
- an over-supply of teachers leading to the need to establish schools to provide a form of self-employment;
- private tuition costs (as discussed above in this chapter); and
- the language of instruction in many private schools in India is English, which many parents see desirable.

So, are low-fee private schools actually of better quality than state schools? Certainly, given the strong increase in numbers attending them, there has been a perception among many parents that low-fee private schools offer a better option, but what is the evidence? As we saw in chapter 2, there is no agreed definition of quality in education and there is conflicting evidence on this question. For example, Woodhead et al (2013, p. 66) and Walford (2011, p. 404) cite evidence from India, Nigeria and Ghana that low-fee private schools have better pupil test scores, better resources, facilities and infrastructure and better teaching activity and teacher attendance than government schools. Srivastava (2013, pp. 22-25) reviews the evidence in relation to inputs and achievement from Kenya, Ghana, India and Pakistan. The research presents a mixed picture on some indicators, such as toilets and buildings, but, generally, state schools had better trained and qualified teachers and low-fee private schools paid lower salaries than state schools, though the pupil–teacher ratio tended to be higher in state schools than private ones. However, as Srivastava notes, some have questioned whether it is better to have less qualified teachers who actually turn up in private schools because they are more accountable (i.e. they can be fired more readily) or to have better qualified but less accountable teachers who frequently absent themselves? In terms of the evidence on achievement, Srivastava concludes that

> low-fee private schools may be better in some areas under
> certain conditions than state schools, but not in others. The
> question then becomes not whether low-fee private schools are
> uniformly better, but in what circumstances, and owing to
> which background characteristics do students in different
> school types achieve higher results?

Thapa (2013) adds some useful evidence to the debate on quality with findings from Nepal that suggest that the existence of private schools in an area also has a positive impact on the quality and performance of government schools. He explains this partly as the result of competition between government and private schools and partly because competition leads to inefficient or poor-quality private schools exiting the market, thereby leaving the better schools to compete with government schools.

However, it does seem to be the case that low-fee private schools manage to charge low fees mainly because they pay lower salaries than state schools and employ untrained and unqualified teachers (Walford, 2011, p. 404). Although fees in low-fee private schools are lower than elite schools, they are still more than in government schools and, while the poor may be making increasing use of them, there is some doubt as to whether the very poorest in society can afford them. Also, while such schools may be numerous in urban areas, they are much less widespread in rural areas (Kingdon, 2007). UNESCO (2012, p. 77) cites survey data from eight developing countries that shows that per capita spending on children in private primary schools is $220 compared with $36 in their public school counterparts. It further notes that sending a child to a private school in a slum area of Lagos, Nigeria for a year would cost the equivalent of four 50kg bags of rice, which would feed the average family for seventy days. Harma (2009) found that even though private education was widespread in a relatively poor, rural area in India, only half of the population could afford it. For the poorest households, the cost of educating a single child in a private school amounted to a fifth of their income, an unsustainable amount given the number of children and other financial commitments. When they do send a child, it tends to be a boy. The overall view of parents was that, while they recognise that private schools offer something better than state schools, what they really want is a better state system. Similarly, in both Ghana (Akyeampong, 2009) and Malawi (Chimombo, 2009), issues of affordability limit the extent to which low-fee private schools can help to achieve Education for All goals – indeed, in Malawi it would require parents to spend at least 30% of their income to send one child to a private school. Lewin (2007) concludes that households that access low-fee private schooling are likely to be drawn from the lower-middle and working classes; they are unlikely to the most disadvantaged or from the poorest 20%.

One way of mediating the cost for the poorest families recommended by proponents of the growth of low-fee private schools is the provision of state- or donor-financed vouchers for the poorest members of the community to spend in private schools of their choice (e.g. Tooley & Dixon, 2006; Tooley, 2009). However, UNESCO (2012, p. 77) points out a number of problems with this. First, many low-fee schools are not officially registered and would thus not be able to participate. Second, vouchers can be a politically unpopular choice – in Chile students protested over the perceived inequitable outcomes of the country's well-established voucher programme. Third, there is the issue of whether a voucher system can be implemented on the necessary scale to help the most disadvantaged. In Pakistan there has been a programme since 2006 that provides vouchers for children from disadvantaged backgrounds so that they can go to low-fee private schools. So far it has only managed to reach 80,000 pupils out of 5.1 million school children. In relation to vouchers and low-fee private schooling UNESCO comes down firmly on one side of the debate:

> Governments have a choice between investing their scarce
> resources to arrest the decline in public school quality or
> subsidising households to send children to private schools
> through voucher programmes. Vouchers may appear to be a
> quick fix, but investing in public schools is likely to be the
> best way to reach the poorest. (2012, p. 77)

Interestingly, however, India began to implement an act of parliament in 2011 in which all private schools must provide 25% of their places free of charge to socially and economically disadvantaged children until they complete their elementary education. Schools will be reimbursed by the amount the state spends on education or the amount of the tuition fee, whichever is less. However, research on those accessing private schools in Delhi, India under this act showed that it was the relatively more advantaged who secured free places at private schools considered to be more prestigious or in middle-class areas and, once in the schools, the

Clive Harber

costs – transport, private tuition, other fees – were higher than those for fee-paying households accessing local low-fee private schools closer to the slum area of the study (Srivastava, 2013, pp. 14, 19-20).

So, even though low-fee private schools may offer, or be perceived to offer, a better alternative to state schools for children from poor backgrounds in many contexts, given the issues of affordability discussed above, there are nevertheless still significant implications for the different dimensions of inequality in the wider society. One longitudinal study in India, for example, concluded that

> Parents' ability, or indeed willingness to reallocate scarce household resources away from other areas to private education seems to be mediated by location ... gender norms, wealth, parental education levels and aspirations, as well as sibling age and gender and birth order of child. The risk is that recent trends result in an increasingly divisive education system in which private school 'choices' reinforce traditional social, economic and cultural divisions. At the same time, many government schools are becoming 'ghettoized' – attended mainly by those from the poorest, most disadvantaged and marginalised groups in society, which will serve to reinforce wider structural inequalities. (Woodhead et al, 2013, p. 72)

Aikman and Rao succinctly put it, 'private schools ... create a new segregation, with girls, scheduled castes and scheduled tribes increasingly confined to the state schools, leading to a rise in educational inequalities by gender and social group' (cited in Bangay & Latham, 2013, p. 247).

Conclusion

The existence and expansion of forms of non-state provision of education results from a number of key factors – the inability of many developing countries to afford education for all, the wider political and economic context of neoliberalism and the preference for private provision, and the poor quality of sections of state provision. In this chapter we have looked at three broad and different types of non-state provision which all have their pros and cons and their ideological proponents and opponents. Most parents, in developing countries and elsewhere, will seek to obtain what they regard or perceive as the 'best' education for their children if they are in a position to do so, whether this is public or private. The problem for the wider society is that such choices and behaviour inevitably have implications for, and impacts on, social and economic inequality and the pursuit of fair opportunities for all.

References

Akyeampong, K. (2009) Public–Private Partnership in the Provision of Basic Education in Ghana: challenges and choices, *Compare*, 39(2), 135-150.

Bangay, C. & Latham, M. (2013) Are We Asking the Right Questions? Moving beyond the State vs Non-state Providers Debate: reflections and a case study from India, *International Journal of Educational Development*, 33(3), 244-252.

Bano, M. (2008) Non-profit Education Providers vis-à-vis the Private Sector: comparative analysis of non-governmental organisations and traditional voluntary organisations in Pakistan, *Compare*, 38(4), 471-482.

Bray, M. (1996) *Decentralisation of Education: community financing*. Washington, DC: The World Bank.

Bray, M. (1999) Community Financing of Education: cultural variations and policy dilemmas in less developed countries, in F. Leach & A. Little (Eds) *Education, Cultures and Economics: dilemmas for development*. London: RoutledgeFalmer.

Bray, M. & Lillis, K. (1988) *Community Financing of Education: issues and policy implications in less developed countries*. Oxford: Pergamon Press.

Bray, M. & Lykins, C. (2012) *Shadow Education: private supplementary tutoring and its implications for policy makers*. Mandalyulong: Asia Development Bank and Comparative Education Research Centre.

Chimombo, J. (2009) Expanding Post-primary Education in Malawi: are private schools the answer?, *Compare*, 39(2), 167-184.

Harna, J. (2009) Can Choice Promote Education For All? Evidence from Growth in Private Schooling in India, *Compare*, 39(2), 151-166.

Kingdon, G. (2007) The Progress of School Education in India, *Oxford Review of Economic Policy*, 23(2), 168-195.

Lewin, K. (2007) The Limits to Growth of Non-government Private Schooling in Sub-Saharan Africa, in P. Srivastava & G. Walford (Eds) *Private Schooling in Less Economically Developed Countries: Asian and African perspectives*. Oxford: Symposium Books.

Phillipson, H. (2008) *Low-cost Private Education: impacts on achieving universal primary education*. London: Commonwealth Secretariat.

Rose, P. (2009) NGO Provision of Basic Education: alternative or complementary service delivery to support access to the excluded?, *Compare*, 39(2), 219-234.

Sobhy, H. (2012) The De-facto Privatisation of Secondary Education in Egypt: a study of private tutoring in technical and general schools in Egypt, *Compare*, 42(1), 47-67.

Srivastava, P. (Ed.) (2013) *Low-fee Private Schooling: aggravating equity or mitigating disadvantage?* Oxford: Symposium Books.

Thapa, A. (2013) Does Private School Competition Improve Public School Performance? The Case of Nepal, *International Journal of Educational Development*, 33(4), 358-366.

Tooley, J. (2009) *The Beautiful Tree*. Washington, DC: Cato Institute.

Tooley, J. & Dixon, P. (2006) De facto Privatisation of Education and the Poor: implications of a study from sub-Saharan Africa and India, *Compare*, 36(4), 443-462.

Tooley, J., Dixon, P. & Gomathi, S.V. (2007) Private Schools and the Millennium Development Goal of Universal Primary Education: a census and comparative survey in Hyderbad, India, *Oxford Review of Education*, 33(5), 539-560.

UNESCO (2012) *Youth and Skills: putting education to work*. EFA Global Monitoring Report. Paris: UNESCO.

Walford, G. (2011) Low-fee Private Schools in England and Less Developed Countries: what can be learnt in comparison?, *Compare*, 41(3), 401-414.

Woodhead, M., Frost, M. & James, Z. (2013) Does Growth in Private Schooling Contribute to Education for All? Evidence from a Longitudinal, Two Cohort Study in Andhra Pradesh, India, *International Journal of Educational Development*, 33(1), 65-73.

Further Reading

Carney, S. & Bista, M.B. (2009) Community Schooling in Nepal: a genealogy of education reform since 1990, *Comparative Education Review*, 53(2), 189-211.

Compare, 39(2) (2009), Special Issue on Non-State Provision of Education: evidence from Africa and Asia.

Compare, 36(4) (2006), Special Issue on The Private Education Sector: towards a reconceptualization.

Tahir, A., Das, J. & Ijaz Khwaja, A. (2008) A Dime a Day: the possibilities and limits of private schooling in Pakistan, *Comparative Education Review*, 52(3), 329-355.

Uribe, C., Murnane, R., Willett, J. & Somers, M-A. (2006) Expanding School Enrollment by Subsidising Private Schools: lessons from Bogota, *Comparative Education Review*, 50(2), 241-277.

Discussion and Activities

1. 'Education is a product that consumers and producers should be able to buy and sell in the same way as any other product'. Discuss.
2. Historically, the self-help, 'harambee' school movement in Kenya was quite widespread. Find out more about it – what were its strengths and weaknesses? What has happened to it in recent years?
3. You take a teaching job with an internationally funded NGO in a developing country. How is your job likely to be different from that of a teacher in a local government school?
4. 'State schools in developing countries tend to be a mixture of the bureaucratic and the inefficient whereas NGO and private education is more flexible and efficient.' How true do you think this statement is?

CHAPTER 13

Employment, Skills
and Vocational Education

Education has often been hailed as the solution to Africa's
problems ... [but] ... [t]here is a whole generation of Ugandans
who have got their qualifications and exams and who want to
go to work in an office, but there are no jobs. Then they have
their families relying on them to bring in an income that their
education promises. (Norman, 2010, p. 42)

Introduction

In chapter 3 we discussed the ambivalent nature of the relationship
between education, economic development and economic growth, and in
other chapters we acknowledged and explored some of the non-
economic ways in which education can contribute to society and
individuals. However, in this chapter we focus more specifically on the
relationships between education and employment and, in particular, the
skills for employment that education may or may not provide. This is an
important issue for developing countries as providing formal education
is expensive for both governments and individuals, and if more
education simply leads to more unemployment among young people,
which it often has, then this can have serious and negative social
consequences. UNESCO (2012, pp. 13, 14) put it that

> Young people are more numerous than ever, and their
> numbers are increasing rapidly in some parts of the world. In
> developing countries alone, the population aged 15-24 reached
> over one billion in 2010. But jobs are not being created fast
> enough to meet the needs of this large youth population.
> Around one in eight people aged 15 to 24 are unemployed.
> Young people are about three times as likely as adults to be
> unemployed ... To accommodate the growing youth
> population in the Arab states, South and West Asia and sub-
> Saharan Africa, an additional 57 million jobs need to be
> created by 2020 just to prevent unemployment rising above the
> current level.

But it is not just a problem of unemployment, there is also the issue of low-quality, poorly paid employment:

> Globally, an estimated 152 million young people – 28% of all
> young workers – are paid less than $1.25 per day. In countries
> such as Burkina Faso, Cambodia, Ethiopia and Uganda,
> working below the poverty line is a much more widespread
> phenomenon than not working at all. (UNESCO, 2012, p. 18)

In this chapter we see employment as not only existing in the formal, wage-earning sector but also in agriculture and self-employment, including the 'informal' sector of small traders and small-scale entrepreneurs such as tailors, carpenters and taxi drivers. Indeed, UNESCO (2012, p. 13) recognises that many young people working in the private, informal sector or farming often earn wages below the poverty line because they lack skills and that 'Providing them with opportunities to escape from low skilled, low paid work should be at the core of every skills development strategy'. However, education itself only creates relatively few jobs directly – in teaching, school meals, cleaning and building when a new school is being constructed and, indirectly, when schools order resources from state and private providers. If education doesn't create jobs, then the key issue is what is the role of education in equipping young people with skills that may be useful to them in making them more employable in the labour market?

Skills for Employment

UNESCO (2012, p. 14) distinguishes between three main types of skill that it considers all young people need in relation to employment, which it terms foundational, transferable and technical and vocational skills. We shall discuss each in turn.

Foundational skills are basic skills such as literacy and numeracy which allow an individual to be in a position to seek better forms of employment and to function in a wider range of social and economic contexts. Literacy here can mean speaking, reading and writing and may not be in the individual's own language. When I was working in KwaZulu Natal, South Africa in the late 1990s, one of my research students asked a sample of Zulu-speaking school pupils what they thought might be the most useful school subject for getting a job. He expected answers like 'we should learn more about electrics or tourism or car mechanics'; instead, the almost universal answer was 'English', as fluency in this was perceived as providing potential access to a whole range of occupations.

Transferable skills are those generic, work-related or pre-vocational skills which might be useful across a whole range of workplaces – for example, problem solving, communication, creative thinking, critical reading, use of information technology and organisational and presentational skills. Both foundational skills and transferable skills help to make a young person generally employable to an employer, who may well then train them to do a particular job while they are employed, i.e. on-the-job training. *Technical and vocational skills*, on the other hand are those required for, and of use in, a particular job such as a bricklayer, computer technician, car mechanic or market gardener.

This raises the question of where, when and how such skills can and should be provided and at what point vocational specialisation takes place. Foundational and transferable skills can be the consequence of a good-quality general, academic education in primary and secondary schools, though often this is not the case if schooling is not available or is of poor quality. In 30 of the 59 countries studied by UNESCO, for example, at least half of the 15-19-year-olds lacked foundational skills (2012, p. 15). It is also the case that in many academically oriented schools there are nonetheless subjects on the curriculum such as metalwork, woodwork or agriculture that are designed to provide appreciation and experience of manual work. More specifically vocational skills – or training for a particular job – can be provided in a number of ways and at a number of levels. This is often referred to as Technical and Vocational Education and Training (TVET), or sometimes just VET. The emphasis that has been given to providing general primary education for all since the global education conferences at Jomtien in 1990 and Dakar in 2000 has led to a renewed interest in vocational education as more and more primary (and secondary) school pupils and their parents ask the question, education for what? What happens when formal, academic education ends? (King, 2008).

Vocational education and training can be organised in a variety of ways but the earliest such training starts is usually at the secondary school level and either it can be based on separate academic and vocational schools or separate vocational and academic streams can exist within the same school. Alternatively, vocational education can take place in separate institutions run by a private provider. Vocational training can also be based on an apprenticeship in a business where the young person learns on the job and may or may not get some time released to continue academic learning at a local educational institution. Conversely, a vocational course might exist in a further education college where students get some academic learning alongside vocational training as well as relevant job placements in local companies. In his study of seven African countries (Egypt, Botswana, Ghana, Senegal, Seychelles, Tunisia and Zimbabwe) Oketch, for example, found that

> In some cases, TVET forms a separate system that parallels the general education system with its own institutions, teachers' programmes and curriculum. In such cases, the issue is mostly on the proportion of academic content in the courses offered

and the level of specificity in the vocational courses on offer.
In many cases, however, TVET is offered alongside general
education in integrated schools forming a dual tracked school
system, (2007, p. 224)

In the next section we examine whether the secondary level is an appropriate place for some students to begin vocational specialisation.

The 'Vocational' and the Vocational School Fallacy

In many postcolonial countries there has been a deep suspicion of vocational education because during the colonial period it was seen as a way in which the colonial power steered local people away from aspiring to white-collar jobs (Bacchus, 1988). In 1965, in the immediate postcolonial period, Phillip Foster wrote what became a seminal paper on secondary education in Ghana in which he coined the term the 'vocational school fallacy' (Foster, 1965). In this he examined the argument that schools in predominantly agricultural and industrially and commercially less developed societies should prepare young people primarily with practical, agricultural and technical skills. Could more emphasis on these vocational skills help with youth unemployment in newly independent countries like Ghana? Foster argued that the failure of many such schemes, when they are provided in specialised, vocational secondary schools in parallel to academic schools, was because they were not popular with parents and pupils and thus there was little demand for them. This was essentially because parents and pupils understood that the academic secondary school was, in fact, *itself vocational*, providing access to the more desirable types of better paid, higher status and more secure bureaucratic, white-collar jobs, either directly at the end of secondary school or, more often, through access to higher education after secondary school. If a young person aspired to be an architect, a lawyer, a civil servant, an accountant, a doctor, a journalist or a teacher then they would have to continue with academic education.

The reason that vocational secondary education was unpopular and unsuccessful, then, was that parents and pupils were realistically reading the signals of the labour market and acting accordingly. It wasn't that Ghanaians or any other Africans were afraid of getting their hands dirty with practical work; the real success or not of the type of education provided was the perceived reward given to each type of training in the economy. Hence, if offered a choice between vocational or academic secondary education, however good the quality of the former, pupils will overwhelmingly opt for the latter. Even if they might fail in their academic education or fail to get into a career of their choice during or after higher education, they would rather take that risk than go into vocational or practical education. Therefore, any attempt to use the curriculum to try to change attitudes towards, for example, bricklaying, carpentry or motor mechanics, through more vocational education in school was doomed to be wasteful and ineffective. However, the corollary of this is that if technical or practical occupations became better rewarded in the labour market, then vocational education would become more popular and successful, especially if there was a clear link to major employers – as there was, for example, in Kenya in the 1970s and early 80s (Lauglo & Narman, 1987).

There are other problems associated with providing vocational education at secondary school level as well. First, practical subjects such as those cited above are expensive to provide, requiring workshops, tools and machinery, which can make them vulnerable when there is a serious financial problem for education, as there often is. Studies in Ghana, Kenya and Botswana, for example, suggest that there is a need for specialised facilities, equipment, consumables and smaller instructional groups (Lauglo, 2010, p. 227). Second, they require specialised teachers who may or may not be available, depending on the demand and level of payment for their skills in the labour market. Also, being a good car mechanic does not necessarily mean that you are a good teacher of car mechanics. Third, it can be argued that secondary school, and particularly lower secondary school, is too early to specialise, even in a developing country where only a small minority might go on to further and higher education. In the two or three years that a young person specialises in a particular trade or craft the demand can change considerably because of changes in the economy or changes in technology, leaving them more vulnerable to unemployment or underemployment than if they had continued with a broader-based, more general education. As Oketch (2007, p. 221) puts it, 'many view general education as a more suitable type of education that is capable of responding to economic and labour force changes in society'. This can be mitigated somewhat if a school offers a more lightly vocationalised curriculum which still remains largely academic but which offers some vocational subjects for four to five hours a week, thereby keeping the possibility of further and higher education open but creating a sort of mental readiness to work in small-scale enterprises in the private sector (King & Martin, 2002). McGrath et al summarise these problems facing VET in this way in their study of southern Africa:

> VET provision is costly and many graduates do not get formal employment. Some VET curricula are very old and some infrastructure is even older and more worn-out. The range of programmes often appears to have little to do with existing and potential labour market conditions. (2006, p. 89)

Another, fourth, issue is the lower status often attributed to vocational education. It is often seen as being for those who are perceived as being academically less able or academic failures, and these pupils are often in practice from poorer socio-economic backgrounds. This is also in part because it is perceived as being terminal in nature and not leading to higher education. As UNESCO put it:

> Pushing low performing students into technical and vocational training can cement social inequality and result in employers devaluing these programmes. In eighteen of the twenty-two countries in the 2009 PISA survey, students streamed into vocational schools had lower socio-economic status, on average, than their peers in general education. (2012, p. 23)

McGrath et al (2006, p. 99), for example, note that the low-status nature of VET continues to be a problem in countries such as Lesotho, Mauritius and Swaziland. A fifth issue is that there is also some suspicion that VET has been used as a political tool. If a government provides training in vocational or pre-vocational skills in schools and yet school leavers still end up unemployed, then whose fault is it? In other words, it is a way of shifting blame from the state to the individual:

> VET reform must be seen in part as an ideological project ... because then politicians can be seen to be doing something about issues such as employment and competitiveness. (McGrath et al, 2006, p. 89)

Such problems have led to a low and declining proportion of TVET in secondary education in Africa, as 'the attitudes that were held in 1965 when Foster exploded the vocational school fallacy have continued to this day' (Oketch, 2007, pp. 229-230).

So, it was perhaps not surprising that Foster was against vocational training in the school system. He thought that

> Vocational skills ought to be taught with close connection to their work application. Training would then be more realistic; and a better balance could be achieved between the supply and demand of skills. (Lauglo, 2010, p. 226)

The Informal Sector and Non-school Vocational Education

A particular issue in developing countries is the type of employment that students are being trained for and the way that such training takes place. The informal sector, based on micro-businesses often operating in an unregulated manner with few records, frequently forms a large part of the labour market in developing countries – the International Labour Organisation estimates it at 1.53 billion businesses globally and it accounts for as much as 70% of non-agricultural employment in some sub-Saharan African countries and over 50% in the poorer countries of South America, as well as being the main employer for many workers in south and west Asia. Such businesses include street vending, cooking, sewing, car repair, farm work and waste-picking (UNESCO, 2012, p. 26). Lauglo argues that in many sub-Saharan countries, and especially in western Africa, a common path to becoming a small-scale entrepreneur in the informal sector has been through a long-term apprenticeship. This is partly because, though schools can provide some relevant pre-vocational skills, there is a lack of provision of successful vocational skills training for the informal sector either by government or non-governmental organisations (NGOs) (Lauglo, 2010, p. 233). In Africa, informal apprenticeships have often taken place at artisan workshops owned by master craftsmen/women in such trades as carpentry, masonry, auto-mechanics, welding, photography and tailoring (Oketch, 2007, p. 223). McGrath et al (2006, p. 97) add that despite the informal sector being the destination of many VET graduates in southern Africa, there is 'often limited understanding of skills required in the informal economy and a lack of systematic addressing of the skills needs of both those already in the informal economy and those likely to enter it'.

One exception to this lack of training provision for the informal sector is India: it is one of the few countries to develop a strategy on this which states that India's 10 million street vendors should receive training to upgrade their technical and business skills so that they can increase their income and look for alternative work (UNESCO, 2012, p. 26). Here we review two examples of vocational training outside of mainstream formal schooling that help to prepare students for the informal sector, both of which have implications for the capabilities of students beyond simply or solely training for employability and a job.

Powell (2012) describes further education and training colleges in South Africa as existing at the crossroads between the end of compulsory education, higher education and the world of work. Partly as a response to growing youth unemployment and underemployment in South Africa, they aim to provide disadvantaged communities with access to good-quality training and skills required for employability, including training for entrepreneurship and for the informal economy, as well as providing second-chance and non-traditional access routes to higher education. Half a million students per year are enrolled in the colleges. In her study of students at such colleges, Powell found that, unlike Foster's school students, students at this level had positive views of vocational education. They did not regard VET as terminal or feel that they had been labelled as a 'vocational student', and the majority wanted to go on to higher education. While they spoke of the skills and attitudes that prepared them for work, the students also spoke strongly about the empowerment role played by the college and the skills training in

> enabling respect, self-confidence and personal pride ... They
> are far more than the unemployed youth and the future worker
> preparing to meet and address critical skills shortages. They

are concerned with relationships with family members and with members of their community, their spiritual development, their personal dignity and with the social and economic challenges faced by their families and other members of their community. For these students, colleges are not simply an opportunity to access the labour market; colleges are an opportunity to gain satisfying work in workplaces where they will be respected and where they can make a contribution. (2012, p. 650)

Blaak et al (2013) examine the work of two NGOs offering non-formal vocational education for the informal sector to early school leavers in Uganda. The wider question was whether this type of non-formal vocational education can go beyond education for employment to education for empowerment, human capability and self-reliance as advocated in the work of Paulo Freire, Amartya Sen and Julius Nyerere (see chapters 5 and 7). The authors define non-formal education as including all organised types of intentional education outside the formal school system, as opposed to informal education, which is unintentional learning which takes place as a side-effect of daily experiences. Formal education in Uganda is characterised by high intake but low completion rates due to a series of problems: lack of interest in the curriculum on offer, pregnancy, marriage, inability to pay school fees, the need to work, family responsibilities, suspension due to disobedience and high indirect costs such as school uniforms, text and exercise books and writing equipment. On the other hand, non-formal education can offer an alternative to school drop-outs because, as discussed in chapter 12, it has the potential to be more creative, adaptive, flexible and participatory in training for work-related and other skills. The study found that while the two case-study NGOs do reach out to educationally marginalised learners through low fees, adaptive teaching and relevant content, there were also problems of lack of facilities for practical exercises and no optimal fit between curriculum content and labour market requirements. The authors conclude that the participants in the study did think that non-formal vocational education can prepare someone to be financially independent and through this stand strong against exploitation and be able to support relatives and the community.

However, whether non-formal education currently contributes to outcomes beyond human capital is questionable. Where empowerment, human capability and self-reliance came out of the theoretical exploration as potential outcomes of education, the reality of non-formal vocational education in Uganda seems to reflect a narrower outcome: self-reliance through economic independence. .., however, even in this narrow perspective participants do not feel completely equipped by the programme to become self-reliant; personal strategies are not always clear and conditions like capital or job opportunities are not always within reach. (Blaak et al, 2013, p. 95)

Conclusion

So, while 'There is no automatic connection between school, skill and work' (King, 2008, p. 76), what does the discussion in this chapter suggest might be done to provide a better preparation for the world of work or to enhance general employability, including employment and self-employment in the informal sector? First, schools need to provide the foundational skills of literacy and numeracy for all that they are supposed to, which, as we saw in chapter 2, is not always the case. Second, while for some academically more successful students general secondary education *is* vocational because it leads to access to various higher status professions, usually via higher education, there is also a need to provide the learning experiences necessary for the development of the sort of transferable skills set out above in this chapter. Such transferable skills, as with all skills, are learned by doing and practice but if pupils are to develop better skills of, say, communication, problem-solving, use of information technology and independent working, then the traditional, teacher-centred teaching methods described in earlier chapters will need to change in a more participatory direction. Third, schools could provide more experience of work for pupils through short-term placements in various forms of business enterprise. There is also a need to provide good-quality vocational and pre-vocational training for those who have missed out on, or dropped out from, school. This might be through non-formal education under government or NGO auspices and involve direct experience of the workplace. Beyond school, further education can provide valuable vocational training without necessarily cutting off access to higher education. At all levels and types of education, quality is important, as is an attempt to combine education for vocational employability with wider considerations of capability and empowerment.

References

Bacchus, K. (1988) The Political Context of Vocationalisation in the Developing Countries, in J. Lauglo & K. Lillis (Eds) *Vocationalizing Education: an international perspective*. Oxford: Pergamon.

Blaak, M., Openjuru, G.L. & Zeelen, J. (2013) Non-formal Vocational Education in Uganda: practical empowerment through a workable alternative, *International Journal of Educational Development*, 33(1), 88-97.

Foster, P. (1965) The Vocational School Fallacy in Development Planning, in A. Anderson & M.Bowman (Eds) *Education and Economic Development.* Chicago: Aldine.

King, K. (2008) Education, Skills, Sustainability and Growth: complex relations, in L. Chisholm, G. Bloch & B. Fleisch (Eds) *Education, Growth, Aid and Development: towards education for all.* Hong Kong: Comparative Education Research Centre.

King, K. & Martin, C. (2002) The Vocational School Fallacy Revisited: education, aspiration and work in Ghana 1959-2000, *International Journal of Educational Development*, 22(1), 5-26.

Lauglo, J. (2010) Revisiting the Vocational School Fallacy: a tribute to Philip Foster, *Comparative Education*, 46(2), 223-235.

Lauglo, J. & Narman, A. (1987) Diversified Secondary Education in Kenya: the status of practical subjects and effects on attitudes and destinations after school, *International Journal of Educational Development*, 7(4), 227-242.

McGrath, S., Akoojee, S., Gewer, A., et al (2006) An Examination of the Vocational Education and Training Reform Debate in Southern Africa, *Compare*, 36(1), 85-104.

Norman, L. (2010) Job Dearth Blights Pupil Success, *Times Educational Supplement*, 15 January, p. 42.

Oketch, M. (2007) To Vocationalise or Not to Vocationalise? Perspectives on Current Trends and Issues in Technical and Vocational Education and Training (VET) in Africa, *International Journal of Educational Development*, 27(2), 220-234.

Powell, L. (2012) Reimagining the purpose of VET: expanding the capability to aspire in South African further education and training students, *International Journal of Educational Development*, 32(5), 643-653.

UNESCO (2012) *Youth and Skills Putting Education to Work.* EFA Global Monitoring Report. Paris: UNESCO.

Further Reading

Bennell, P., Mukyanuzi, F., Kasogela, M., Mutashubirwa, F. & Klim, M. (2006) Artisan Training and Employment Outcomes in Tanzania, *Compare*, 36(1), 73-84.

International Journal of Educational Development, 32(5) (2012), Special Issue on Skills and Development.

King, K. & McGrath, S. (2002) *Globalisation, Enterprise and Knowledge: education, training and development in Africa.* Oxford: Symposium Books.

King, K. & Palmer, R. (2013) Post-2015 Agendas: northern tsunami, southern ripple? The Case of Education and Skills, *International Journal of Educational Development*, 33(5), 407-425.

Discussion and Activities

1. Reflecting on your own education so far, what aspect has most prepared you for the world of work?

2. 'Education can be the solution to youth unemployment.' Discuss.

3. What do you think are the specific key skills that education can provide to enhance employability?

4. Workers are also citizens and vice versa. What are the implications for vocational education and training?

CHAPTER 14

Education and Corruption

I thought I was prepared to face the temptations and
diversions that would be thrust on my path throughout Africa
and Asia, but realised later that I was not fully prepared for
either its magnitude or its frequency. Rarely a year has gone by
over the past four decades without some direct or indirect
attempt to influence my decisions, from my employers,
contractors, consultants or clients.
(Nicholas Bennett, 2001 – Educational Planning Consultant
with experience in a wide range of developing countries)

Introduction: corruption and development

Transparency International defines corruption as 'the abuse of entrusted
power for private gain', adding that grand corruption consists of acts
committed at a high level of government that distort policies or the
central functioning of the state, enabling leaders to benefit at the expense
of the public good. Petty corruption refers to everyday abuse of entrusted
power by low- and mid-level public officials in their interactions with
ordinary citizens, who often are trying to access basic goods or services
in places like hospitals, schools, police departments and other agencies.
While corruption is a global problem affecting all countries, it is a
particularly serious problem in developing countries. Such corruption
harms development because it is a major obstacle to democracy and the
rule of law, depletes national wealth, denies communities of investment
and necessary services, undermines trust in social institutions and can
harm the environment through lack of enforcement of regulations in, for
example, mining and forestry. In their 2012 corruption perceptions index
Transparency International found that the 10 countries perceived as
being least corrupt were largely 'developed' and the 10 most corrupt
were largely 'developing'. The least corrupt were (in order): Denmark,
Finland, New Zealand, Sweden, Singapore, Switzerland, Australia,
Norway, Canada and the Netherlands. The countries perceived as being
most corrupt were, in order, to the most corrupt: Haiti, Venezuela, Iraq,
Turkmenistan, Uzbekistan, Myanmar, Sudan, Afghanistan, North Korea
and Somalia (http://cpi.transparency.org).

Sims et al (2012) have examined reasons why corruption is more widespread in developing countries. They define corruption as 'the misuse of public office for personal gain and include such practices as bribery, kickbacks, coercion and related activities that provide an unfair advantage to one party' (p. 90). They suggest that the higher the level of human development (i.e. as measured by the United Nations Development Programme's Human Development Index), the lower the level of corruption because of the country's ability to enhance transparency in public administration. It is also suggested that in more developed countries more abundant resources reduce the motivation for engaging in corruption, that people in such countries tend to be more highly educated and empowered to monitor public behaviour, and that, by definition, countries with a higher level of human development will place a greater emphasis people's right to exercise their free will and realise their maximum potential. More developed countries provide an environment where more individuals collectively seek social justice and enhanced moral standards and where there is an infrastructure available for the public to take control over and punish unethical behaviour.

However, Sims et al (2012) also argue that culture (see chapter 1) provides a significant context for a better or more nuanced understanding of people's behaviour in relation to corruption and development within particular countries. They use Hofstede's (1997) four-dimensional comparative analysis of cultures to examine macro-level statistical relationships between cultural characteristics of developing countries and levels of corruption. Of these, two dimensions had a significant relationship with corruption: (1) power distance:

> As human development increases, the desire and capability of a country's people to question and oversee those in power increases. In a low power distance culture, citizens expect that those in power will act legitimately and fairly exercise their authority. People expect to be treated equally and unearned privileges are not accepted ... Yet in a high power distance culture, citizens are accustomed to accepting self-serving behaviours from those in power. This holds true even if the capability to question and oversee those in power increases. The questioning of authority is less acceptable in some cultures, regardless of the level of human development present. Proportional increases in human development lead to less change in corruption in high power distance cultures than they do in low power distance cultures. (p. 93)

The second is individualism:

> the relation between human development and national corruption is stronger in cultures that are higher on the individualism dimension. When high levels of human

development are present, citizens have the capability to question and oversee those in power and are more likely to do so if they live in an individual culture that supports independent thinking and speaking one's mind. This differs from collective cultures that support being cooperative and maintaining harmony between people. Even with high levels of human development and the capability to question and oversee those in power, citizens in a collective culture may be unwilling to create the disharmony likely to occur should one question those in power. Therefore, proportional increases in human development lead to less change in corruption levels in collectivist cultures than in individual cultures. (2012, p. 94)

A further possible aspect of culture that can have a bearing on corruption is the interplay between the norms and values of traditional social, economic and political systems and those of modern, bureaucratic ones, as previously discussed in chapter 4. For example, in many traditional cultures officials would not be paid salaries from a central fund but would get a 'prebendary' income, that is, income accrued by taking a portion of the tributes, rents, etc. collected before passing the remainder on up the chain of command. Riggs (1964, p. 44) notes that

the general public, long accustomed to paying officials directly for services rendered, cannot be expected to abandon this practice suddenly. Thus the opportunities and temptations for officials to augment their incomes on a prebendary basis remain overwhelming unless very sharply curtailed by the ruler or new political and judicial control systems.

Corruption also affects education in many developing countries. This has serious consequences because when education is corrupt it loses its impartiality, quality and fairness. UNESCO (2009, pp. 138-139) notes that

Tackling corruption in education is important for the sector and for society in a broader sense. Education receives a large share of public expenditure – in most countries it is the largest area of government activity and the largest public employer. Efforts to limit corruption in general are not likely to succeed if they do not address the education sector in particular. Moreover, lack of integrity and unethical behaviour within the education sector is inconsistent with one of the main purposes of education itself, which is to produce 'good citizens' respectful of the law, human rights and of fairness ... Corruption has adverse consequences for efficiency and equity. Efficiency suffers because corrupt practices mean part of the benefit of public investment is captured in the form of private rent. Equity suffers because corruption acts as a regressive tax that hurts the poor the most.

What does Corruption in Education Look Like?

In earlier chapters of this book we have come across some instances of corruption in education under different topics (e.g. modernisation, gender and private tutoring). In this chapter corruption in education is the main focus of our discussion. Heyneman (2009, p. 1) defines corruption in education as 'the abuse of authority for both personal as well as material gain'. We begin this section of the chapter by describing a series of concrete examples of corruption in education across a range of developing countries before further categorising and analysing corruption in education in the next section.

Lebanon: cheating in examinations

Vlaardingerbroek et al (2011) discuss what they term 'open cheating', that is, cheating with the compliance of invigilators who are all themselves teachers. They found in roughly a quarter of the examination events that they studied that invigilators turned a blind eye to cheating and in 10-15% invigilators were reported as quietly assisting individual candidates. Also, in about 15% of the cases invigilators reportedly allowed candidates to discuss questions among themselves, in conjunction with a high incidence of wilfully ignoring obvious cheating. Invigilators made some candidates assist others, took answer books from strong candidates and gave them to weak ones and gave out answers. The main reason for this was a desire to help based on the empathy felt by the invigilators towards the candidates. The following are some quotations from the invigilators:

> The official exam represents a crucial stage in the student's life. They enter the exam room nervously. It is good to allow them to cheat just a little.

> Sometimes the students need just a hint to enable them to answer questions. It's alright to allow that, it's not really cheating.

> The students have been studying hard all year. They're good students but may come across a question they can't answer. It would be unfair to fail them for that, so we make things easier for them.

> In some centres, cheating is allowed and others it is not. This is unfair, all students should have the chance of equal success.

Examination invigilators in Christian areas hear that students at examination centres in Muslim areas are allowed to cheat, so why shouldn't we allow our students to cheat too?

Teacher Absenteeism and Lack of Professionalism: Nepal, Ghana, Chad, Cameroon and Ethiopia

In many developing countries, low levels of teacher professionalism result from the cultural factors discussed above as well as poor training, lack of resources, low or unpaid salaries and low levels of continuing and professional development (Harber, 2012). The following extracts from Bennett (2001) provide a useful personal insight based on experience of how this can manifest itself:

> Visiting primary schools in Eastern Nepal one Monday, we were surprised to find that none of the schools were operating. School after school was closed. It was difficult to find out why, as most of the villagers were out working in the fields. Finally we found a group of parents, and they explained to us that their school had two teachers, in common with most of the schools in the area. One would work on Tuesdays and Wednesdays, and the other on Thursdays and Fridays. Both would take a long weekend from Saturday to Monday. A parents' committee had been to the district education office to complain, but were not made to feel welcome, and came away empty handed. Later we questioned the district official, and he agreed that the teachers were expected to teach six days a week, from Sunday to Friday. He admitted sending the parents' group that came to his office away, as they were 'troublemakers'. If he accepted the parents' complaint he would have to sanction those teachers who were not working as officially expected, which would make him unpopular with his peers. Better children are not taught, than to upset the status quo. Again it is the children who suffer.
>
> Just because the teacher is present does not necessarily mean that any teaching actually takes place. Many is the time that I have visited schools in Ethiopia, Ghana, Cameroon, or Nepal and found the school open, but both the teacher and his students absent. The teacher has taken the children to work on his farm, not as a learning experience as might be obtained from a demonstration plot, but as unpaid child labour for the benefit of the teacher. Not only does this further reduce learning time, but discourages parents from sending their children to school.

Clive Harber

Privatisation is one of the current mantras of development gurus, and no civil servants had taken this mantra so much to heart as those in Cameroon. Teachers sold places in the front rows of their overcrowded classrooms, parents had to pay if they wanted their child's exercise books to be corrected, and the only way a child could complete the curriculum in an examination year was through private tuition with the same teacher. An Inspector's main function on visiting a school was to be fed. Poor food and drink would result in a poor report. Headmaster's posts were sold, those in the larger schools by the highest officials in the Ministry of Education. In Chad the Parent Associations were imposing significant and unsanctioned levies, without which the schools could not operate. Students who could not or did not pay the levy were sent home. A similar situation existed in Ghana, and elsewhere in Africa. Again in Ghana the going price for a place in a Teacher Training College, which was a guarantee of future employment, was 5,000 Cedis ($80 at that time) and a goat. All of these forms of petty corruption teach children that everything has its price, and that the idea of 'basic education for all' is a concept alien to many cultures.

Bangladesh: 'red tape' as corruption

Choe et al (2013) investigated the extent to which corrupt teachers and schools used procedural or bureaucratic methods to gain financially from what should be free educational services. Examples include paying to have a child admitted to a school, paying for extra tuition, paying to influence examination results, paying to receive a stipend for their child and payment of extra fees without a receipt. Choe et al conclude that

> A corrupt teacher (or school) creates multiple layers of red tape that obstruct a household's access to their child's education service which is otherwise free. Facing the red tape, the household can choose to pay a bribe, or use informal relationships with influential people who can influence the bribe-taker on behalf of the household. Those households that find neither of the above options available would either have their child receive sub-quality education or take their child out of school altogether. The latter households are more likely to be from economically disadvantaged groups. Thus our results indicate that the burden of corruption is disproportionately borne by the poor, lending support to the positive relation between corruption and inequality. (2013, p. 239)

Iran: teacher recruitment,
promotion, deployment and remuneration

Atashak (2011) writes of corruption among teachers in Tehran, Iran in the areas of recruitment, appointment and promotion, which are based on subjective criteria, and involve such practices as payment of bribes; fake diplomas; a position being already filled, but declared vacant by head teachers in order to get more teachers; women faking marriage in order to get a transfer; misallocated teachers; teacher exchanges between regions, based on private agreements and involving payments; teachers seconded without official clearance from teaching to administrative duties; illegal replacement of teachers based on private agreements and involving payments; payment of bribes to be admitted to in-service training programmes; incorrect or double salary payments; teachers having to pay back part of their salaries to the person in charge of giving it to them – either local administrators or head teachers; ghost teachers; forging of documents and bribing of officials by educational staff to secure larger retirement cheques than they are entitled to, and/or to retire before the customary age; and taking leave, in which teachers have not returned to their jobs but are still paid.

Egypt: private tutoring

In addition to the private tutoring practices discussed in chapter 12, Sobhy (2012) adds a range of associated corrupt practices. Members of the Ministry of Education curriculum-setting committee are often also private textbook authors who then write much better private textbooks while at the same time authoring poor official textbooks, thereby forcing students to rely on and buy the private books. It has been estimated that Egyptians spend 1.5 billion Egyptian pounds on such books each year. Sobhy adds that

> The highly profitable tutoring and private textbooks
> businesses became part of a powerful web of corruption and
> patrimonial relations across the system. Often described as a
> 'mafia' in the media, this web of interests has gained
> considerable leverage over key centres of decision-making in
> the Ministry of Education. Examination, curriculum and
> teacher pay reforms that may undermine the private market for
> education are routinely blocked and resisted. (2012, p. 54)

Misappropriation of Large-scale Funds: Nicaragua and Brazil

UNESCO (2009, p. 139) provides two interesting examples of the large-scale misappropriation of funds from Central/South America. In Nicaragua the monitoring of six major school upgrades and repair

---

Clive Harber

projects compared buildings before and after completion and revealed widespread irregularities. Substandard materials and overpricing contributed to substantial financial losses. In Brazil about 13% of a fund meant for teacher salaries and training was lost in the course of transfer from the federal budget to municipal bank accounts, rising to 55% for some municipalities. This was caused by the inability of local councils charged with monitoring the grants to ensure that they were properly received and used.

Sexual Violence and Corruption: Nigeria

We discussed the problem of sexual harassment and violence in education in chapters 6 and 10. Here we simply add a case study that emphasises the corrupt dimension of such practices in the sense of using power and authority in an unfair manner to gain something that one is not entitled to. Bakari and Leach (2009) studied a college of education in northern Nigeria where female students in interviews estimated that 45-65% of male lecturers forcefully sought favours from students. It was generally acknowledged that many female students had to choose between accepting the lecturers' advances or not gaining admission to the college, failing or repeating assignments, not getting approval for a final-year project, having marks lowered, or withdrawing from the college. The result was that transactional sex, as discussed further below, had become part of the institutional life of the college.

Types and Causes of Corruption in Education

There are different ways in which corruption in education can be classified. Heyneman classifies corruption in four ways:

- first, through educational functions such as the assessment of students, student selection for training and university accreditation;
- second, through the supply of goods and services – private appropriation of government monies supposedly for textbooks, buildings and writing materials;
- third, professional misconduct such as taking bribes or rewards in exchange for good grades, awarding good grades or desired places based on family or other private requests, awarding grades based on ascriptive characteristics such as ethnicity or gender, forcing pupils to take private lessons in order to pass, sexually exploiting students, ordering particular educational products because of gifts or incentives and ignoring the misconduct of colleagues; and
- fourth, property and taxes, where public educational facilities are leased for private gain (2009, pp. 2-4).

222

Hallak and Poisson (2005), in Table V, categorise specific types of corruption in education and spell out some of the direct consequences.

Areas	Corrupt practices	Impact on education
School building, rehabilitation	Fraud in public tendering Embezzlement School mapping	Access Quality *Example*: bad location of schools; too high or too low use; demand for places unattended
Equipment, textbooks, food	Fraud in public tendering Embezzlement Bypass of criteria	Equity Quality *Example*: school meals free to the rich and not available for the poor; lack of consistency between textbooks and curricula
Teacher appointment/ management	Favouritism Nepotism Bribes	Quality *Example*: less qualified teachers appointed
Teacher behaviour	'Ghost teachers' Bribes (for school entrance, exams, assessment, private tutoring, etc.)	Equity Ethics *Example*: disparity in staffing by schools; discrimination against the poor
Examinations and diplomas	Selling of information Favouritism Nepotism Bribes Academic fraud	Equity Ethics *Example*: unjustified credentials available to students who can afford to pay bribes
Information systems	Manipulating data Selecting/suppressing information	Equity Ethics Policy priorities *Example*: omitting data on repetition/dropout; less priority on quality improvement
Specific allowances (fellowships, subsidies, etc.)	Favouritism Nepotism Bribes	Access Equity *Example*: inflating

	Bypass of criteria	enrolment figures to increase financial transfers
Finance	Transgressing rules/procedures Inflationof costs and activities Opacity of flow Leakage of funds	Access Quality Equity Policy priorities *Example*: less resources for quality improvement: textbooks, materials, etc.

Table V. specific types of corruption in education some of the direct consequences. Source: Hallak & Poisson (2005, pp. 5-6).

Corruption in education in developing countries is caused not just by obvious individual motives such as greed and personal desire for gain, but also by a wider, surrounding cultural and socio-economic system of corruption. This, in part at least, stems from the 'developing' nature of the social, economic and political system, as we discussed at the beginning of the chapter. While certain individuals do hold out against corruption, if a critical mass of people in a society or educational system are corrupt it can be difficult for ordinary people to survive without being involved in corruption from time to time. We also saw in chapter 4 on modernisation theory how 'prismatic' cultures and institutions can create contexts for corrupt and unprofessional behaviours in education. Other cultural factors may be specific to a region or country. Collins (2009), for example, argues that in sub-Saharan Africa transactional sex in which men and women exchange material goods and sex is a widespread cultural practice and that 'Researchers have documented that most sexual relationships in many regions of sub-Saharan Africa have a transactional element, from short- and long-term relationships, non- and extra-marital partnerships, to marriage' (p. 26). When these cultural patterns occur in a modern educational setting, such as the college of education in Nigeria described above, the resulting behaviour is then perceived as professional misconduct and corruption.

Such cultural factors can negatively affect the effective and proper functioning and operation of educational organisations and processes and, in turn, their resulting ineffectiveness itself facilitates corruption. The following summary of educational factors that both result from and facilitate corruption in education is from Atashak on Iran (2011, p. 462) but many aspects of this list can be found in a wide range of developing countries:

> The Root Causes of Corruption among teachers are: Lack of specialized supervision and quality management. Lack of transparency in certification of examination results and not being based on verifiable criteria. Inadequate documentation

or absence of examination requirements, conditions and assessment criteria. Inadequate salaries, irregular or delayed payment. Inadequate regulation of examination procedures. Lack of human resources, technical infrastructure and rooms required to ensure the development of fraud-free examinations systems and the conducting of fair examinations. Lack of checks and controls for the authenticity of certificates by institutions and employers. Lack of or inadequate enforcement of professional code of conduct for teachers. Absence of legal basis to prevent students being forced to take private lessons, or existing legislation is not enforced. Absence of requirements to document the contents and course of lessons or to disclose information relevant for lessons to students and parents.

What Can be Done about Corruption in Education?

However, while cultural factors may help to explain corruption, they do not excuse it and it is important for those in positions of authority in education to make efforts to combat corruption. Heyneman (2009, p. 6) groups anti-corruption measures into four categories:

1. Structural reforms to reduce the opportunity for corruption, such as the establishment of an autonomous examination and accreditation agency, clear ownership of educational property, tax differentiation between for-profit and not-for-profit educational institutions and the freedom for non-profit educational institutions to seek monetary support without being subject to taxation.
2. Mechanisms for adjudication and management – the establishment of professional boards in education, public ombudsmen, and teacher/student codes of conduct boards to hear cases of infraction and to recommend consequences.
3. Preventative mechanisms – annual reports to the public on education corruption, public access to financial statements of educational institutions, codes of conduct for teachers, students and administrators, anti-corruption commissions and a free and active education press.
4. Sanctions – criminal penalties for economic and professional misconduct, public exposure, dismissal from employment, fines payable to the victim for professional misconduct and withdrawal of licence to practice.

What might such anti-corruption initiatives look like in practice? Here we describe examples from three continents – Asia, Latin America and Africa. Hallak and Poisson (2005, pp. 7-10) provide two examples of successful experiments in improving transparency and accountability and reducing corruption. The first concerned the use of codes of conduct for teachers in Bangladesh, India and Nepal in order to provide self-disciplinary guidelines for members of the profession by creating norms of professional conduct; and ensuring that the community supports and has confidence in the profession by emphasising the social responsibilities of the profession towards the community. A comparative study revealed that all the actors in the educational sector saw codes as useful instruments and that codes had a positive and significant impact in attempts to improve the commitment, professional behaviour and performance of teachers and staff. The situation was seen to improve in regard to abuses of the school admission system, fairness in promotion and appointments, teacher absenteeism, malpractice in examinations, embezzlement of school funds and private tuition. Hallak and Poisson conclude that:

> 1. Adherence to ethical standards and to codes of conduct can greatly contribute to the establishment of a more favourable educational environment, thus directly influencing the quality of education. 2. The successful enforcement of these codes requires: (i) a clear definition of their aims (not limited to professional development); (ii) the wide dissemination of the codes; (iii) the establishment of both social or professional controls for their implementation; (iv) a strict sharing of responsibilities among the different stakeholders involved in their monitoring; and (v) the training of education personnel. 3. To ensure their credibility and ownership, teacher codes of conduct should be established through a participatory process involving the teaching profession. Minimum targets to achieve are the undertaking of sensitisation exercises, the sharing of information, capacity building, and efforts towards 'mainstreaming participation'. (p. 9)

The second example concerned Colombia. Between 1998 and 2003 the costs of providing more places for pupils in schools in Bogota, Colombia was drastically reduced because of the design of a more transparent system of teacher management. This included reforming management, introducing a new information system, cleaning and continuously updating the list of employed teachers, more transparent procedures for transferring teachers, correcting distortions in the payment of salaries, and better control over medical assurance and pension funds. Perhaps the most important aspect was the 'cleaning up' of the list of employed teachers, which required:

- making an accurate estimate of the required number of teachers by region and institution;
- checking the existing stock of teachers employed and eliminating double counting, 'ghost teachers', etc.;

- taking into account budgetary constraints in defining the maximum amount available for salaries;
- estimating the number of teachers to be deployed and/or redeployed from one region to another and between schools;
- involving as much as possible representatives of the teaching profession (unions); and
- using a formal administrative act to validate the final list of teachers eligible to receive salaries from the Ministry of Education.

Hallak and Poisson drew the following conclusions:

1. More transparency in teacher management entails the setting of clear and objective criteria and the design and implementation of well-defined and transparent procedures for the recruitment, posting and transfer of staff.
2. Automation of personnel functions works against the traditional scheme of favours, replacing it with fixed, widely publicised procedures, in which the only condition for being recruited, promoted or transferred is that the requirements made are met.
3. The involvement of trade unions, combined with easy access to information both from within the system and in response to requests from the citizens, together with a communication strategy to disseminate accurate and timely information to the public at large, can contribute to a transparent management system and help build an ethical culture among the various levels of the education administration.

We conclude with two examples of the fight against corruption in education in Africa. The first concerns Chad:

> Chad has amongst the highest paid teachers in Africa in relation to its GDP per capita, the highest level of teacher absenteeism, and some of the largest classes I have ever seen. Teachers were being paid with six to nine months of arrears. At the same time there were large numbers of graduates of teacher training colleges who were unemployed. Primary school enrolment rates were low, and most children in school were learning very little because of teacher absenteeism. Schools were rarely, if ever, inspected, as the inspectors had no transport, and nowhere comfortable to stay if they ever arrived at a village school. We convinced the Government to move away from the employment of civil service teachers, and instead to send money to the Parent Committees to employ teachers, with a minimum qualification, on contract, paying about one third what the civil servant was paid. Because the teachers were contacted and employed by the parent community, and were only paid if they were present in the

classroom, they tended to teach the whole academic year. It was one of the most popular measures that I have ever been involved in. Rural primary schools were revitalised, and three times as many unemployed and qualified teachers were recruited each year as was previously the case. The children were the ultimate beneficiaries. (Bennett, 2001, p. 4)

In Uganda, Reinikka and Svensson (2005) report on a newspaper campaign that was aimed at reducing the amount of money taken by local government officials and politicians from capitation grants for non-wage expenditure dispensed by central government. The government did this by publishing data on monthly transfers of grants to local districts in the national newspapers and their local language editions. Thus, parents and others were informed of what monies should be available and were more able to monitor the handling of grants by local officials. Reinikka and Svensson conclude that this had a positive impact and that

both enrolment and test scores increased significantly more in schools in areas with higher newspaper penetration, and thus in schools with more funds. Since schools were free to spend their grants on whatever non-wage items they needed, be it textbooks, school meals, school uniforms, or flipcharts (or even to boost wages since funds generated by the schools themselves are fungible i.e. can be used for other things), these findings suggest that experimentation and evaluation of the processes and institutions that improve voice and accountability, and thus indirectly enhance the learning environment in schools by ensuring that entitlements actually reach their beneficiaries as intended, should be high on the policy and research agenda. (2005, p. 267)

Conclusion

In this chapter we have explored why corruption is a particular problem for developing countries and how and why this can and does affect education. Although there are possible cultural and institutional explanations for corruption in education, this is not to condone it and its negative effects on quality and inequality in education. While the problem is not likely to go away in the immediate future, it is not a completely intractable issue. In recent years there has been increasingly open recognition of, and publication on, corruption in education and this has paved the way for strategies to reduce both its level of occurrence and its impact. We have discussed some of these strategies as well as some innovative ideas for combatting corruption in particular contexts.

References

Atashak, M. (2011) Identifying Corruption among Teachers of Tehran, *Social and Behavioural Sciences*, 29, 460-463.

Bakari, S. & Leach, F. (2009) I Invited Her to My Office: normalising sexual violence in a Nigerian college of education, in S. Heyneman (Ed.) *Buying Your Way into Heaven: education and corruption in international perspective*. Rotterdam: Sense Publishers).

Bennett, N. (2001) Corruption in Education Systems in Developing Countries: what it is doing to the young.
http://www.10iacc.org/content/phtml?documents=112&art=126

Choe, C., Dzhumashev, R., Islam, A. & Khan, Z. (2013) The Effect of Informal Networks on Corruption in Education: evidence from the household survey data in Bangladesh, *Journal of Development Studies*, 49(2), 238-250.

Collins, J. (2009) When Schools Fail to Protect Girls: school-related gender-based sexual violence in sub-Saharan Africa, in S. Heyneman (Ed.) *Buying Your Way into Heaven: education and corruption in international perspective*. Rotterdam: Sense Publishers.

Hallak, J. & Poisson, M. (2005) Ethics and Corruption in Education, *Journal of Education for International Development*, 1(1), 1-16.

Harber, C. (2012) Contradictions in Teacher Education and Teacher Professionalism in Sub-Saharan Africa: the case of South Africa, in R. Griffin (Ed.) *Teacher Education in Sub-Saharan Africa: closer perspectives*. Oxford: Symposium Books.

Heyneman, S. (2009) Education Corruption in International Perspective: an introduction, in S. Heyneman (Ed.) *Buying Your Way into Heaven: education and corruption in international perspective*. Rotterdam: Sense Publishers.

Hofstede, G. (1997) *Culture and Organisations: software of the mind*. New York: McGraw-Hill.

Reinikka, R. & Svensson, J. (2005) Fighting Corruption to Improve Schooling: evidence from a newspaper campaign in Uganda, *Journal of the European Economic Association*, 3(2-3), 259-267.

Riggs, F. (1964) *Administration in Developing Countries: the theory of prismatic society*. Boston, MA: Houghton Mifflin.

Sims, R., Gong, B. & Ruppel, C. (2012) A Contingency Theory of Corruption: the effect of human development and national culture, *The Social Science Journal*, 49(1), 90-97.

Sobhy, H. (2012) The De-facto Privatisation of Secondary Education in Egypt: a study of private tutoring in technical and general schools in Egypt, *Compare*, 42(1), 47-67.

UNESCO (2009) *Overcoming Inequality: why governance matters*. EFA Global Monitoring Report. Paris: UNESCO.

Vlaardingerbroek, B., Shehab, S. & Alemeh, S. (2011) The Problem of Open Cheating and Invigilator Compliance in the Lebanese Brevet and Baccalaureat Examinations, *International Journal of Educational Development*, 31(3), 297-302.

Clive Harber

Further Reading

Cheung, H. & Chan, A. (2008) Corruption across Countries: impacts from education and cultural dimensions, *The Social Science Journal*, 45(2), 223-239.

Hallak, J. & Poisson, M. (2007) *Corrupt Schools, Corrupt Universities: what can be done?* Paris: UNESCO.

Hallak, J. & Poisson, M. (2006) *Governance in Education: transparency and accountability.* Paris: Institute for Educational Planning.

Heyneman, S. (2004) Education and Corruption, *International Journal of Educational Development*, 24(6), 637-648.

Suryadarma, D. (2012) How Corruption Diminishes the Effectiveness of Public Spending on Education in Indonesia, *Bulletin of Indonesian Economic Studies*, 48(1), 85-100.

Discussion and Activities

1. Check the most recent corruption perceptions index. Do you think there is a correlation between national levels of development and perceptions of corruption?

2. Do you have any sympathy for the views of the teacher invigilators in Lebanon about why they allow cheating in examinations to take place?

3. Read the novel *No Longer at Ease* by the Nigerian writer Chinua Achebe. What insights on reasons for corruption does this provide?

4. 'There are no circumstances in which I would ever give a bribe or inappropriate payment to anybody in education in a developing country.' Discuss.

CHAPTER 15

Education, Health and HIV/AIDS

It is of some concern that a quarter of all children eligible to be in school are malnourished and that children in developing countries frequently carry an additional burden of infectious diseases. It is estimated that 60 million school-age children suffer from iodine deficiency disorders, 85 million are at risk from acute respiratory disease and other infections because they are deficient in vitamin A, and 210 million suffer from iron deficiency anaemia. Parasitic worms (including hookworm, roundworm, whipworm and schistosomiasis) are a major source of malnutrition with an estimated 880 million school-age children infected. Malnourished children become even more malnourished when they are infected with worms, which interfere with nutrient uptake and are a major cause of anaemia. (Pridmore, 2007, p. 1)

Introduction

We saw in chapter one that life expectancy is one of the indicators used to compose the United Nations Development Programme's Human Development Index. The general health of the population is therefore an important indicator of development, and poverty can mean that curable and preventable diseases such as malaria and diarrhoea can have a devastating impact on life expectancy and child health. Education both affects, and is affected by, health issues. The educational level of parents affects the health and mortality of their children; the existing health of a child affects both their ability to attend school and their chances of success within it; school can provide both negative and positive health experiences and can provide teaching that directly tries to improve health-related understanding and behaviour. In relatively recent times HIV/AIDS has in particular provided a serious challenge to education both in terms of its impact on the education system and in terms of what education might do to help to combat the spread of the disease. We begin by examining the general relationships between education and health before discussing HIV/AIDS in the second part of the chapter.

Clive Harber

What Roles Can Education Play in Improving Health?

One significant and long-established factor in the health and mortality of children is the educational level of parents – the more years of education the parents have, the lower the mortality and better the health of the children. While educated parents are often better off financially, education remains an important separate factor even when socio-economic status is controlled for. The education of mothers is often seen as particularly important because of their traditional nurturing role within the family (Caldwell, 1979; Caldwell & Caldwell, 1985). Pamuk et al note that there is an 'impressive body of evidence supporting a strong positive effect of greater maternal education on child health after adjustments for household economic resources' (2011, p. 638). Moreover, their own study of 43 low- and middle-income countries also found that the female parental educational level was independently associated with lower infant mortality and that the general level of education had a wider effect on all mothers in the community regardless of their own educational attainment. One estimate cited by UNESCO suggested that improvements in female education accounted for half the reduction in child deaths between 1990 and 2009. UNESCO further comments that for sub-Saharan Africa, 'If the average child mortality rate for the region were to fall to the level for children born to mothers with some secondary education, there would be 1.8 million fewer deaths – a 41% reduction' (UNESCO, 2011, p. 35).

However, Aslam and Kingdon (2012) note that studies in Indonesia, Bangladesh and the Philippines have found that the educational level of fathers can also play an important role in the health of their children. Indeed, their own research in Pakistan found that fathers' (and mothers') education level had an impact on the health of their children. So important is the link between parental education and child health that Aslam and Kingdon note that 'it has even been argued that education has contributed more to mortality decline than the provision of health services' (2010, p. 2014).

This, then, raises the question of what causes this relationship – how does the education of parents translate into better health and lower mortality of infants? There are many ways that such a relationship might take place – greater literacy and numeracy may improve understanding of illness and access to, and administration of, medicines and the self-management of disease; education might empower people (especially women) to demand better treatment for children and to negotiate over resources in the household; and education might make parents more aware of immunisation programmes. UNESCO (2011, p. 36), for example, provides clear evidence of a relationship between the level of the mother's education and the percentage of one-year olds that have received basic vaccinations across 44 developing countries in Africa, the Middle East, Asia and the Pacific, and Latin America and the Caribbean.

Aslam and Kingdon's study of Pakistan (2012) found that the main pathways through which parental education may impact on child health outcomes were through higher household income, greater exposure to the media, literacy, better health knowledge, mother's participation in the labour market (and thus social discussion of illness) and the extent of maternal empowerment within the home.

So, simply providing more education, particularly for females, is one way in which education can make an important contribution to the health and life expectancy of the next generation in developing countries. However, those children who continue to suffer from poor health are still at a major disadvantage educationally in terms of both access to schooling and their ability to take advantage of the education on offer.

> Recent studies have found sizeable and statistically significant impacts of school child health and nutrition on educational outcomes. Further, analyses show that there is strong evidence to suggest that school-aged children who suffer from protein-energy malnutrition, hunger, or who lack certain micronutrients in their diet (particularly iron, iodine or vitamin A) or who carry a burden of diseases such as malaria, diarrhoea or worms do not have the same potential for learning as healthy, well-nourished children, and that they are more likely to repeat grades, drop out early and fail to learn adequately due to poor attention, low motivation and poor cognitive function. (CREATE, 2008, p. 2)

Here the school can play a role in feeding and de-worming programmes and the provision of micronutrients. The need for such programmes is now recognised in the 'Focus Resources on Effective School Health' (FRESH) framework developed jointly by UNESCO, the World Health Organisation (WHO), the United Nations Children's Fund (UNICEF) and the World Bank. This emphasises the need for clean water, proper sanitation and good nutrition in schools, which is not always the case. In Cambodia, for example:

> Despite unprecedented levels of investment into sanitation systems, it was still widely reported by the district education advisers that toilets were not used correctly. School directors often kept them locked or made them only accessible to staff to ensure they remained clean. When toilets were open they were often unhygienic, lacking water or any cleaning and therefore not used. (Courtney, 2007, p. 627)

Indeed, one obvious way in which schools could help to improve the health of children would be to stop or reduce the negative practices that go on within them that have been discussed in chapter 6 – for example, bullying, corporal punishment and sexual harassment – and to provide a better quality education overall. On a more positive note, schools can provide taught health education programmes in the curriculum. UNESCO (2005, pp. 150-151) has estimated that in between a quarter and a third of countries globally, health education is required during primary and lower secondary school. The content varies considerably and can include family planning, HIV/AIDS prevention education, sex education, drug prevention and personal hygiene. (One further area that might usefully be added is traffic safety education, as road traffic injuries in developing countries have been termed the 'neglected epidemic'. In the late 1990s, for example, more than 85% of all deaths and 90% of disability resulting from traffic accidents happened in developing countries. Among children aged 0-14 years the number of fatalities from road accidents per 100,000 population in low-income countries was about six times greater than in high-income countries [Nantulya & Reich, 2002].)

In a study of health education courses in India, Uganda and Zambia, Hawes notes the increased interest in health education globally and in official aims and syllabuses in the three countries concerned, but 'Would that such concern were translated into action. It is not. Programmes are uncoordinated, unfocused and often widely shy of the mark in terms of their relevance to learners' needs and conditions' (2003, p. 8). Hawes suggests a number of reasons why health education programmes are difficult to plan and deliver in practice. One is that health education does not necessarily fit neatly into the existing school curriculum, being essentially cross-curricular and community related. Subject teachers may or may not tackle aspects of it, and when they do it is in an uncoordinated and fragmentary manner. A second problem is that health education deals not only with personal health but wider issues of health and society, which inevitably leads on to controversial social issues concerning values and attitudes as well as knowledge and which subject teachers may not be comfortable with, or trained for. A third problem is a problem of assessment because there is a need to measure health education in terms of health competencies and action, not only marks in tests, and they need to be evaluated here and now and not only at examination time. (Also, while it is possible to test knowledge and even competencies, testing changes in actual behaviour is much more difficult because of problems of proving cause and effect and of the possibility of there being only long-term changes in behaviour.) Hawes found that the net result was that schools and curriculum developers tend in practice to leave health education to someone else, such as the Child-to-Child health education non-governmental organisation (NGO), for example, which is active in many developing countries. Sometimes such NGO programmes operate in schools with teachers in spare curriculum time or work outside the classroom, or even away from the school rather than within it.

Such general problems with the implementation of health education programmes via schools are also reflected in the role of education in a major global health challenge of the last three to four decades that has particularly affected developing countries – the spread of HIV/AIDS – and it is to this that we now turn.

Education and HIV/AIDS

HIV/AIDS

By 2000, AIDS had become a full-blown development crisis presenting a grim picture with glimmers of hope. (UNESCO, 2012, p. 84)

As the epidemic worsened, many hard-won development gains were eroded or threatened. This is because HIV/AIDS reduces life expectancy, increases child mortality, leaves large numbers of children without adult care, places extra burdens on health-care systems, negatively affects economic development, and impoverishes households. (Castle & Richmond, 2012, p. 34)

While there has been some success in combating the spread of HIV/AIDS, the problem has far from gone away. The number of new HIV infections globally fell by a fifth between 1999 and 2009 and HIV prevalence fell by more than a quarter from 2001 to 2009 in 33 countries, including 22 in sub-Saharan Africa. Nevertheless, it remains a significant problem. In 2010, 34 million were infected globally and 2.7 million were infected that year. In 2009, 41% of all new infections were of people aged 15-24, and 71% of all young people living with HIV are in sub-Saharan Africa. Within the region, infection rates are highest in southern and eastern Africa (UNESCO, 2012, p. 84). Moreover, in some countries in Eastern Europe and Central Asia infection rates have gone up by as much as 25% (Biggs, 2012, p. 22). While antiretroviral drugs have played a key role in the reduction in HIV/AIDS, there are now major global programmes concerned with education for HIV/AIDS prevention (Castle & Richmond, 2012, pp. 34-40) and education has played a role in reducing the rate of infection. However, HIV/AIDS has also had a major impact on access to, and provision of, education and there are significant issues surrounding the ways in which education might or might not help to combat HIV/AIDS, not least because of the sexual way in which the HIV virus is predominantly transmitted and the stigma attached to it.

AIDS Orphans and Education

One impact of high rates of HIV/AIDS in the wider society is the creation of AIDS orphans or children made vulnerable by AIDS; that is, children of school age who have lost one or both of their parents. By 2010 between 30 and 40% of children in the high-prevalence countries of southern and eastern Africa were estimated to be orphaned, with even larger numbers affected because their adult caregivers were ill or caring for the ill (Kendall & O'Gara, 2007, p. 5). This affects school attendance because of the increasing difficulty of paying school fees and purchasing necessary materials such as books, paper and writing instruments, and because children need to stay at home to care for a parent or to look after younger siblings. A further disincentive to attending school may be the stigma that is attached to coming from a family where somebody has HIV/AIDS.

Such children have considerable needs stemming from their vulnerability to psychological trauma, poverty and neglect. Schools, however, are widely distributed and are tasked with the healthy development of children, and so potentially offer AIDS orphans protection and a safe space. However, the findings of a study of three countries seriously affected by HIV/AIDs – Kenya, Malawi and Zimbabwe – were 'soberingly different' from international and state policy statements about the very positive role that education plays in tackling AIDS. In a context of increasing numbers of children and decreasing resources per pupil, none of the schools studied were involved with outreach, tracking or meeting the particular needs of vulnerable children. The impact of the epidemic on the school and its target communities was not acknowledged, and instead:

> Schools focused tightly on government-tested subjects like maths, English, language and science, doing little to address subjects that were more likely to be of everyday use to vulnerable children. They followed a colonially-inherited model of schooling designed to 'weed out' children that is inherently contradictory with the goals of Education For All and support for vulnerable children. The schools had not changed their schedules, regulations concerning student or teacher behaviour, pedagogical approaches or relations with communities in response to the epidemic. In the Zimbabwe and Malawi cases, school was sometimes a site of humiliation and stigma for vulnerable children. (Kendall & O'Gara, 2007, p. 17)

Elsewhere, one of the authors of the above study argues that children affected by HIV/AIDS are less likely than other children to be well served by schools, as the main focus of the response to the epidemic has simply been to get orphaned children into schools as they currently exist but

'The question of what types of schooling might better serve students has, however, for the most part been ignored' (Kendall, 2008, pp. 375, 381).

A further study of children affected by HIV/AIDS and poverty in Namibia and Swaziland (Nordtveit, 2010) also found a gap between official education frameworks for the protection of vulnerable children and actual implementation. It found that the official curriculum did not contain much preparation in life skills (further discussed below) and did not effectively address the needs of children's current and future lives. Moreover, the hidden curriculum of schools was often a hostile one because of beatings and ostracism by teachers and peers, adding to the reasons why such pupils drop out, along with the costs of schooling and the need to work. This is not to say that schools cannot, with the requisite effort and resources, help orphaned and vulnerable children. An intervention study in Zimbabwe specially trained teachers to be able to provide psychological support to AIDS affected children who had been showing signs of withdrawal, short temper, crying and bullying. As a result, the schoolwork of the children improved, as did confidence, self-esteem, interaction with peers, attendance and their trust of others (Chitiyo et al, 2008).

Impact on, and Effect of, Education

A second impact of HIV/AIDS is on the education system itself. Teachers themselves have become infected with HIV and become sick as a result. In some countries, they are considered a high-risk group. In 2002 in Zambia, for example, the infection rate among teachers was 70% higher than that in the general population (cited in Biggs, 2012, p. 25). However, in a study of 48 African countries Bennell (2003) found that teachers were no more at risk than other occupational groups but they were still at risk. Teachers who are ill as a result of HIV/AIDS become less able to teach consistently or well. A higher mortality rate because of HIV/AIDS means that education systems have been facing serious issues of continuity and teacher supply in those countries affected by the epidemic.

Does overall level of education help to reduce the risk of HIV infection? Whereas studies prior to 1996 in sub-Saharan Africa tended to find that the most educated were at higher risk because of greater affluence and mobility, studies since then have tended to find a lower risk amongst the more educated. It is thought that this is because education promotes the literacy skills to read information and improves confidence and coping skills (Castle & Richmond, 2012, p. 41). It may also be that exposure to more education reduces risky behaviour because of an increased sense that that there is a future worth living for and a decreased sense of simply living for the here and now. Poverty increases the possibility of HIV/AIDS infection for the very same, but opposite,

Clive Harber

reasons. However, as discussed in chapters 6 and 10 for example, it has to be remembered that sexual harassment and violence in schools can also contribute to the spread of HIV/AIDS.

HIV/AIDS, the Curriculum and Teaching

Many countries now explicitly include education about HIV/AIDS in their school curriculum, but there are some concerns about the teaching of HIV/AIDS in schools. One is that some evaluations have found that teaching tends to focus almost exclusively on knowledge and facts rather than attitudes, values and behaviours (Castle & Richmond, 2012, p. 42). Another problem is that the topic of HIV/AIDS is fraught with controversy and sensitivity because of its relationships to, for example, sex, drugs, gender and prostitution. Many teachers are not trained to teach controversial issues in the classroom and are afraid to do so, hence their reliance on a more knowledge-based approach (Harber & Serf, 2006; Chikoko et al, 2011). Mirembe's research in Uganda, where considerable effort has been put into HIV/AIDS education, found that teachers put emphasis on control of pupils and the passing on of knowledge. Lessons were teacher-centred, denying young people a chance to produce knowledge and to be in charge of their learning. Mirembe describes the school she witnessed as authoritarian, with little exploration of values – an approach, she argues, that is unlikely to change behaviour even if knowledge is increased. Little was done to try to challenge through discussion and interrogation dominant patterns of male dominance and sexism in education and society, a major factor in the spread of HIV/AIDS. Condom use, for example, assumes partnership and negotiation. This situation was not helped by the national curriculum, as HIV/AIDS education did not contribute significantly to grades and therefore was seen as a waste of time by teachers and pupils.

In the wake of the HIV/AIDS epidemic, retraining of teachers to teach about HIV/AIDS in Kenya and Tanzania has tended to be 'sporadic and patchy' (Juma, 2001, p. 79). However, starting in 2001 Education International and its partner organisations ran two separate programmes on Education for All (EFA) and HIV/AIDS education. In 2006 they merged to become the EFAIDS Programme, which involves a strong element of AIDS teacher training and is a partnership between Education International, the WHO and the Education Development Center. It has been implemented by 46 teacher unions in 35 countries in Africa, Asia, Latin America and the Caribbean – from India to Haiti and from Peru to Tanzania. Between 2001 and 2005, 150,000 teachers were trained in 20,000 schools in 17 countries. An evaluation of the programme reported that there had been a significant increase in

teachers' knowledge of HIV prevention, teachers' acquisition of skill in using participatory learning exercises to train peers

and students, teachers' guidance to students in obtaining
further support and assistance and the active role that
motivation plays in HIV prevention. (Castle & Richmond,
2012, p. 47)

However, there are further obstacles, as teachers may also hold religious
beliefs concerning sexual practices which they feel makes it difficult for
them to teach the topic, and this is particularly so in the case of
homosexuality. They may also believe (against the evidence) that courses
which involve sex education actually encourage promiscuity (UNESCO,
2012, pp. 87-88). For example, at an in-service training session for 200
teachers in South Africa who were given a talk on sexually transmitted
diseases, half walked out because of the explicit nature of the slides.
When the next lecturer spoke about contraception and sexual protection
the remainder of the audience, except for about eight people, got up and
left the hall. One of the few teachers that remained said, 'I couldn't
believe it. How can we expect to teach our children about the realities of
a national crisis when we want to ignore those realities ourselves'
(Dyanti, 1999). Finally, contextuality can also be a problem. Even when
HIV/AIDS is taught about, it tends to focus on the heterosexual
transmission of the virus, yet in Asia, for example, the three main
behaviours leading to HIV transmission are unprotected sex in the
context of sex work, unsafe injection of drugs, and unprotected anal sex
between men (Castle & Richmond, 2012, p. 43). Education against
HIV/AIDS can only hope to be effective if it tackles the actual causes of
the epidemic in a given context.

Knowledge Levels

Thus, while level of education may help to reduce the risk of HIV/AIDS
and courses on the topic are now far more widespread, there are still
problems with resulting levels of knowledge. The Southern and Eastern
Africa Consortium for Monitoring Educational Quality (SACMEQ)
devised the HIV/AIDS Knowledge Test (HAKT) which was administered
to pupils and teachers in 2770 schools in late 2007. The results were
analysed according to whether respondents had a 'minimal' level of
understanding, defined as mastery of half of the official HIV/AIDS
curriculum. Whereas almost all teachers (98-100%) in all countries
reached the minimal level, the pupils did not have the same level of
understanding. The resulting percentages of pupils with a minimal level
of knowledge were: Botswana 32%; Lesotho 19%; Malawi 43%;
Mozambique 40%; Namibia 36%; South Africa 35% and Swaziland 52%
(www.sacmeq.org). In the Caribbean the equivalent levels were also
relatively low: Antigua and Barbuda 48%; Barbados 50%; Belize 50%;
Cuba 58%; Dominican Republic 39%; Guyana 45%; Haiti 36%; Jamaica

Clive Harber

40%; St Kitts and Nevis 52%; St Lucia 59%; St Vincent and the Grenadines 49%; and Suriname 41% (Clarke, 2012, p. 119).

Life Skills Education

However, as UNESCO (2012, pp. 85-86) points out, even where young people have good knowledge about HIV/AIDS, this does not necessarily mean that they will change their behaviour. Values and attitudes need to change and skills need to be developed so people are empowered to say no to sex or negotiate condom use. This requires HIV/AIDS education to take place in a wider context of life skills programmes. The Health and Family Life Education programme (HFLE) in the Caribbean, for example, aims to:

– enhance the potential of young persons to become productive and contributing adults/citizens;
– promote an understanding of the principles that underlie personal and social well-being;
– foster the development of knowledge, skills and attitudes that make for healthy family life;
– provide opportunities to demonstrate sound health-related knowledge, attitudes and practices;
– increase the ability to practise responsible decision-making about social and sexual behaviour; and
– aim to increase the awareness of children and youth of the fact that the choices they make in everyday life profoundly affect their health and personal development into adulthood (Clarke, 2012, p. 121)

Of the 99 countries that responded to a survey on this topic, 23 countries reported providing life-skills-based HIV education, including high-prevalence countries such as Kenya, South Africa and Zimbabwe, and a review of 25 evaluations of life skills programmes for HIV prevention among young people from 17 countries found that effective interventions had positive effects (UNESCO, 2012, pp. 85-86). In 15 Caribbean countries the provision of such life skills courses varied from 0% in Suriname and 6% in the Dominican Republic to 100% in Barbados, Cuba, Grenada, Guyana and St Vincent and the Grenadines (Clarke, 2012, pp. 118-119).

Nevertheless, if such courses are to be successful they need to be exploratory, participatory, interactive and cooperative, and to use a variety of learning and teaching methods including role-play, drama and critical discussion. While UNESCO (2012, p. 87) does provide positive examples of teacher education courses in Papua New Guinea and Botswana that provide the type of training necessary for this way of teaching, it has to be said that the majority of teacher education courses

240

in developing countries probably do not (Harber & Mncube, 2012, pp. 119-123). Moreover, as we have also seen in the earlier chapters of this book, the dominant pattern of classroom teaching in schools does not necessarily facilitate the more participant approach required by a life skills approach. In the Caribbean, the HFLE programme faces barriers such as a lack of teacher training, lack of teacher confidence, lack of time and resources, social taboos regarding sexuality and lack of legitimacy because the subject is not tested as part of the curriculum. Perhaps not surprisingly, an impact evaluation found no pattern of significant positive effects of the HFLE curriculum on the self-reported attitudes, behaviour and skills in the health domain of form 3 students (Clarke, 2012, pp. 121-122). As a result of these sorts of problems, in many countries life skills courses are often implemented by NGOs on an extracurricular, voluntary and small-scale basis rather than in mainstream classroom teaching (UNESCO, 2012, p. 89). In Kenya and Tanzania, for example, it has been suggested that working outside the formal school setting with various youth clubs and religious groups is more productive because participants take part freely 'without any coercion' (Juma, 2001, p. 10).

Given the difficulties facing teachers and taught programmes, including life skills, one positive way forward might be, in the tradition of Child-to-Child mentioned above, to facilitate student-organised, peer education methods such as the HIV/AIDS clubs that exist in Ugandan secondary schools. These use drama, popular culture and community outreach to consider and discuss HIV/AIDS related issues and provide unusual opportunities for female students to raise gender issues and develop leadership skills (Norton & Mutonyi, 2007). However, even if life skills courses or other educational approaches aimed at HIV/AIDS prevention are successful in influencing the knowledge, skills and attitudes of participants, the extent to which individuals can implement their knowledge in behavioural terms may be limited by cultural, social and economic factors. Unequal gender roles, the use of violence, and poverty may remove choice from people nominally empowered by an education programme.

Conclusion

The health of the population is a crucial development issue for any country. One of the often-stated outcomes of formal education is improved health, whether directly through the education of young people in schools or more indirectly through the education of parents caring for their children. As this chapter has shown, there is evidence to support this but the picture overall is not clear-cut. Health education doesn't necessarily fit into traditional school curricula and timetables in a neat and tidy way and teaching about health soon leads into areas of values and morals and therefore social and political controversy. No area of health education is more fraught with controversy and has larger implications for classroom teaching and learning methods and teacher education than HIV/AIDS. This is partly why, despite significant efforts on a global scale, levels of knowledge about HIV/AIDS can still be disappointingly low. However, despite its shortcomings, education remains a key potential weapon in the fight against many diseases and health education continues to be a key aspect of debates about the role of education in development.

References

Aslam, M. & Kingdon, G. (2012) Parental Education and Child Health: understanding the pathways of impact in Pakistan, *World Development*, 40(10), 2014-2032.

Bennell, P. (2003) The AIDS Epidemic in Sub-Saharan Africa: are teachers a high-risk group?, *Comparative Education*, 39(4), 493-508.

Biggs, N.A. (2012) Global Overview, in N.A. Biggs (Ed.) *Education and HIV/AIDS*. London: Continuum.

Caldwell, C. (1979) Education as a Factor in Mortality Decline: an examination of Nigerian data, *Population Studies*, 33(3), 395-415.

Caldwell, J. & Caldwell, P. (1985) Education and Literacy as Factors in Health, in S. Halstead, J. Walsh & K. Warren (Eds) *Good Health at Low Cost*. New York: The Rockefeller Foundation.

Castle, C. & Richmond, M. (2012) International Responses to HIV/AIDS and Education, in N.A. Biggs (Ed.) *Education and HIV/AIDS*. London: Continuum.

Chikoko, V., Gilmour, J., Harber, C. & Serf, J. (2011) Teaching Controversial Issues in England and South Africa, *Journal of Education for Teaching*, 37(1), 5-21.

Chitiyo, M., Changara, D.M. & Chitiyo, G. (2008) Providing Psychosocial Support to Special Needs Children: a case of orphans and vulnerable children in Zimbabwe, *International Journal of Educational Development*, 28(4), 384-392.

Clarke, D. (2012) The Education Sector Response to HIV and AIDS in the Caribbean, in N.A. Biggs (Ed.) *Education and HIV/AIDS*. London: Continuum.

Courtney, J. (2007) Does Partnership and Sustainability Really Happen? A Case Study of an In-service Health Education Programme Implemented in One Province in Cambodia, *International Journal of Educational Development*, 27(6), 625-636.

CREATE (2008) Impact of Health on Education Access and Achievement. Policy Brief no. 3, University of Sussex.

Dyanti, A. (1999) No Sex Education, Please ... Teachers Walk out of Aids Lecture, *Saturday Star* (Johannesburg), 31 July.

Harber, C. & Mncube, V. (2012) *Education, Democracy and Development: does education contribute to democratisation in developing countries?* Oxford: Symposium Books.

Harber, C. & Serf, J. (2006) Teacher Education for a Democratic Society in England and South Africa, *Teaching and Teacher Education*, 22(8), 986-997.

Hawes, H. (2003) Health Curriculum and School Quality: international perspectives, *Compare*, 33(1), 5-14.

Juma, M. (2001) *Coping with HIV/AIDS in Education.* London: Commonwealth Secretariat.

Kendall, N. (2008) 'Vulnerability' in AIDS-affected States: rethinking child rights, educational institutions, and the development of paradigms, *International Journal of Educational Development*, 28(4), 365-383.

Kendall, N. & O'Gara, C. (2007) Vulnerable Children, Communities and Schools: lessons from HIV/AIDS affected areas, *Compare*, 37(1), 5-22.

Mirembe, R. (2002) AIDS and Democratic Education in Uganda, *Comparative Education*, 38(3), 291-302.

Nantulya, V. & Reich, M. (2002) The Neglected Epidemic: road traffic injuries in developing countries, *British Medical Journal*, 324, 1139-1141.

Nordtveit, B.H. (2010) Schools as Agencies of Protection in Namibia and Swaziland: can they prevent dropout and child labour in the context of HIV/AIDS and poverty?, *Comparative Education Review*, 54(2), 223-242.

Norton, B. & Mutonyi, H. (2007) 'Talk what others think you can't talk': HIV/AIDS clubs as peer education in Ugandan schools, *Compare*, 37(4), 479-492.

Pamuk, E., Fuchs, R. & Lutz, W. (2011) Comparing Relative Effects of Education and Economic Resources on Infant Mortality in Developing Countries, *Population and Development Review*, 37(4), 637-664.

Pridmore, P. (2007*) Impact of Health on Education Access and Achievement: a cross-national review of the research evidence.* CREATE Pathways to Access Research Monograph 2, Institute of Education, University of London.

UNESCO (2005) *Education for All: the quality imperative.* EFA Global Monitoring Report. Paris: UNESCO.

UNESCO (2011) *The Hidden Crisis: armed conflict and education.* EFA Global Monitoring Report. Paris: UNESCO.

UNESCO (2012) *Youth and Skills: putting education to work.* EFA Global Monitoring Report. Paris: UNESCO.

Further Reading

Baxen, J. (2008) Using Narratives to Develop a Hermeneutic Understanding of HIV/AIDS in South Africa, *Compare*, 38(3), 307-320.

Boler, T. & Archer, D. (2008) *Politics of Prevention: a global crisis in AIDS and education.* London: Pluto Press.

Bloom, D. (2005) Education and Public Health: mutual challenges worldwide, *Comparative Education Review*, 49(4), 437-451.

Penn, H. (2005) *Unequal Childhoods: young children's lives in poor countries.* Abingdon: Routledge.

Pridmore, P. & Stephens, D. (2000) *Children as Partners for Health.* London: Zed Books.

UNESCO Global Initiative on Education and HIV/AIDS (EDUCAIDS) – this is an important source of information and can be accessed via UNESCO/EDUCAIDS websites.

Discussion and Activities

1. Child-to-Child is a health education programme active in over 70 countries that emphasises children working together and with their families at home. Visit their website, www.child-to-child.org. What do you think are the good points about their approach to health education? What drawbacks might there be? (See also Pridmore and Stephens [2000] above.)

2. Why might road traffic be a particular health danger for school-aged children in developing countries? What might educational authorities, schools and teachers be able to do to reduce the risk?

3. What do you think would be the main characteristics of (a) a school and (b) a classroom that was ideal for dealing with, and helping to reduce, the HIV/AIDS epidemic?

4. What does the HIV/AIDS epidemic teach us about the 'contextuality' of education? (Previously discussed in chapter 1.)

5. 'It is easier to change knowledge about health than to change behaviour.' Why might this the case?

CHAPTER 16

International Aid to Education

[G]iven the current state of global poverty and inequality ...
One would have hoped that 60 years of international aid
would have led to clear improvement. However, the best that
anyone can say is that the situation could have been a lot
worse than it is now had there been no aid. (Klees, 2010, p. 15)

Introduction

Built in to debates about development is the idea that the wealthier
countries of the world will help the poorer ones through financial and
other forms of assistance – aid. Hence there are 'donor' countries and
'recipient' countries, though not all donor countries are necessarily from
the richer, industrialised 'North'. Aid can be given for a number of
reasons: the moral reason of the need to help those worse off than
yourself; the economic reason that such investment also provides
opportunities for business in your own country; and the
diplomatic/strategic reason that there are certain countries that need to
be supported in order to stop them being a threat to yourself and others.
Aid can be provided to a whole range of development sectors –
agriculture, roads, the police, water supply, the military, good
governance or education. Aid can be in the form of grants, or gifts, or can
be loans to be paid back at rates lower than the market rate. Some aid
donors to education are multilateral organisations and these pool aid
from a number of sources and distribute it internationally to many
different recipients. Or aid to education can be bilateral, between one
country and another. Aid from multilateral and government sources is
often referred to as ODA – official development assistance. Aid can be
aimed at medium- to long-term development, or can be provided for
emergencies. In this chapter we shall largely concentrate on the former,
as education and emergencies was the topic of chapter 11. Aid to
developing countries has its critics as well as its supporters and this will
be also be discussed.

Clive Harber

The Aid Agencies and Donors

Aid to education can be given by large, multilateral agencies such as the World Bank or the various other branches of the United Nations. In the case of the World Bank, although it is a United Nations institution and is owned by over 180 countries, the largest shareholder is the USA and it is very closely connected to the US Treasury. It is also located in Washington, DC. It works closely with the International Monetary Fund (IMF), which evaluates the economic viability and stability of countries that wish to take out a loan. Both the World Bank and the IMF have been advocates of capitalist, free-market economics in relation to education and have made the introduction of free-market reforms conditions of loans, as discussed in more detail in chapter 7.

The other big multilateral aid agency is the United Nations (UN), and in particular the United Nations Educational, Scientific and Cultural Organisation (UNESCO), which specialises in education and is based in Paris; the United Nations Development Programme (UNDP), which specialises in development issues and which is based in New York; and the United Nations Children's Fund (UNICEF), concerned with the well-being of children and which is also based in New York. UNESCO, in particular, has been at odds with the World Bank and the IMF over their commitment to a neoliberal approach to educational funding. In the 1980s, under Mrs Thatcher and Ronald Reagan, Britain and the USA pulled out of UNESCO because it was perceived as being too left wing, though Britain rejoined in 1997. The UN agencies have played a significant role in setting international agendas for education and development since the end of the Second World War:

> As the core of multilateral education, they powerfully reflect
> the UN's historic grounding in peace, human rights and
> economic and social development as its primary drivers. There
> can be no doubting the power and influence of the agencies in
> shaping key ideas and policies about education futures;
> further, with the exception of UNESCO, their financial clout
> across the developing world cannot be questioned. (Jones &
> Coleman, 2005, p. 2)

As well as the multilateral aid agencies, a large number of non-governmental organisations work internationally (often known as INGOs). Some well-known examples involved with education include Save the Children and Oxfam, but others are Christian Aid, the International Red Cross and Red Crescent Societies and Médecins Sans Frontières. These are independent of nation-states but are influential in both donor and recipient countries. Another major source of aid is national government aid agencies – often separate government ministries or parts of ministries such as the Foreign Office. In Britain, for example, it is the Department for International Development (DfID), in the USA,

246

the United States Agency for International Development (USAID), in Canada, the Canadian International Development Agency (CIDA) and in Sweden, the Swedish International Development Agency (SIDA). The UN has set a target of 0.7% of gross domestic product that wealthier countries should donate towards poorer ones.

Finally, there are the large philanthropic donors, who are wealthy individuals and their foundations. Two well-known examples are the Bill and Melissa Gates (of Microsoft) Foundation, which donates to organisations working with HIV/AIDS and the Soros Foundation, set up by George Soros, who made his money investing on the stock exchange. The Soros Foundation set up the Open Society Foundations, which promote democratic governance, human rights, the rule of law and economic and social reform. Srivastava and Oh (2010) argue that there is a 'burgeoning hope that private foundations will be significant actors in plugging the holes left by the chronic underfunding of official development assistance' but that

> it cannot be used as a substitute for actual ODA. This is
> because ODA is a structured system of aid, supported by
> international agreements and legal frameworks. Despite its
> faults, it is meant to be a concerted, coordinated effort that
> holds countries accountable. (2010, p. 470)

They also point out that included in philanthropic aid should be the large sums of money which are remitted by nationals from developing countries working abroad and which the World Bank see as one of the strongest poverty reduction forces in poor countries (Srivastava & Oh, 2010, p. 465).

As a result of the financial crisis in 2008 in richer countries, official development assistance to all sectors decreased in real terms by 3% from 2010 to 2011. Some countries made severe cuts – Spain over 30%, Japan 11% and Norway, France and Canada also made cuts. In the United Kingdom aid decreased only slightly but Australia, Germany, New Zealand, Sweden and Switzerland continued to increase their aid budgets (UNESCO, 2012, pp. 149-51). However, there is now also a growing group of new aid donor countries, particularly the BRICS countries – Brazil, the Russian Federation, India, China and South Africa – meaning that some aid is South–South rather than just North–South in development terms. As the economic growth and power of China in particular has increased, so has its role in aid. China plays the largest role of the BRICS countries in terms of aid, contributing $2 billion to aid in 2010 and particularly to Africa. However, some have argued that many of the loans it extends do not really qualify as aid as the interest is at market rates. Unlike some Western donors, who have insisted on conditions attached to loans and aid such as free-market reforms, better human rights and greater transparency (see chapters 5 and 7), China has adopted a policy of 'friendship and non-interference'. The only condition that China seems to attach to aid is that African countries support its one China and peaceful reunification policy (Nordtveit, 2011, p. 107).

Critics of Aid

The giving of aid, including aid to education, has many critics and the area is fraught with controversy. Klees (2010) provides a useful discussion of such critics of aid. He starts with a book published in 1972 by Peter Bauer called *Dissent on Development* which argued that aid, rather than helping, simply created dependency, distorted priorities, fostered corruption and interfered with the market. Dichter (2003), in his book *Despite Good Intentions: why development assistance to the Third World has failed*, added the criticism that the aid 'industry' had become a business whose main stake was its own survival, which was why it persisted despite a record of failures. He admitted that aid had had some successes, such as increases in literacy and the eradication of certain diseases, but these were exceptions and that developing countries would develop better if they adopted the free market and private sector rather than if they relied on development assistance. A further critic is William Easterly in his 2006 book, *The White Man's Burden: why the West's efforts to aid the rest have done so much ill and so little good.* Easterly is very critical of international aid as not achieving what it should do. He describes it as a:

> tragedy in which the West spent $2.3 trillion on foreign aid
> over the last five decades and still had not managed to get
> twelve-cent medicines to children to prevent half of all
> malaria deaths. The West spent $2.3 trillion and still had not
> managed to get four-dollar bed nets to poor families ... The
> West spent $2.3 trillion and Amartech (an Ethiopian girl) is
> still carrying firewood and not going to school. (p. 4)

Easterly rejects planning and social engineering and puts his faith in more markets, less government and a much-reduced role and scope for foreign aid.

Perhaps the most recent critic in this vein is Dembisa Moyo (2009), who wrote a book entitled *Dead Aid: why aid is not working and how there is a better way for Africa.* Moyo is a Zambian economist who spent two years at the World Bank. Her argument is that after enormous aid expenditures on Africa the recipients of aid are actually worse off – aid has made the poor poorer and growth slower – largely because it has fostered corruption, increased conflict, distorted the market, decreased savings and investment, increased inflation and hurt exports. The result is a culture of 'aid dependency' or 'aid addiction' which is fostered by an international aid complex employing half a million people. It also encourages laziness on the part of African policy makers in relation to finding ways of remedying Africa's problems.

A critic coming from a different direction is Roger Riddell, a former International Director of Christian Aid who wrote *Does Foreign Aid Really Work?* (2008). His criticisms concern the extent to which aid is tied to the political and commercial interests of donor countries, particularly the way aid money is tied to spending on goods and products in the donor country. He was also critical of the degree to which the amount of aid depends on the political interests of the donor country so that, in the case of the USA for example, large amounts of the aid budget are devoted to Iraq, Afghanistan and Pakistan. (Equally, Penn [2005, p. 67] points out that the aid of ex-colonial powers such as France, the Netherlands, Spain and the United Kingdom tends mainly to go to its ex-colonies.) However, Riddell also concludes that aid has saved lives and led to tangible benefits for millions of poor people and poor-country economies and societies even though some aid interventions have been failures or not had a long-term systemic and sustainable impact. (See also Mason [2011, pp. 447-448] on critics of aid.)

Klees's own critique is different again. Far from spending too much money on ODA, he thinks that rich countries have spent nowhere near enough. He asks what kind of development do rich countries think they can buy for less than 1% of GDP, even if all countries spent the 0.7% they are supposed to, which many don't. He points out that in 2008 the total amount of aid to the whole of Africa was $35 billion – less than the bailout of the American car industry. He also notes that

> the Marshall Plan for reconstruction after World War Two
> spent as much on Europe as the rich countries do on total
> ODA for all developing countries now ... Developing countries
> need a much more intense effort than the Marshall Plan. The
> point is that we haven't been throwing money at our social
> problems; instead we've been miserly ... Attempts to cost what
> it would take to achieve the Millennium Development Goals
> have produced estimates of an additional $120 to $190 billion
> a year, and that may well be an underestimate. (2010, p. 17)

He argues that education, like other social sectors, has been a victim of the neoliberal 'onslaught' of cuts in public expenditure and that more money for education is desperately needed as there are still 75 million children of primary school age out of school in developing countries, and they need teachers, classrooms and learning materials. To achieve this requires an extra $16 billion of expenditure per year from aid and other sources, which at the moment is not forthcoming.

Aid and Education

It is important to remember that, despite the contribution of international aid, national spending by governments remains the largest contribution to spending on education in most countries. For example, although India receives the second largest amount of aid in absolute terms globally, this only amounts to 1% of total spending on education. However, aid amounts to as much as a fifth of education budgets in low-income countries overall and in some countries it is considerably more. In Mozambique, for example, between 1999 and 2010 the numbers of out-of-school children fell from 1.6 million to 0.5 million and during much of the period 42% of the education budget was funded externally (UNESCO, 2012, p. 144). Increases in aid have generally contributed significantly to progress towards Education for All since the early 2000s but there are signs that this will not continue, with total aid falling in 2011 for the first time since 1997. In 2010 aid to education stagnated, but in the period from 2002 until 2010 aid to basic education increased considerably, though not necessarily to the countries with the most need. During that period aid to sub-Saharan Africa, the region in most need, increased by 27% whereas it increased to the Arab states by more than three and a half times. In 2010 funding for basic education was increased for 16 low-income countries, but 55% of this went to Afghanistan and Bangladesh, and funding for 19 low-income countries fell (UNESCO, 2012, pp. 147-148).

As this difference between sub-Saharan Africa and the Arab states (as well as Afghanistan and Bangladesh) suggests, trade (including oil) and perceived strategic security interests play a role in aid to education as well as aid generally. Indeed, Novelli (2010) has argued that aid to education has been increasingly politicised and tied to security issues so that it is also increasingly directed to conflict and post-conflict countries. In 2007, 38.4% of official development assistance went to conflict and fragile states. Development, Novelli argues, is now seen as part of counter-terrorism and counter-insurgency strategy by both the USA and European Union – by solving problems and reducing poverty in targeted countries, so the terrorist threat to donor countries is reduced. Educational provision is part of this strategy to win the 'hearts and minds' of local populations. The net result is that social provision such as education can be perceived and portrayed as part of a war effort against occupying forces and is thus seen as a legitimate military target, as has been the case with the Taliban in Afghanistan where education, and education for girls in particular, has been subject to violent attacks.

There has also been much criticism of the way in which donors have tended to dictate terms and conditions for aid to developing countries in a rather one-sided manner. The imposition of loan conditions by the World Bank's neoliberal structural adjustment policies were discussed in chapter 7. However, this can also be the case with national development agencies. Brock-Utne (2007), for example, is very critical of the way in which traditionally independent Norwegian bilateral aid to education was strongly influenced by World Bank free-market thinking and policies on education and developments such as privatisation and school fees – 'usually imposed uniformly irrespective of local conditions and preferences' (2007, p. 1).

In 2005 and 2008, however, important changes took place in the principles governing the relationships between aid donors and recipients. This was in response to a perceived need for greater partnership and equality in aid relationships.

> The Paris Declaration (of 2005) promised that donor agencies would align themselves behind the objectives for poverty reduction set by developing countries themselves; utilising local systems to deliver and track aid resources, coordinating and sharing information amongst themselves to avoid duplication, and securing mutual accountability between donor and recipient authorities for the results achieved. Three years later at a follow-on conference in Accra, it was further agreed that donors would provide information on their planned programmes between three and five years in advance, they would use country systems to deliver aid, rather than donor systems, and they would not impose their own conditions on how and when the aid resources would be used – rather they would use conditions based upon recipient countries' own development targets and aspirations.
> (Colclough & Webb, 2012, p. 263)

The idea was that aid should move from a top-down, donor-controlled process to greater partnership, cooperation, harmonisation, mutual accountability and management for results. As UNESCO has pointed out, these principles have particular relevance to education, which needs long-term, sustainable development in schools, teacher recruitment and training (2012, p. 152). However, Mason (2011) has argued that there are limits in practice to a completely equal relationship in aid to education in developing countries and that there remains a need for Northern donors to still insist on conditions to aid in order to enhance effectiveness, minimise corruption and make sure that aid given for one purpose is not diverted to another. As he says, 'It is no doubt hard to construct an equal partnership when one party controls the purse strings' (2011, p. 453).

Colclough and Webb (2012) provide a useful case study of the attempt to apply the Paris/Accra principles in aid to education in Kenya. They point out a number of background obstacles – that the budgetary timetables of donor aid agencies are often determined by their own national parliament; that government ministers responsible for aid in donor countries have to defend the outcomes of their expenditures and many developing country budgetary systems make this difficult; and that developed country aid lobbies and officials often have strongly held views about the best ways of reducing poverty in developing countries. Thus, 'it may be that the admirable aspirations of Paris and Accra represent a triumph of hope over reason' (p. 264). After substantial withdrawal of aid to Kenya in the 1990s because of corruption and political repression, aid resumed with the election of a new government in 2002. Aid to education took the form of a Sector Wide Approach (SWAp) – that is, where all major donor funding to the education sector supports a single-sector policy and expenditure programme under national government leadership. The new aid programme was launched in 2005 and since then the following features have emerged in relation to the Paris/Accra principles:

- Donor preferences to support the primary education sub-sector were influential in the definition of Kenya's priorities.
- The funding and experience brought by donor organisations meant that they were influential in the allocation of funds for specific programmes.
- Donors remained unconvinced that there were credible systems of accountability and transparency that would safeguard their resources if channelled to national budget support.
- Donor agencies were not speaking with one voice because they were not fully coordinating and sharing information with each other.
- Most of the responsibility for accountability was still with the Government of Kenya – indeed the whole notion of conditionality presupposes that direction of responsibility.

Colclough and Webb conclude they while the programme was cooperative and was believed by participants to have increased efficiency, nevertheless the aid process fell short of Paris/Accra ideals in the above ways.

On the other hand, some countries have minimised the impact of donors on their education policy. The Government of India has been very sensitive about national autonomy for its education policy, and Colclough and De (2010) discuss how for over twenty years India has used donor aid to education to both get external endorsement for its education policies and also to blame donors when progress has faltered or where there has been criticism of the government. Aid also helped to put education at the centre of the domestic stage politically and could be used to provide advocacy of the government's own policies. The donors' advice was used and incorporated in ways chosen by the government. Nevertheless, and similarly to Kenya, 'it has had a significant direct impact on management practice, financial reporting, accounting procedures and monitoring arrangements. These changes probably improved the efficiency, and certainly the accountability, of the educational process' (2010, p. 506).

Nevertheless, however much aid relationships have changed towards a more equal partnership since Paris/Accra, UNESCO (2012, p. 154) points out that in the tightened circumstances following the financial crisis of 2008-09, governments and taxpayers in donor countries want to see what their money is being spent on and whether it achieves its stated aims. Donors are therefore increasingly turning to results-based funding linked to specified outcomes. The World Bank, for example, has introduced a 'Program-for-Results' financing scheme whereby loans will only be given once prior specified results have been achieved. UNESCO also provides the example of the UK DfID's aid to education in Ethiopia. In 2012-14 DfID has made a grant to the Ethiopian Ministry of Education for additional students who sit or pass the grade 10 examination. The unit grant for each girl will be higher than for each boy, as will it be for each additional student sitting the examination from a poorer region. UNESCO comments that 'Putting more emphasis on outcomes such as children's learning is welcome and necessary. Results-based aid could also increase country ownership over policies because governments would take responsibility for their own decisions' (2012, p. 154).

UNESCO notes, however, that there are three risks facing results-based aid to education that need to be considered in any new scheme. The first is that if circumstances beyond their control prevent recipients from reaching agreed outcomes – a not uncommon situation – then withholding funds could put governments in a difficult financial position. Second, there is the problem of skewing behaviour because of working to targets. Where funding is contingent on standardised test results there is a high risk that teachers teach to the test and neglect other forms of learning. In Chile and Mexico, paying teachers by results led them to focus on the best-performing students, raising issues of widening inequality. Third, poorer countries need aid upfront, so if education aid is only disbursed once young people have graduated, who will pay for the school buildings and teacher salaries to improve the conditions that allows them to graduate?

Finally, in terms of South–South aid, at the time of writing BRICS aid to education is quite small compared to traditional donors (UNESCO, 2012, p. 153) . Nevertheless, China, for example, has been providing aid to Kenya for fifty years and in recent years there has been a growth of interest in China as a destination for short- and long-term training for Kenyans and there is also increasing interest among Kenyans in learning Chinese. These educational developments cannot be separated from China's involvement (as elsewhere in Africa) in business, investment, infrastructure development and Chinese migration to East Africa (King, 2010). China also has economic ties with Cameroon where it has been increasingly active in providing four types of aid to education – Confucius Institutes which provide language and culture-related training; longer-term scholarships and shorter-term training for Africans; school construction; and stand-alone education projects such as inter-university collaboration. However, whereas in Kenya China has not tended to harmonise its procedures with other major donors, in Cameroon it has been increasingly present and visible at donor coordination meetings organised by UNESCO, the World Bank and the Cameroonian government and, according to one commentator, there is a risk that in future, 'China will run the risk of being perceived as an aid donor rather than its preferred role of being seen as a larger developing country involved in the best of its ability in South–South cooperation with other developing countries' (King, cited in Nordtveit, 2011, p. 167).

Conclusion

International aid, including aid to education, is a large-scale affair involving a great deal of money and employing a great many people, but is also an area of considerable controversy. Aid has obviously not solved all the problems of developing countries and there are many issues with both the priorities and mechanisms of disbursement of aid. However, there are many young people in developing countries now in education who wouldn't have been before and they are receiving a better education and with better outcomes than would have been the case without aid. Despite its critics, international aid is unlikely to be abandoned in the near future, though its scope, modalities and priorities are likely to change as the global political and economic contexts that shape it also change.

References

Bauer, P. (1972) *Dissent on Development.* Boston, MA: Harvard University Press.

Brock-Utne, B. (2007) Worldbankification of Norwegian Development Assistance to Education, *Comparative Education*, 43(3), 433-449.

Colclough, C. & De, A. (2010) The Impact of Aid on Education Policy in India, *International Journal of Educational Development*, 30(5), 497-507.

Colclough, C. & Webb, A. (2012) A Triumph of Hope over Reason? Aid Accords and Education Policy in Kenya, *Comparative Education*, 48(2), 263-280.

Dichter, T.W. (2003) *Despite Good Intentions: why development assistance to the Third World has failed.* Amherst, MA: University of Massachusetts Press.

Easterly, W. (2006) *The White Man's Burden: why the West's efforts to aid the rest have done so much ill and so little good.* Oxford: Oxford University Press.

Jones, P. & Coleman, D. (2005) *The United Nations and Education: multilateralism, development and globalisation.* London: RoutledgeFalmer.

King, K. (2010) China's Cooperation in Education and Training with Kenya: a different model?, *International Journal of Educational Development*, 30(5), 488-496.

Klees, S. (2010) Aid, Development and Education, *Current Issues in Comparative Education*, 13(1), 7-28.

Mason, M. (2011) What Underlies the Shift to a Modality of Partnership in Educational Development Cooperation?, *International Review of Education*, 57(3-4), 443-455.

Moyo, D. (2009) *Dead Aid: why aid is not working and how there is a better way for Africa*. New York: Farrar, Straus & Giroux.

Nordtveit, B. (2011) An Emerging Donor in Education and Development: a case study of China in Cameroon, *International Journal of Educational Development*, 31(2), 99-108.

Novelli, M. (2010) The New Geopolitics of Educational Aid: from cold wars to holy wars?, *International Journal of Educational Development*, 30(5), 453-459.

Penn, H. (2005) *Unequal Childhoods: young children's lives in poor countries*. Abingdon: Routledge.

Roger Riddell (2008) *Does Foreign Aid Really Work?* Oxford: Oxford University Press.

Srivasta, P. & Oh, S. (2010) Private Foundations, Philanthropy and Partnership in Education and Development: mapping the terrain, *International Journal of Educational Development*, 30(5), 460-471.

UNESCO (2012) *Youth and Skills: putting education to work*. EFA Global Monitoring Report. Paris: UNESCO.

Further Reading

Ashford, R. (2009) Negotiating Donor Participation in the Sri Lankan Educational Sector, *Comparative Education Review*, 53(3), 355-378.

Benavot, A., Archer, D., Mosely, S., et al (2010) International Aid to Education: moderated discussion, *Comparative Education Review*, 54(1), 105-124.

Chisholm, L. & Steiner-Khamsi, G. (2009) *South-South Cooperation in Education and* Development. New York: Teachers College Press.

International Journal of Educational Development (2010) 30(5), Special Issue on The New Politics of Aid to Education.

Karpinska, Z. (2012) *Education, Aid and Aid Agencies*. London: Continuum.

King, K. (2013) *China's Aid and Soft Power in Africa: the case of education and training*. Woodbridge: James Curry.

King, K. (2007) Multilateral Agencies in the Construction of the Global Agenda on Education, *Comparative Education*, 43(3), 377-391.

McCormick, A. (2012) Whose Education Policies in Aid-receiving Countries? A Critical Discourse Analysis of Quality and Normative Transfer through Cambodia and Laos, *Comparative Education Review*, 56(1), 18-47.

Clive Harber

Discussion and Activities

1. Read the debates on aid to education in the special edition of *Current Issues in Comparative Education*, 13(1), on 'Aid, Development and Education' and Benavot et al (2010), in Further Reading above. What do you think is the best way forward for aid to education?

2. Go to the websites of two national development agencies such as DfID, USAID or SIDA. Are there differences in their policies, priorities and in the countries they deal with in relation to education? Why might this be the case?

3. Traditionally, aid and aid to education have been seen in terms of a North to South donor relationship. However, new donors have emerged such as the BRICS countries and South Korea. What difference might there be between South–South aid and North–South aid to education? (See, for example, Chisholm & Steiner-Khamsi [2009] and King [2013] in Further Reading above.)

CHAPTER 17

Literacy and Language

It is believed by many researchers and policy makers that
literacy is the starting point of development. For centuries
some have considered reading and writing key for achieving
democracy, economic growth and stability, social harmony
and, most recently, competitiveness in world markets. School
has been promoted as the institution responsible for the
education of new readers and writers who, according to this
view, will learn the basic skills necessary for entering the work
force, vocational or professional training and, eventually,
placement in the job market ... The ability to read new
material, understand, synthesise and use information, and
produce written documents was once only expected of an
educated elite. The goal of universal, mass literacy is indeed a
recent one. (Kalman, 2008, pp. 524, 534)

Language is by no means an uncontroversial issue in any
education system ... (Kamwendo, 2013, p. 115)

Introduction

The fourth of the Education for All goals that form part of the
Millennium Development Goals included achieving a 50% improvement
in levels of adult literacy by 2015. Literacy is accorded a high priority in
the development of countries and is seen to bring both personal benefits
to the individual and developmental gains for the society in terms of, for
example, economic modernisation and growth, democratic participation
and citizenship and general levels of health. Yet, 'On a global scale, few
illiterate adults live in rich countries' – illiteracy is a much more serious
issue in developing countries (UNESCO, 2012, p. 91). Illiteracy means
that millions of people in developing countries have restricted access to
important information about health and social, economic and political
issues. However, literacy, despite widely being seen as an obviously
positive thing for individuals and societies, nevertheless involves more
than the ability to read and write and is a contested and controversial
area in terms of its definition, measurement, outcomes and language of

use. In the first part of this chapter we explore these themes but we begin by presenting some data on literacy rates as a background context for a discussion of the nature of literacy and its role in education and development. The second part of the chapter examines the role of language in relation to literacy in more detail.

Literacy

To be literate has been defined differently over time as someone able to:

1. Sign his/her name
2. Read/write a simple sentence describing his/her daily activities
3. Read/write by him or herself
4. Pass a written reading comprehension test at a level comparable to that achieved by an average 4th grade student
5. Engage in all those activities in which literacy is required for effective functioning in his/her community. (Kalman, 2008, p. 525)

UNESCO itself has long defined literacy as 'The ability to read and write, with understanding, a short simple statement related to one's daily life'. However, this understanding now also includes functional literacy – an individual's ability to engage in all activities in which literacy is required for the effective functioning of their group or community and also for enabling them to continue to use reading, writing and calculation for their own and the community's development (UNESCO, 2012, p. 312). In 2010 it was estimated that there were still 775 million adults who could not read or write, two-thirds of whom were women. The global youth rate for illiteracy was 10% in 2010, meaning that illiteracy will not be eradicated by the target date of 2015. Though there is adult and youth illiteracy in high-income countries, it is proportionately much lower than in developing countries. Over half of all illiterate adults live in South and West Asia and one-fifth in sub-Saharan Africa. Some 28% of youth in sub-Saharan Africa and 19% of youth in South and West Asia are illiterate – 45 million and 62 million people respectively (UNESCO, 2012, p. 91).

However, caution must be exercised about such figures. Global literacy figures are based on national surveys about whether the respondent or household members have been to school and are literate rather than on direct assessments of literacy. Not only might respondents not admit to being illiterate on a questionnaire, but also, completing primary school is not a guarantee of literacy. Indeed, evidence from surveys in 10 low-income countries (Nigeria, Ghana, Zambia, India, Kenya, Timor-Leste, Cambodia, Tanzania, Haiti and Nepal) showed that a considerable proportion of young adults who had six years of primary school were still illiterate or semi-literate (UNESCO, 2012, p. 96). This reflects problems with the quality of education, discussed in chapter 2. In Ghana, for example, even among those with nine years of schooling in 2008, 21% were illiterate and about a quarter only partially literate (UNESCO, 2012, p. 97). Another problem is how we judge terms such as 'literate', 'semi-literate' and 'illiterate' — where the boundaries are and what is considered 'enough' to be literate may depend on local meanings, needs and practices (Maddox et al, 2011, p. 577). Moreover, in cross-national comparisons of literacy rates the language of literacy is rarely specified and it is difficult to know if figures for a country are for literacy in a single official language, several official languages or non- or semi-official languages (Bartlett, 2008, p. 739). Shiohata (2010, p. 243) points out that in some studies in countries in Africa literacy is defined solely in terms of skills in the colonial language and respondents who can read and write in their own language are counted as illiterate.

Another issue is the nature of literacy, or perhaps more accurately, 'literacies'. Although literacy is clearly concerned with reading and writing, these can be used in different ways and in different contexts. Maddox et al (2011, p. 577), for example, suggest there are academic literacies, digital literacies and vernacular literacies, languages and scripts. (The word 'literacy' is also often appended to other areas of life such as financial literacy, media or health literacy.) They also suggest that certain forms of literacy, for example, academic or schooled literacies, tend to be given a more privileged status. They use the example of a large number of 'out-of-school' children in Nigeria who were actually in Quranic school, not recognised by global and national policy makers and statisticians as legitimate educational institutions, though pupils spent 8-10 years in such institutions. Thus, Western education and literacy is privileged over Islamic literacy.

Another problem with the way literacy is measured is that how it is used and understood differs from context to context. In terms of the uses of literacy, direct studies of actually measuring literacy carried out by UNESCO in Jordan, Mongolia, Palestine and Paraguay found that although they have all achieved a relatively high literacy rate, there were large differences in the percentage of adults who reported reading for pleasure, those who reported using computers and those who reported reading bills, invoices or budget tables (UNESCO, 2012, p. 94). In terms of what factors help a community to acquire and sustain a literate environment, UNESCO found that in Jordan, Mongolia, Palestine and Paraguay, public lighting, street names and dwelling numbers, newsstands and public libraries were important characteristics.

Moreover, there are those who question whether literacy can really be best understood primarily as an individual's set of information processing cognitive skills or should rather be seen as primarily to do with social relationships — that is, the ways in which words and deeds are actually used, and the meanings ascribed to them, in different contexts and cultures. In this social understanding of literacy, setting tests to assess or measure tasks such as reading a bus timetable or understanding consumer instructions may bear little relation to people's day-to-day activities. As Hamilton and Barton (cited in Bartlett 2008, p. 741) put it, 'Once a real life text such as a bus timetable is wrenched out of its real life context it ceases to be a timetable and becomes a test item'. Thus:

> The messy social construction of literacy becomes naturalised and reified through its measurement; literacy is transformed from social process to social fact ... Literacy practices are so contextual and so variable that it would never be possible, a priori, to invent a measurement that would be able to account for their diversity. (Bartlett, 2008, p. 742)

Being literate in the social sense, therefore, means the ability to use written language to participate in the social world. Literacy involves 'learning how to manipulate and create with written language – text genres, meanings, discourses, words and letters – in a calculated and intentional way in order to participate in culturally valued events as a means for relating to others' (Kalman, 2008, p. 527).

Others, however, ask further questions about the social purposes of literacy. Is it to provide individuals with the reading and writing skills to be able to cope and survive in society as it is or is it a means of helping to transform unjust and unequal relationships by reading the world in a more critical way? Is developing literacy seen as just a 'neutral', technical exercise achieved through rote, copy and dictation or is it a more overtly political one of either oppressing the poor to accept their lot or of encouraging learners to use their literacy skills to participate and engage with issues of oppression, fairness and social justice in the manner advocated, for example, by Paolo Freire (Freire & Macedo, 1987)? Bajaj (2009), for example, compares an alternative private school in Zambia that used Freirean approaches to literacy and education, including greater use of local languages, with government schools where use of the local language was punished.

Linked to the purposes of literacy is the question of possible outcomes or benefits – does it, for example, actually improve job prospects and levels of political engagement? Bartlett (2008, p. 744) notes that UNESCO's 2006 Education for All Global Monitoring Report selected literacy as its key theme but that throughout the report frequent use is made of tentative language such as 'may', 'probably reasonable to assume' and 'has the potential to' in terms of the economic and political benefits of literacy. Her study of literacy programmes in Brazil (2008) found that the economic mobility of students on literacy programmes resulted from the relationships and networks they cultivated through and in schools rather than the actual literacy they learned in school. While several of the literacy programmes had little effect on political participation, only one of the literacy programmes, specifically organised on Freirean lines, did seem to have some effect, though it was not literacy per se that accomplished this but rather the rhetoric in class urging participation. She concluded that

> literacy is a tool taken up by students with their own histories and literacy ideologies. The impact of literacy programmes on the students who participated in my study was filtered through their specific cultural definitions of education, their social networks, and their positioning in larger social structures. (2008, p. 751)

Language, Literacy and Education

> It is not possible for learners to learn if they do not understand lessons; and they cannot understand lessons if they do not understand the language in which the lessons are taught. This is also the case with teachers. They cannot teach effectively if they have problems in expressing themselves in the language of instruction. (Afitska et al, 2013, p. 154)

This section of the chapter examines more closely the question of literacy in what language and at what stage of education. Which language should children be learning in and when? This is an important issue in many developing countries because of the legacy of a colonial language such as English, French, Portuguese or Spanish which has often been adopted as the national language to unite diverse ethnic groups, each with their own language. In Zambia, for example, English was adopted as the national language 'For the sake of communication between Zambians whose mother tongues differ and in order to promote the unity of the nation (Paran & Williams, 2007, p. 3). Amongst those who research and study the use of language in education there is general agreement that the most effective language as a medium of instruction for both literacy and subject content is the learner's first, local or home language rather than the colonial language. On this basis children would continue to learn in their first language as the medium of instruction through primary school and into secondary school, though at some point in upper primary school or secondary school they would also take the colonial language as a subject of study. It would not be until higher education, or perhaps not even then, that the medium of instruction would be the colonial language. However, this is not necessarily the case in practice and many countries continue to use the colonial language in primary or secondary school as the medium of instruction despite evidence that this is not an effective way to learn.

Paran and Williams (2007, p. 3) note that

A wealth of research supports the view that teaching in a
language already known to the learners, typically their mother
tongue, is more likely to succeed than teaching children in a
language children meet for the first time as they enter the
classroom.

Benson (2002), in examining bilingual education in four countries –
Guinea-Bissau, Niger, Mozambique and Bolivia – sets out some reasons
why learning in the first language has significant advantages. First, it
provides content area instruction in a language which children
understand. If the medium of instruction is the second, colonial language
teachers rarely have any strategies to get beyond 'chalk and talk' and
eliciting rote responses. Teachers can also get a much better idea of what
students are learning if use is made of the first language. Second, using
the first language greatly facilitates the achievement of literacy in
reading, writing and speaking in that language through meaningful
interaction. This then greatly helps in learning the second, official
national language through transferring the literacy skills they have
learned when children have mastered their mother tongue. Benson also
argues that there is evidence that test scores improve when the first
language is the medium of instruction, that there is increased pride in
the local language, that parents are more willing to participate in school
matters, that there are friendlier relationships between teachers and
pupils and there is more active participation by learners in classes. In a
study of language use in education in Tanzania and Ghana Afitska et al
(2013, p. 161) add that when African languages are used in primary
school they have certain obvious and visible benefits – they can reinforce
home–school links, strengthen local cultures, teach traditional skills,
increase community cohesion outside the school, help gain initial
literacy more easily than learning through a European language, improve
academic achievement, increase learner motivation and increase parental
participation.

Poor levels of understanding of European languages where the
European language is the medium of instruction are linked with low
levels of academic achievement in countries such as South Africa,
Tanzania, Uganda, Kenya, Nigeria, Burundi, Mali and Malawi (Paran &
Williams, 2007, pp. 3-4). Moreover, Afitska et al (2013) argue that
teachers themselves may not have a fluent grasp of the language of
instruction and this limits teachers to using only a limited range of
teaching strategies and to using 'Safetalk' whereby they avoid topics they
don't feel linguistically competent enough to teach. Their own
Tanzanian study found that teachers used a wider range of pedagogical
techniques when working in an African language – they explained
concepts more clearly, used more questions and prompts, used a wide

range of feedback to learners and a wider range of assessment strategies as well as providing more opportunities for group work, and that teachers also simply spoke less (Afitska et al, 2013, p. 158). However, at secondary level in Tanzania the language of instruction is English, but teachers are not trained to teach classes where the learners have difficulty with the language of instruction with the result that in practice much teaching at secondary level is learner-centred and relies on code switching (i.e. moving back and forth between the European language of instruction and either Kiswahili or the local African language) and Safetalk. In Malawi, where English is the medium of instruction from Standard 5 of primary school onwards, Kamwendo (2013, p. 116) found that pupils have problems switching to English, having been previously learning in Chichewa, and that

> teachers have a number of strategies that help them to cope with the English as a medium of teaching/learning problem. The first strategy involves the teachers' use of simple English words. To this end, the teacher tries as much as possible to avoid using complex vocabulary. However, it is not easy to stick faithfully to this practice all the time. There are times when the use of complex vocabulary becomes inevitable. As a second strategy, teachers code switch between English and Chichewa/or any other appropriate indigenous language. The third strategy amounts to the use of some school-based language policies and/or practices that are perceived to promote pupils' competence in English. One of such school practices is to hold debates – the aim being to improve pupils' oral proficiency in English. In addition, as part of what can be called school-based language policy, some teachers reported that in their schools/classrooms, they impose a 'speak English only rule'. That is, pupils are required to speak solely in English. A pupil who breaks the rule by speaking Chichewa or any other indigenous language attracts punishment.

It may also not be an ex-colonial language that is the problem. In the Lao People's Democratic Republic, Lao has been the official language of instruction since 1975 but in the North-western district of Nalae children speak Kmhmu rather than Lao language so teachers move in and out of Kmhmu and Lao in their interactions with children in order to bring into play the children's strongest language resources (Cincotta-Segi, 2011).

So, if overall the benefits of using a local language (and the problems of using an ex-colonial language) as a medium of instruction are so clear-cut, why do so many ex-colonial countries still use the colonial language as the medium of instruction in primary and secondary schools? Part of the pressure comes from parents who are aware of the cultural capital and potential jobs and economic rewards that a language like English, French or Spanish can confer. They are also keen for their children to gain access to a language that is a national and international means of communication. This tends to override the contrasting view that high levels of understanding classroom content are important. Hence, parents, despite the evidence to the contrary, can support an 'earlier the better' and 'as much as possible' approach to learning the European language: 'This has led parents in South Africa to opt for English-medium schooling as early as possible; in Tanzania it is one reason for choosing English-medium private schools' (Afitska et al, 2013, p. 162).

Afitska et al (2013, pp. 162-163) found that teachers in Tanzania were also concerned that Kiswahili was not sufficiently developed to function as the medium of instruction throughout schooling and that it did not have the international standing to prepare learners for the job market. In Ghana both teachers and parents wanted English in both primary and secondary schools and said that one further reason was that there was a general lack of resources written in African languages. Afitska et al conclude, 'Thus the common-sense view of these respondents – that learners learn best in a language they understand – is trumped by the perceived benefits attached to fluency in a European language' (2013, p. 163). Parents in both Uganda and Kenya have also resisted first language as the medium of instruction in primary schools, preferring English (Qorro, 2009).

Another reason that the local language is not used is resources. There is a shortage of teaching materials written in local languages, partly due to the cost of producing them, so that many countries find it more practical to import teaching resources that have been produced in, for example, English. Qorro (2009, p. 60) quotes a Minister of Education in Tanzania who talked about improving the quality of education but claimed that the government did not have the money to 'waste' the few resources it had for education on the language of instruction. A proposal to introduce more indigenous languages (i.e. the dominant language/s of a school's catchment area) was made in Malawi in 1996 but remains unimplemented due to a lack of resources (Kamwendo, 2013, p. 115). Of course, this might be putting the cart before the horse: 'If the policy were changed, the textbook publishers who are dependent on a market for their product, would publish' (Brock-Utne & Holmarsdottir, 2004, p. 72). Policy makers may also fear moving away from English will restrict access to science and technology and inhibit investment and aid from Western countries though, as Perry (2008, p. 63) points out in relation to southern Africa, while these are potentially serious consequences, they are not ones that necessarily put children's literacy learning interests first.

Finally, self-interest may play a role in protecting the privileged position of European languages, as language can play a significant role in social and economic reproduction. If the political and economic elite in a country works mainly in English (and uses the language at home with their children), for example, then those who do not have access to fluency in the ex-colonial language are restricted from access to power and privilege – use of the English language in schools and universities serves as a sifter or gatekeeper which allows the children of the elite to succeed in school and others to fail or do less well. This way, the position of the powerful is protected (Bamgbose, 2000). In Tanzania, for example, where Kiswahili is the medium of instruction in primary schools, the government has also allowed English-medium private schools, and many of the elite have sent their children to them. This helps the elite because their children are already better able to manage in English and this reinforces their advantages for the future (Qorro, 2009).

However, another obstacle to using a local language as the medium of instruction is that the language situation in schools is more complex in some countries than others. In Tanzania, there is a dominant, widely used African language – Kiswahili – that can be used as a medium of instruction in primary schools and potentially in secondary schools. In Malawi 70% of the country speak Chichewa (Kamwendo, 2013, p. 115). In other developing countries it is less obvious which language should be used. In Eritrea there are nine equal official languages using different scripts (Asfaha & Kroon, 2011). In southern Africa, Botswana has two official languages out of 25 languages spoken in the country; Zambia has seven official languages out of 31 spoken there and South Africa has 11 official languages out of at least 28 spoken there (Perry, 2008, p. 62). Moreover, it is possible in these countries for pupils in one school to come from a wide range of first-language backgrounds, especially in urban areas. This can lead to some difficult and complex language choices concerning which language to use as a medium of instruction and which to incorporate into the curriculum as a subject.

In South Africa, for example, although schools can choose to teach in African languages, in practice English is used as the medium of instruction from Grade 4 onwards. While this causes many of the problems for learners and teachers discussed above, and there is certainly more that could be done to encourage teaching and learning in learners' first language (Brock-Utne & Holmarsdottir, 2004), the situation in some schools is complex and language choice and implementation is not necessarily straightforward:

> Matatiele Primary School in KwaZulu Natal is an ex-Griqua community school, which was a single-medium Afrikaans school. Subsequently, it changed to a parallel/dual medium school offering English and Afrikaans as the two languages of instruction and is currently phasing out Afrikaans. The school offers two languages as subjects, English (first and second language) and Afrikaans (first and second language). However,

the social and linguistic profile of its pupils has changed
dramatically in the last three years, with 55% now speaking
either Sesotho or isiXhosa in almost equal numbers. Neither of
the two indigenous languages is dominant in the province of
KwaZulu Natal where isiZulu predominates but both are
prevalent in the Matatiele/Kokstad district. (Brown, 1998,
cited in Harber, 2001, p. 34)

For many children the language of instruction, even if it is a local one,
may only be a third or fourth language. So, even if a local language is
chosen as the medium of instruction, the one that is used can be a matter
of culture and power rather than an uncontroversial choice and may only
be the dominant language rather than one that is used universally in that
country or region of a country. This is a further reason why policy
makers often opt for the ex-colonial language.

Conclusion

There is no doubt that literacy is at the heart of education – not being
able to read or write does not make life impossible but it makes it
considerably more difficult and restricts access to many activities that
might improve the quality of life. There is also little doubt that it is much
more a feature of 'developing' countries than the higher income countries
of the global north. Yet, literacy is not straightforward and, as we have
seen, its nature, measurement, extent and purposes are all controversial.
A major area of controversy in literacy debates, especially in postcolonial
countries, is policy and practice in relation to the language of literacy in
primary and secondary schooling. Despite very strong evidence of the
benefits of learning in a local language, the ex-colonial languages
continue their domination of formal education and the higher up the
system one progresses, the more this is the case. While there are genuine
problems facing greater implementation of first languages as media of
instruction, there is much that could still actually be done to improve the
experience and outcomes of children who do not have immediate
familiarity with the dominant language nationally. Many in education in
developing countries support greater use of local languages and work
towards overcoming the sort of barriers and obstacles discussed in this
chapter.

References

Asfaha, Y.M. & Kroon, S. (2011) Multilingual Education Policy in Practice:
    classroom literacy instruction in different scripts in Eritrea, *Compare*, 41(2),
    229-246.
Afitska, O., Ankomah, Y., Clegg, J., et al (2013) Dilemmas of Language Choice in
    Education in Tanzania and Ghana, in L. Tikly & A. Barrett (Eds) *Education*

Quality and Social Justice in the Global South: challenges for policy, practice and research. London: Routledge.

Bajaj, M. (2009) 'I have big things planned for my future': the limits and possibilities of transformative agency in Zambian schools, *Compare*, 39(4), 551-568.

Bamgbose, A. (2000) *Language and Exclusion: consequences of language policies in Africa.* Hamburg: Lit Verlag.

Bartlett, L. (2008) Literacy's Verb: exploring what literacy is and what literacy does, *International Journal of Educational Development*, 28(6), 737-753.

Benson, C. (2002) Real and Potential Benefits of Bilingual Programmes in Developing Countries, *International Journal of Bilingual Education and Bilingualism*, 5(6), 303-317.

Brock-Utne, B. & Holmarsdottir, H. (2004) Language Policies and Practices in Tanzania and South Africa: problems and challenges, *International Journal of Educational Development*, 24(1), 67-84.

Cincotta-Segi, A. (2011) Talking in, Talking around and Talking about the L2: three literacy teaching responses to L2 medium of instruction in the Lao PDR, *Compare*, 41(2), 195-211.

Freire, P. & Macedo, D. (1987) *Literacy: reading the word and the world.* London: Routledge & Kegan Paul.

Harber, C. (2001) *State of Transition: post-apartheid educational reform in South Africa.* Oxford: Symposium Books.

Kalman, J. (2008) Beyond Definition: central concepts for understanding literacy, *International Review of Education*, 54(5-6), 533-538.

Kamwendo, G. (2013) Malawi: contemporary and critical issues, in C. Harber (Ed.) *Education in Southern Africa.* London: Bloomsbury.

Maddox, B., Aikman, S., Rao, N. & Robinson-Pant, A. (2011) Literacy Inequalities and Social Justice, *International Journal of Educational Development*, 31(6), 577-579.

Paran, A. & Williams, E. (2007) Editorial: Reading and Literacy in Developing Countries, *Journal of Research in Reading*, 30(1), 1-6.

Perry, K. (2008) Primary School Literacy in Southern Africa: African perspectives, *Comparative Education*, 44(1), 57-73.

Qorro, M. (2009) Parents and Policy Makers' Insistence on Foreign Languages as Media of Education in Africa: restricting access to quality education – for whose benefit?, in B. Brock-Utne & I. Skattum *Languages and Education in Africa: a comparative and transdisciplinary analysis.* Oxford: Symposium Books.

Shiohata, M. (2010) Exploring the Literacy Environment: a case study from Senegal, *Comparative Education Review*, 54(2), 243-269.

UNESCO (2012) *Youth and Skills: putting education to work.* EFA Global Monitoring Report. Paris: UNESCO.

Clive Harber

Further Reading

Brock-Utne, B. & Skattum, I. (2009) *Languages and Education in Africa: a comparative and transdisciplinary analysis.* Oxford: Symposium Books.

Compare, 41(2) (2011), Special Issue on Multilingual Literacies in the Global South: language policy, literacy learning and use.

Compare, 39(4) (2009), Special Sub-issue on Literacies in Comparative Perspective.

International Journal of Educational Development, 31(6) (2011), Special Issue on Literacy Inequalities and Social Justice.

Street, B. (2001) *Literacy and Development: ethnographic perspectives.* London: Routledge.

Discussion and Activities

1. 'Being literate is about more than just being able to read and write.' Discuss.

2. Identify one postcolonial, multilingual developing country. What are its main languages? What is its official policy towards language use in primary and secondary school? Do these encourage learning in a local, first language or not?

3. Are you familiar with a second language from your schooling? What problems would you face if the course on education and development that you are following was in that language? How would you and your teachers try to cope?

Index